"This is an inspiring and unusual book by two 'Church Doctors' who have helped a huge number of individual churches move significantly forward. By quoting a very large number of examples from churches located in both the UK and US, it gives practical advice and HOPE that situations can change."

—Peter Brierley, Brierley Consultancy, Tonbridge, England

"Holy Spirit genius! If you lead a church and have holy discontent about the way it is versus the way it could be, you need to read this book. If you lead a church and don't have a holy discontent, you need to hit yourself on the head with this book, and then open it and make notes on every page!"

—Anthony Delaney, strategic leader, Ivy Church, Manchester, England

"Is there anything more important than the church of Jesus becoming all it's meant to be? I love Kent's heart and commitment to seeing this happen, and I love this book. Buy one for yourself and one for each of your church leaders. You won't regret it!"

—Andy Hawthorne, the Message Trust, Manchester, England

"*Who Broke My Church?* has hit the bull's-eye of the church's greatest need, fulfilling the Great Commission of making disciples! This book by Church Doctors Kent Hunter and Tracee Swank provides a Bible-based explanation of what the modern church must do to break through all hindrances to healthy biblical activity and growth. Every concerned Christian should read this book."

—Dennis L. Kutzner, general overseer, CMIGLOBAL, Fort Wayne, Indiana

"When you are reading a book and you find yourself having difficulty putting it down, that means you are reading a really, really GREAT book! That's exactly what happened to me as I read *Who Broke My Church?* I am going to make Kent and Tracee's book required reading for all of my church leaders."

—Walt Kallestad, lead pastor, Community
Church of Joy, Glendale, Arizona

"In this book, Kent Hunter provides a necessary corrective with the concept of 'thriving.' A healthy organism displays a comprehensive picture of growth. The authors explore the essential dimensions and provide welcome research data to demonstrate the progress made by churches that embrace the concepts."

—Eddie Gibbs, author of *The Rebirth of the
Church: Applying Paul's Vision for
Ministry in Our Post-Christian World*

"If you and your church need a breakthrough, what are you waiting for? Start reading now...and get ready. Breakthrough is on the way! If you desire to see God's Kingdom advance, dive into this book and expect a BREAKTHROUGH!"

—Mark Zehnder, senior pastor,
King of Kings Lutheran
Church, Omaha, Nebraska

"Kingdom culture changes everything. That's what Kent Hunter taught me in his new book, *Who Broke My Church?* If you are ready to move past mediocrity, sameness, and survival mode, this new book is for you. Filled with insights and challenging lessons, we are reading this book as a staff, and I'm recommending it to all my coaching networks."

—Nelson Searcy, lead pastor,
the Journey Church, and founder,
www.ChurchLeaderInsights.com

"Kent Hunter is indeed the 'Church Doctor.' I know of no one more adept at bringing clear diagnosis and field-tested prescriptions to the challenges churches face. No matter how difficult your church's situation, you can and will experience heaven-sent breakthrough—if you heed the Church Doctor's advice!"

—David Shibley, founder and world
representative, Global Advance

"Kent Hunter is known as an effective church consultant and has written many helpful books to revive and grow your church. His latest book, *Who Broke My Church?*, is the result of many years of working with local churches to overcome growth barriers and expand their outreach."

—Elmer L. Towns, cofounder and
vice president, Liberty University

"In this book, Kent Hunter's love for the church emanates from every page. I am certain that God will use this book to motivate Christians around the world to renew our passion and desire to see the bride of Christ thrive in our generation."

—Tim Tucker, CEO, the
Message Trust, South Africa

"Dr. Kent Hunter's newest book simply sizzles with brave insights and hope-filled faith for the church. As one of the world's top church consultants, Dr. Hunter also offers meticulously studied and practical insights for bringing spiritual health to the local church. This is an essential resource for all church leaders."

—Dr. Arlen Salte, author and founder,
Break Forth Ministries, Break Forth, Canada

"I have known Kent Hunter as a friend and mentor for thirty years. This book is the culmination of Kent's wisdom, experience, and giftedness. These ideas work! My congregation and personal ministry are living proof that these strategies can change everything!"

—Robert W. Shriner, senior pastor, St. John
Lutheran Church, Kendallville, Indiana

"Our church has used Kent Hunter and the Church Doctor Ministries as a consultant over many years and in many, many circumstances. In this new book, Kent shares seven 'Breakthrough Strategies' that can help your church experience a new level of health and vitality. I recommend it to every serious student of church health and growth."

—Chris Scruggs, senior pastor, Advent
Presbyterian Church, Cordova, Tennessee

"A missional masterpiece! I encourage all congregational leaders and members to read, study, discuss, pray over, and implement the invaluable wisdom shared in this book."

—Jon Vollrath, pastor, Our Savior's
Lutheran Church, Eyota, Minnesota

"As I read this book, I could not put it down. I have had the privilege of knowing Kent for many years. God called me to do a church plant, and I implemented all of Kent's recommendations that I possibly could. IT WORKS!"

—Mike Albaugh, pastor, Destiny Family
of Faith, Kendallville, Indiana

"This book will be a blessing to those who sense something is wrong and yet aren't quite sure what it is or what to do about it. [Dr. Hunter's] guidance on building a Kingdom culture is invaluable."

—Dr. Michael Hiller, senior pastor, Peace With
Christ Lutheran Church, Aurora, Colorado

"When Kent Hunter writes a book, I read it immediately! His latest release uniquely equips us to connect our culture with Christ."

—Mitch Kruse, author of *Street Smarts from Proverbs: How to
Navigate through Conflict to Community*

"This book is the culmination of [Kent's] many years of experience and research and will help anyone who reads it to experience some holy discontent. There is a great hope and a future for the local church—as we let the Holy Spirit lead in God's direction for transformation into a people alive in the fullness of Christ."

—Gerry Hartke, pastor, Prince of Peace
Lutheran Church, Oregon, Ohio

"Once in a while, a book comes along that challenges the boundaries of popular thought. *Who Broke My Church?* is one of those books. It's a game-changer for the health, vitality, and future of the local church...your local church. Do yourself a favor and put this one on your must-read list."

—Rev. Alan Chandler, consultant, Church
Doctor Ministries, and ordained elder,
Free Methodist Church—USA

"For the parish pastor who is in the trenches every day with the gnawing feeling that the church could and should be more for the Kingdom, *Who Broke My Church?* is a must-read. Dr. Hunter gives words and knowledge to the discontent that pastors feel. *Who Broke My Church?* can make a difference in your church. It has in mine."

—Rev. Robert D. Suhr, pastor, Christ
Church, Mequon, Wisconsin

"In *Who Broke My Church?* you can experience the insights of practitioners who have observed, connected with, and continually learned about what makes congregations healthy and thriving. The book you hold in your hand or see online is a treasure of wisdom. Do not just flip through it. Do not just read it. Ingest it into your soul."

—George W. Bullard Jr.,
www.BullardJournal.org

"CAUTION: This book will cause you to become so fired up, it may keep you awake at night! Certainly, it will make you rethink everything you've ever thought about your church. I highly recommend this to anyone ready to take a fresh look at what it takes to truly make one's church fire on all cylinders. The Church Doctor has truly given us the right diagnosis and prescription."

—Dr. Jeff King, author and host of the
nationally syndicated radio show
Everyday Encouragement

"I LOVE this book! *Who Broke My Church?* is one of those books that you need to keep on your bookshelf. I know I will continually reread this book to keep me focused on the important tasks of the church. Each of the seven ceilings are areas that I have struggled and still struggle with as a pastor and leader."

—James Cho, president, Great Commission
Research Network, English track director
and professor, Grace Mission University, and
missions pastor, Community Christian
Center, Los Angeles, California

"Kent and Tracee have their fingers on the pulse of the movement, and this book will help the church break through barriers that have hindered the great work of God. We need to know what we are up against, and we need the strategies in this book to break down these barriers."

—Ron Pennekamp, senior pastor, St. Paul
Lutheran Church, Lakeland, Florida

"The organized church in America has reached a tipping point. Kent Hunter has predicted this for quite some time. This book not only diagnoses the problems that churches are facing but systematically lays out the solutions that are needed to help them thrive in this twenty-first century."

—Pastor Jon Bjorgaard, director of ministries,
Shepherd of the Desert Lutheran Church and
School, Scottsdale, Arizona

"*Who Broke My Church?* is not an autopsy for dying churches. In this day of great spiritual and social upheaval, it is a game-changing reminder of how Jesus *continues* to build his church today. As Kent and Tracee have done for me and the churches where I served as pastor over the past thirty-six years, I know they will do for you in this book. This book brings fresh hope, courage, and know-how to thrive in both your personal and church life."

—Jon Trinklein, Lutheran pastor

"Using inspiring examples, Dr. Hunter and Tracee speak about the holy discontent and encouragement about how we can reach people. *Who Broke My Church?* provides direction about how it can be done—through low control, loving, serving, showing hospitality—as we allow the Holy Spirit to be the real controlling factor."

—Khurram Khan, leader, People of
the Book Ministries International,
Outreach to Muslims

"To say that my friend and mentor Kent Hunter knows churches is an understatement. To say that he has the answers to help churches is also an understatement! This book is a must-read to 'unbreak' the local church and restore Kingdom culture!"

—Dr. Barry L. Kolb, teacher, consultant,
and missionary, Branson, Missouri

"Kent Hunter and Tracee Swank have given the church a great gift: seven ceilings churches face and seven strategies for health and growth. They provide a word of hope in challenging times with a solid biblical foundation. Thanks, Kent and Tracee, for inspiration for God's great work."

—Richard Burkey, senior pastor,
Christ Lutheran Church,
La Mesa, California

"The potential of your church can be unleashed by following the writings of Dr. Hunter. Your church can become a Kingdom culture church. God can change your church by applying the principles found in this book. Get ready for your church to be transformed."

—Dennis Kruse, Indiana State senator, Auburn, Indiana

"In this incredible book, Hunter and Swank assess, then address, the biggest challenge that keeps the church from becoming all that God intends it to be. They reveal the challenge our churches face isn't the lack of a program but rather the lack of a Kingdom culture. You're gonna love this."

—Mike Burnidge, lead pastor, North Ridge Community Church, Cave Creek, Arizona

"Having successfully used Dr. Hunter as a consultant for our church, I thought I had sponged up all the knowledge he could offer. I was wrong. In this book, there is an underground river of fresh concepts that I've tapped into, and I'm happily using them to water the landscape of our ministry."

—Larry Gember, pastor, St. James Lutheran Church, Greenfield, Indiana

"*Who Broke My Church?* by Dr. Kent R. Hunter is a dynamic tool to guide us here in Cambodia. I thank God for a servant like Dr. Hunter, who is gifted in a special way cross-culturally."

—Setan Aaron Lee, president and CEO, TransformAsia

"Years of research and experience, coupled with a diligent study and knowledge of the Holy Scriptures, have given Kent and Tracee a powerful perspective into the DNA of healthy congregations and HOW these churches THRIVE! *Who Broke My Church?* is a must-read for church leaders who CARE about their congregations and desire to be faithful followers of Christ. Here is undeniable, practical, and powerful TRUTH that will convict, heal, and TRANSFORM."

—Rev. David P. E. Maier, president, Michigan district, Lutheran Church—Missouri Synod

"Remarkable insights, penetrating critique, surgical precision. This book is one that many of us have been waiting to read for a very long time. Kent Hunter and Tracee Swank have put into words what many of us have thought about, and felt, but didn't know how to describe. I don't know anyone, or any agency, that has done this kind of work that represents the vast majority of congregations in America."

—Rev. Mark Vander Tuig, service coordinator,
Lutheran Congregations in Mission for Christ

WHO BROKE MY CHURCH?

Also by Kent R. Hunter

WHO BROKE MY CHURCH?

7 PROVEN STRATEGIES FOR RENEWAL AND REVIVAL

KENT R. HUNTER

WITH TRACEE J. SWANK

Faith
Words

New York   Nashville

Cover design by Edward A. Crawford
Cover photography by Jake Olson/Trevillion and Getty Images
Cover copyright © 2017 by Hachette Book Group, Inc.

FaithWords
Hachette Book Group
1290 Avenue of the Americas, New York, NY 10104
faithwords.com
twitter.com/faithwords

First Edition: September 2017

FaithWords is a division of Hachette Book Group, Inc. The FaithWords name and logo are trademarks of Hachette Book Group, Inc.

The publisher is not responsible for websites (or their content) that are not owned by the publisher.

The Hachette Speakers Bureau provides a wide range of authors for speaking events. To find out more, go to www.hachettespeakersbureau.com or call (866) 376-6591.

Library of Congress Control Number: 2017942514

ISBN: 978-1-4789-8930-1 (trade paperback), 978-1-4789-8931-8 (ebook)

Printed in the United States of America

LSC-C

10 9 8 7 6 5 4 3 2

*Dedicated
to
Craig*

Holy discontent with a vision for healthy churches

CONTENTS

Contents

Building the Right Culture
the Right Way

Restoring your church to the healthy, transforming, divine organism God intended is similar to the way novelist E. L. Doctorow described his writing process: "It's like driving a car at night: You never see further than your headlights, but you can make the whole trip that way." Trust God. He has great plans for you!

Kent R. Hunter and Tracee J. Swank.
E. L. Doctorow interviewed by
George Plimpton, *The Paris Review*

INTRODUCTION

During the last twenty centuries, in hundreds of nations, Christianity has flourished—then atrophied. Local churches thrive with vitality for a season. Then, over time, many plateau, decline, and lose impact. Christianity fades and becomes marginalized. Secularization creeps in, and thriving nations become increasingly troubled. The value of life disintegrates.

Likewise, there are many documented movements in which God has reversed the decline among receptive people. It begins with an "awakening," a wake-up call among Christians and their churches. They reclaim the essence of the New Testament church. What follows is often called a "revival." God moves in the land. Christianity spreads rapidly. Many become believers. The nation benefits. How does this movement begin? How can the power of the church be restored?

After four decades of helping Christians and churches become more effective, our team at Church Doctor Ministries has discovered a dramatic and encouraging element for church vitality. God transforms Christians and their churches. They impact their communities and nations.

We have field-tested this discovery in hundreds of churches. We surveyed 75,000 Christians in those churches. We have participated in major movements of God on six continents. For sixteen years, we have closely studied many of the spiritually reenergized churches in England. The movement that started in England twenty years ago is just beginning in North America.

Diagnosing the issues Christians and churches face, we have identified seven ceilings. They greatly hinder the work God intends. We have field-tested seven strategies that effectively remove these ceilings. You might ask, "If it's that simple, why doesn't everyone know this?"

Most Christians—and most churches—suffer from Kingdom

culture drift. Kingdom culture is the spiritual and nonnegotiable climate for the seven strategies. It is found in Jesus' teaching about the Kingdom of God. The power of your church depends on who you are and who you become. This changes everything. The apostle Paul wrote, "Do not be conformed to this world, but be transformed by the renewal of your mind" (Rom. 12:2 ESV).

Kingdom culture is the spiritual DNA that powers healthy, thriving churches. The helix of this DNA has five interconnected elements: values, beliefs, attitudes, priorities, and worldviews. As you focus on Kingdom culture, you grow. These five elements change everything. As you grow, God transforms your church to be more as Jesus intended. Don't be fooled: This is not a quick-fix program. It is recapturing the movement the Holy Spirit birthed at Pentecost.

This dramatic change is not beyond you or your church. Our research demonstrates that God can ignite a core group in any church, improving health, vitality, and effectiveness for outreach and mission. Making disciples is what Jesus commissioned us to do. But first, He commissioned us to be—and become—Kingdom people. He said, "My Kingdom is not of this world" (John 18:36 NIV). This culture makes the difference.

As you will discover, when God revitalizes His movement in any area of the world, it begins with those who have *holy discontent*. It is likely several of those people exist in your church. They love the Lord. They love the church and respect the pastor(s) and staff. They are involved, generously giving of their time and money. They are not the whiners and complainers found in almost every church. They are discontent about the lack of fruit. They are dissatisfied with puny results or business as usual. They know too much from Scripture to accept mediocrity. They will not settle for simply managing the congregation. They believe what Jesus said: The harvest is ripe (see Matthew 9:37). They are deeply troubled that many young adults consider the church irrelevant. They recognize the church exists to make a difference.

Those with holy discontent are the "early adopters" of a move of God: spiritual seeds that represent the organic start of a coming harvest—if they are cultivated and nurtured. You may discover that you are one of them. If not, you may be about to become one. If you choose to take this journey, get ready for the greatest God-adventure of your life.

CHAPTER ONE

The Gift of Holy Discontent

Now the Berean Jews were of more noble character than those in Thessalonica, for they received the message with great eagerness and examined the Scriptures every day to see if what Paul said was true.

—Acts 17:11[1]

Thrive 1. To prosper or flourish; be successful. 2. To grow vigorously.
Survive 1. To live or exist longer than or beyond the life or existence of; outlive. 2. To continue to live after or in spite of: to *survive* a wreck.

Webster's New World College Dictionary

How would you describe your spiritual life? Is it thriving or simply surviving? Is it spiritually prospering? Flourishing? Successful? Is it growing vigorously? *You will never do what God wants you to do unless you become who God wants you to be.* What about your Christian community, your church? *Your church will never do what God wants your church to do unless the people become who God wants them to be.*

Jesus used picture language to make sure his disciples would get it. He said, "I am the vine; you are the branches."[2] He also said, "You didn't choose me, but I chose you. I have appointed you to go, to produce fruit that will last, and to ask the Father in my name to give you whatever you ask for."[3]

Grapes grow when the vine is healthy. A grapevine will be healthy when the *atmosphere* is good—fertile soil, proper levels of rain, and just enough sun. Consider spiritual atmosphere to be *Kingdom culture*. Healthy vines multiply and produce an enormous number of grapes. This occurs not just once, but year after year. Does that describe you? Does it describe your church?

It does describe God's miracle of creation. It is amazing but not surprising. At creation, God did say, "Be fruitful and multiply," right?[4]

If you owned a vineyard, what would you possibly do to increase your harvest? You don't have much control over the atmosphere—the rain, the sun, and the soil. Is there any way you might cooperate with your Creator to experience better results? According to Jesus, the answer is yes. Admittedly, it doesn't make a lot of sense. It is counterintuitive. Much about Kingdom culture is counterintuitive. Most everything Jesus says when He begins, "The Kingdom of God is like…" is not the way humans normally understand the world. Jesus did say, "My Kingdom is not of this world."[5] Get that? Your spiritual life is *not* like this world. Your church is *not* like this world. It is not supposed to be like this world.

With grapes, God does what seems unusual. This is the miracle move with the vine and the branches: They multiply when they are cut back. Really? This is Kingdom culture: Sometimes less equals more.

"For My thoughts are not your thoughts, Nor are your ways My ways," says the Lord.[6] Jesus told the disciples that His Kingdom works differently than the way human kingdoms operate. It is not similar to nations, human cultures, programs, or activities of this world. A young man once asked Oliver Wendell Holmes Jr., "What is the secret of success?" Holmes responded, "Young man, the secret of my success is, at an early age, I discovered I was not God."[7] This is a good reminder for those who call themselves Christians.

After analyzing several hundred churches during the last several decades, it is clear to me that many Christians are surviving, not thriving. Christians are overcome with maintenance of the mundane and are anemic in the movement of mission. Many of the faith communities we call *church* are, in fact, plateaued or declining and aging. Many churches report a median age older than sixty in worship. The following is a typical profile:

Age Distribution

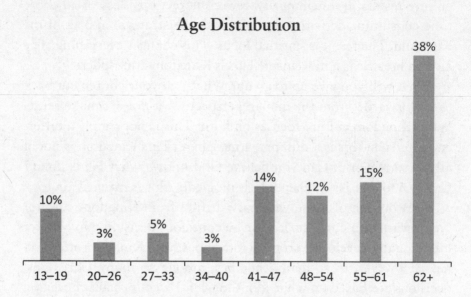

No, this is not a church in a retirement community. It is typical of many churches. Is that thriving? You don't have to be a Church Doctor to see the end in sight. Many Christians and their congregations have shifted into survival mode. Church leaders grasp at straws—the latest program as a "miracle cure" packaged for a quick fix.

The quick fix is another worldly way. Jesus did not build Kingdom atmosphere using a ten-week Bible study. Like many worldly ways, "shortcut Christianity" has seeped into the church. "Just give me a program I can run with," says the pastor. The result? *Kingdom culture drift.* A puny harvest. However, there is a spark of hope, a turning point. God is getting our attention. Christians are showing signs of a holy infection, diagnosed as *holy discontent* or *spiritual restlessness.* Many Christians are wondering, "Is my church surviving or thriving?"

In John 15, Jesus speaks from a Kingdom culture perspective. He says, "He prunes the branches that do bear fruit so they will produce even more."[8] Really? This is Kingdom math. It is different from what you learned in grade school. You learned addition equals more. Kingdom math says subtraction equals multiplication, by God's power. Less is more, but less of what? The impact of Kingdom culture results in less impurity, fewer distractions, less of all those time-consuming activities that diminish the strategic impact of the Kingdom. The result is spiritual focus. This changes everything. The air you breathe is a movement. This is Kingdom atmosphere.

What will you give up to go up? What will your church cut back to go forward? From the human perspective, it doesn't make sense. Why? Kingdom culture focuses on faith. This is not simply a different approach; this is a different atmosphere. This Kingdom is not at all like this world. Can you believe God knows what He is doing? Can you follow Jesus when it feels illogical? This is rarefied air.

Are you one of those who have drifted from Kingdom culture? No, it wasn't on purpose. It wasn't a conscious decision. No believer intentionally develops a strategy to wander from Kingdom effectiveness. However, in so many churches, among so many Christians, decisions are based on what seems logical. Directions are chosen on winning arguments and majority votes. By contrast, Kingdom culture relies on biblical input to discover God's direction.

Many Christians experience death by meetings, not life by discipling. Corporate behavior overcomes focused outreach. The flashy program is more attractive than spiritual formation. *Robert's Rules of Order* trumps prayer to sort out what God wants. Leaders quote the latest fad rather than inspired Scripture. This is the disease of spiritual dry rot. As many churches have discovered, it is terminal. The health of a church is a reflection of the spiritual vitality of the believers within it. Thriving churches are filled with individuals who live Kingdom culture. This is the atmosphere that breathes life into the Christian movement.

Jesus, in this unusual and miraculous Kingdom, developed a body—His body. He is the head. He is the Master. He is the Lord. It is this head, not the church board, who gives health and life abundantly.[9]

> Many Christians experience death by meetings, not life by discipling. Corporate behavior overcomes focused outreach.

The direction of this head can impact churches riddled by drift, suffering from subtle, secular culture. This drift kills churches, but Jesus is the Master of resurrection. His body, in any form, can rise again!

It makes little sense to cut traditional programs and activities, but these activities cause burned-out believers. It is a hard sell to focus on spiritual formation (*re*-formation, transformation). Yes, God's Kingdom isn't anything like the world where we live. It takes serious faith to be sold out to God's plan. It takes trust in Jesus to focus on Kingdom culture and to expect the church to flourish and thrive. It sounds strange. Someone changed the verse to add this insight, "You will know the truth, and the truth will make you . . . 'a little peculiar.' "[10]

What if you pulled the plug on half the programs that keep you so occupied? What if you moved from *doing* toward *becoming*? God created us human beings, not human doings.

What would happen if you focused on Kingdom culture for a year or two? Could that lead to more outreach? More joy? More community impact? The growth of God's Kingdom *inside* people? The growth of God's Kingdom as Christians engage those in social networks? What if you, and others, were full of the King? Would the King's Kingdom become a Jesus epidemic? Would it change your church? Your community? The world? Instead of *belonging* to the church, what would change if you focused on *being* church?

Would you look and act more like a Christ-follower? Would your church look more like the body of Christ? Reggie McNeal in his book *The Present Future* says, "As he hung on the cross Jesus probably never thought the impact of his sacrifice would be reduced to an invitation for people to join and to support an institution."[11] Could your church change complexion from institution to movement? Could it move from being reactive to proactive? Could it be rearranged from a destination to a launching pad? Could Jesus thrive as the head, not just in theory, but also in function?

Do you really believe Jesus when He said, "I will build my church"?[12] Honestly, we work too hard at church. Imagine what would happen if we focused on Kingdom culture. What if we quit doing and began being?

FAITH

It takes faith to take Jesus at His word. It takes faith to believe. It takes faith to practice Kingdom culture. It requires *humility*. Ken Blanchard and Terry Waghorn in *Mission Possible* said, "An attitude of humility is an ingredient of successful change because it permits people to take what they do seriously, while at the same time taking themselves lightly. People with humility don't think less of themselves—they just think about themselves less."[13] How much do you think about Jesus? His Kingdom?

Jesus' Kingdom is so different. From the human perspective, the Kingdom looks weird. It is definitely not like this world. It is not like our experience. It is not supposed to be! God wants your church to thrive, to prosper. Prosperity is having everything you need to accomplish the will of God in your life and in the life of your church. When you think about "everything you need," does your attention drift to the mundane? Do you focus on money, staff, programs, volunteers, and activities? In truth, the real key is Kingdom culture—atmosphere for harvest. You can have the best seeds, the greatest soil, and the right fertilizer, but you won't get a crop if you plant it in Minnesota in January. Why? Programmatic activity is not enough. Atmosphere changes everything!

> From the human perspective, the Kingdom looks weird. It is definitely not like this world. It is not like our experience. It is not supposed to be!

You have faith to believe Jesus for salvation. You can also have faith that Jesus can use you and your church for the salvation of others. You can trust Jesus for the faith that your church can thrive without all the gimmicks and gadgets. You can believe the culture of the King will infect you and make you a contagious Christian. You will transform from "local church" to "lifestyle movement."

In northern Canada, there are two seasons: July to August...and winter. At the end of August, the rains come and the rural roads become ruts. Then, overnight, they freeze. At the place where the pavement becomes a dirt road is a sign that reads, CHOOSE YOUR

RUT VERY CAREFULLY. YOU WILL BE IN IT FOR A LONG TIME. Some churches have been in a religious rut for a long time. Some Christians act like they have been in a rut forever. Someone has said, "The only difference between a rut and a grave is its length, depth, and how long you're in it." What is this rut?

The rut for many Christians is subtle slippage from Kingdom culture. It is quiet, subtle, and often escapes notice. It is like slowly changing temperature. Your spirituality cools, and your church cools to the cause of Christ, one degree at a time. The church veers off its course, one person, one idea, and one activity at a time. It is a slow drift, but it is deadly.

We are warm in the bed of salvation by grace through faith. We've got that nailed! We know we need forgiveness. Our faith is in the Savior who died on the cross for our sins. Our salvation is secure. It is so easy for us to take on the aura of a spiritual country club. To those who don't yet know Jesus, we are an odd group that occasionally invites others to come to our building, eat spaghetti, and donate to a youth mission trip.

RECAPTURING KINGDOM

The idea of recapturing Kingdom culture hits like a cold slap in the face. "Are you telling me I am off base, that our church is less productive? How dare you! We've always done it that way. We have a nice church. The people are friendly. We do nice things for the poor. Part of our budget goes to missions." Yet, you know, in spite of it all, your church may be stalled, aging, and struggling to reach the next generation. You can feel it: more empty seats and less money. On the other hand, your church may be functioning in a way that seems strong, yet the ability to reach non-Christians is far below your potential, and you know it.

Could Kingdom culture really change that? It takes a leap of faith. Why do you think Jesus spent so much time embedding Kingdom DNA in His disciples? Kingdom DNA is the identity imprint of the King. Jesus knows a thriving church is fueled by Kingdom culture. Yes, Jesus came to save the world. He also built an army that breathes air that is out of this world. It is the atmosphere of Kingdom culture. Jesus said it is like yeast in bread. You can't see it, but it changes everything![14]

This culture is spiritual DNA. It represents our *values*—what we identify as important. It includes our *beliefs*—what we demonstrate we believe is true. It reflects our *attitudes*—the way we position our lives before God. It reveals our *priorities*—what we will consistently, always, do first. It mirrors our *worldviews*—the way we see the world and the way the world works.

- Values: What we consider important
- Beliefs: What we demonstrate we believe is true
- Attitudes: How we position our lives before God
- Priorities: What we always do first
- Worldviews: The way we see the world and the way it works

Kingdom culture is so vital to thriving Christianity; Jesus spent most of His ministry pouring it into His disciples. Who would think that focusing most of His attention on a few disciples would launch the greatest movement in history? Who would believe that a few people imprinted with Kingdom DNA could change the world? Who would have ever thought it would last for centuries, change civilizations, and turn around lives by the billions?

Jesus told stories about this culture. He taught through those stories. He made a contrast between this Kingdom and the kingdom of the world, even the world of religious people. Jesus demonstrated Kingdom culture. He fed the hungry. He forgave the guilty. He healed the crippled and cleansed the lepers. He walked on water. He cast out demons. He taught; His disciples learned. He demonstrated; they experienced it. In the process, they caught it. They weren't just people who knew content. They weren't followers obsessed with *doing*. They *became* different people. Then Jesus said, "Whoever believes in me will do the works I have been doing, and they will do even greater things than these."[15] Really? Is that you? Is that your church? Do you think He was joking? Do you think He meant it only for *them*? Honestly, many Christians and their churches act like it!

In the Lord's Prayer, we pray that we want God's will to be done on earth, in our lives, and in our churches, just like it is done in heaven.[16] Our drift from Kingdom culture makes these words empty. We forget that inside the will of God, there is no failure. We forget that outside the will of God, there is no success. We have drifted.

TIME TO CHANGE

Christians everywhere are beginning to sense that it is time, or past time, to change. It is time to do what Jesus says works—as crazy as it looks, as strange as it sounds. It is time to become who Jesus called us to be. It is late, but not too late. It takes guts to leave ruts. It takes faith to believe that through focus on Kingdom culture, God will transform Christ-followers. It takes a leap of faith to believe God will develop thriving people who become thriving churches. This did work, you know, in the first century. It has worked, you know, in many places around the world where great moves of God, revivals, have taken place. Can it work now? Can it work for you?

It was a great leap of faith for the disciples to hang out with Jesus for three years. It took faith to listen to all His stories. It took faith to live in Kingdom culture. Yet the disciples knew. They knew Jesus "taught with real authority—quite unlike their teachers of religious law."[17] There is power in His Kingdom teaching. There is power in Kingdom atmosphere. Kingdom culture changes everything. I wonder if they wondered—I wonder if you wonder—is the power in the teacher or in what He taught? The answer is both!

Starting a movement with twelve ordinary guys seems risky. It demonstrates that Kingdom culture makes a difference. It shows that God's people change. The early church thrived, in every dimension of the definition. The early church prospered. It flourished. It was successful. Your church can be thriving today, centuries later. It can begin with you and spread to others. Oswald Chambers in his book *My Utmost for His Highest* makes the following point:

> When looking back on the lives of men and women of God, the tendency is to say, "What wonderfully keen and intelligent wisdom they had, and how perfectly they understood all that God wanted!" But the keen and intelligent mind behind them was the mind of God, not human wisdom at all. We give credit to human wisdom when we should give credit to the divine guidance of God being exhibited through childlike people who were "foolish" enough to trust God's wisdom and His supernatural equipment.[18]

The church spread to Galatia, Ephesus, Corinth, and Rome. As Christians came together, they formed churches. These churches had impact. The movement multiplied. Then it happened. During the brief history of the New Testament church, they drifted. They wandered, subconsciously, from Kingdom culture. How do we know? The apostles wrote letters to correct the drift. God wanted those early churches to thrive. Read the New Testament letters through the lens of Kingdom drift. You will see the importance of values, beliefs, attitudes, priorities, and worldviews.

Wherever Christianity is flourishing and churches are thriving, ordinary people are living out the culture of the King. My friend Ben Manthei wrote an outstanding book, *In His Majesty's Service*. Ben says, "Success is the reward you gain from being very good at what you do. Significance is using your success to make a difference for eternity. True significance is not what you do for God, but your ability to allow God to accomplish His goals through you."[19] That is Kingdom culture.

> Wherever Christianity is flourishing and churches are thriving, you see ordinary people living out the culture of the King.

God wants to restore that culture in you and in your church. Kingdom culture in you empowers the church to thrive and influence the world. It is an inside job, inside each of us. It restores us to the mission of the Great Commission. Gerhard Knutson wrote the book *Ministry to Inactives*. In that book, Knutson says,

> One of the tragedies of the modern church is the way in which the gospel has been used as an internal balm, comforting the faithful. We hardly recognize the gospel as the power to energize the church to live with faith. We have many comfortable Christians, but few courageous Christians. We have seen the church as the fortress and protector. Seldom have we seen the church as a launching pad, the base camp for witness and ministry in the world.[20]

Kingdom culture brings a courageous mission to life in your church.

Courageous missionaries ignite courageous mission. For this to occur, you have a choice, and it's a big one. Do you really believe Jesus builds His church? Many Christians are ready to see God renew the church and bring life back again. They have watched the church decline for too long. They have unrest in their gut. They can't shake the vision that God could use their church more powerfully. They are people with holy desperation. Someone said, "If you do desperation right, you get inspiration out of it."

Before you read further, turn to the back and take the short self-reflection survey in Appendix I. See if you score at the high end of holy discontent. If you don't, you may not be ready. It might be better to wait, pray, and study Scripture. Listen to God speak and breathe Kingdom atmosphere into your life.

Those with holy discontent and spiritual restlessness are "early adopters" in the move of God to restore His church. They are fertile soil for Kingdom culture. They represent a golden moment, an opportunity for breakthrough. It is the atmosphere for spiritual health. Healthy Christianity ignites holy infection. Healthy churches thrive! God will refresh Kingdom culture in you and in others. The Holy Spirit will reignite your church.

How is your trust in God? Can you embrace Kingdom culture? Do you believe the Lord of the church will embed Kingdom DNA in you? Can you trust God to transform you into a healthy citizen of the Kingdom? Can you fathom that He will, literally, build His church in you and through you?

God is already doing this. The church is growing like wildfire in various areas of the world. His holy fire is springing up in places throughout Europe and in North America. Some call this revival. David Shibley says, "The purpose of revival is to fire the church with divine energy for her divine assignment."[21] As Christians, sometimes we look backward and get fixated on "the good ole days." We cling to familiar styles like a drowning person grasps at straws. Our focus is toward yesterday. However, God is a God of hope. He restores our strength and we "will soar high on wings like eagles."[22] When there is no faith in the future, there is no power in the present. Our trust is in Christ, "who is able, through his mighty power at work within us, to accomplish infinitely more than we might ask or think."[23] If you are willing to grasp Kingdom culture, you are about to experience the dawning of a new day.

Mark Hall of the Christian music group Casting Crowns and Matthew West wrote the song "Thrive" in 2013. In that song, they share these words:

> We know we were made for so much more than ordinary lives.
> It's time for us to more than just survive—we were made to thrive.[24]

LOOKING AHEAD

Chapter two presents what, for many, is a breakthrough thought: Your spiritual health fits God's view of church more than your efforts. If all you do is weighed against who you become, your spiritual health is the most important element in Kingdom culture.

Chapter three expands on this theme. The Kingdom of God is not about what you do but about who you are and who you become. Much of Christianity is focused on what you do. Churches are piled high with programs. Christians strongly committed to their church and God's Kingdom are most often on the brink of burnout. The subtle implication is: The harder you work, the more your church will grow. This is mission-directed works righteousness.

Chapter four explores the unlikely, counterintuitive, unnatural approach Jesus used to launch the most successful movement in history. Jesus focused most of His attention on developing Kingdom DNA in a small group of people. As strange as this feels to human beings, the development of Kingdom culture works. Most active Christians have heard the stories beginning with the words, "The Kingdom of God is like…" yet many have not embraced this culture.

Chapters five through eleven focus on seven strategies that remove Kingdom culture drift. These issues have been identified through forty years of consulting almost two thousand churches. These challenges act as ceilings to the health, vitality, and growth of Christians, their churches, and the Christian movement. These Kingdom culture issues are not on the radar for many Christians or their church leaders. You will discover that these ceilings sound familiar. If you know much about the Bible, you will recognize their power to derail the effectiveness of anyone who is serious about Jesus' Great Commission to make disciples. You will even wonder, "Why do we do what we do? How did we get here?" Breaking through these ceilings will liberate you and your church to join Jesus in His Kingdom work. Spiritual breakthrough allows Christians to impact their world.

Chapter twelve shows how to change your lifestyle and your church. It will speak about breakthrough through change, the way Jesus intended. It is the movement approach. It is at the heart of every revival in history. It is how God moves! He wants to move in you and in your church!

CHAPTER TWO

Health Wins

It [the Kingdom of God] is a Kingdom of obedience to God's will as made known by Jesus, a Kingdom where God is truly made known, accepted as Lord, and obeyed.

—Floyd V. Filson[1]

For four decades, Church Doctor Ministries has been singularly focused on helping Christians become more effective, "to disciple people in all nations."[2] As a ministry, we were formed on the presupposition that for Christians, Jesus' last commission should be our first concern.

What we have learned comes from a long journey of working with hundreds of churches in North America. We have also taught church leaders on six continents, equipping them to be more effective for growing God's Kingdom. This has often placed us in the environment of major revivals. Our definition of a revival is "such exponential expansion of new believers that it is *humanly* unexplainable—impossible to point to any cause-and-effect program or strategic approach." The exponential growth of the Kingdom and rapid multiplication of churches is undeniably a move of God. As we've taught these Christians on several continents, we have also learned. We've experienced spiritual health. We have begun to see the power of Kingdom culture.

While the spark of revival is undeniably the work of the Holy Spirit, there is a definite and fertile *climate* among Christians. The best way to describe it is *spiritual health.* When the spiritual health of God's people is strong, God moves through His people less hindered. Roadblocks or ceilings dissolve. From the human perspective, we have concluded that for Great Commission effectiveness, nothing beats healthy churches. This implies spiritually healthy people. We have also come to understand that this health is directly connected to a culture. It is an

> While the spark of revival is undeniably the work of the Holy Spirit, there is a definite and fertile *climate* among Christians.

issue of who we are, spiritually. It is the culture of Jesus, the King of the universe. It is the culture Jesus taught when He spoke about the Kingdom of God. It is the atmosphere for harvest.

Church Doctor Ministries consults churches looking for help. In the process, we have participated in one-on-one personal and confidential interviews with 5,500 Christians. We have gathered data from 75,000 anonymous surveys analyzing various areas of spiritual DNA. The result includes great insights into how Christians think about their churches, representing sixty-five denominations, fellowships, nondenominational churches, and associations. In 2006, we began to learn something new. We began to see spiritual breakthrough signs we had not seen before in North America. We began to hear Christians share their holy discontent. Increasingly, some of these interviews demonstrated a spiritual restlessness. A common thread among those who shared their feelings included, "I just can't shake the feeling. I love my church. I'm a loyal member. I'm not considering another church. I'm here to stay. But I just can't stop thinking that our church should be reaching more people."

Meanwhile, we began looking at God's movement anywhere in the world from the perspective of the men of Issachar. In 1 Chronicles 12:32, the Bible says, "...Issachar men had understanding of the times to know what Israel ought to do."[3] We call this observational approach "God watching." We began to look for where God is blessing and moving. Our journey led us to what God is doing among some Christians in England. We have been particularly fascinated with the recent history of St. Thomas Crookes in Sheffield, led by Mick Woodhead.

The Sheffield congregation caught our attention for several reasons. It is a good case study for the following reasons: (1) It is an older church. (2) The facilities were worn, and the building looked ancient. (They have since renovated and added new facilities.) (3) The church declined in membership through an organized split with the purpose of planting a new congregation in a different area of Sheffield. (4) The church was left as a shadow of its former self, with most of the top givers, key leaders, and almost all of the younger people leaving for the new church plant. This profile of fewer members, limited finances, and almost no younger people resonates well with many plateaued or declining churches in North America.

Today, STC (as they call it) reflects what God is doing among many churches around England. God has changed this church from decline into a strong, healthy, and growing congregation, with many enthusiastic young adults. STC is an excellent model of how God develops spiritual health and vitality leading to effective disciple-making. We take groups of Christians to England each year. Why? Kingdom atmosphere—culture—is caught more easily than taught. Like any revival, it is contagious. It is a Jesus epidemic.

We have learned much from Mick Woodhead and his staff team, as well as others who are spiritually thriving in the movement occurring in England. We have studied closely the work of Holy Trinity Brompton in London, under the senior leadership of Nicky Gumbel. Nicky expanded and made popular the Alpha course, an outreach tool for inquiring unbelievers used throughout the world. Alpha has become a vehicle to reach tens of millions of people. We have grown from those who lead Worship Central, the worship and music arm of Holy Trinity Brompton. (Worship Central has now moved to Birmingham, England.) We have gained insights from what Holy Trinity calls "desperation church planting." The Vineyard Movement also has a church planting effort in London. Overseas, Holy Trinity Brompton multiplied a new church plant in Kuala Lumpur, Malaysia, a technically Muslim country. This church plant grew from twenty-five to five hundred in worship in six months! Contagious Christians almost anywhere can transplant the contagious spirit of health.

We have also grown in our understanding of how God works

through our relationship with the Message Trust in Manchester, England, led by Andy Hawthorne. This ministry has been able to reach the "least and the lost" in difficult inner-city environments. Manchester, the site of the Industrial Revolution, has suffered from urban disintegration for decades. The incredible work of God through the Message Trust has been a fascinating learning experience. We have been inspired by the work of Anthony Delaney, leader of the Ivy Church in Manchester. This church has developed organic leadership and spontaneous multiplication of church starts, transforming the Ivy Church into a network of congregations. The Ivy Church demonstrates strong focus on making disciples throughout the Manchester area.

Another contribution to our breakthrough understanding of how God is working in the twenty-first century comes from our relationship with Peter Brierley, leader of Brierley Consultancy in Kent, England.[4] Peter has worked as a diagnostician for the Lausanne Movement for world evangelization, founded by Billy Graham. Peter has worked extensively on the cause-and-effect growth of the Kingdom throughout the world. All of this exposure has helped us in our growth and understanding of church health and vitality.

WHY ENGLAND?

Have you visited the beautiful cathedrals of Europe? They are marvelous. Clearly, at some time in history, people were greatly excited about Christianity. They built amazing places for worship. Today, these symbols of faith are primarily tourist attractions. On Sunday mornings, you might see a handful of elderly people faithful in worship. Most often, the crowd consists of tourists with cameras. The European cathedral, as a symbol of Christianity, has become a relic of history. Decades ago, we conducted research on the streets of Paris, Cologne, Brussels, and London. We positioned ourselves within view of a cathedral. We watched for twentysomethings who would know English.

"Hello." They were attracted to our American accent. "Can you tell me, what is that big building over there? What happens there?" The responses were similar almost everywhere. You might call it "irrelevant laughter." "That's a church. A few old people go there, but for us, it means nothing. It is a place for tourists."

"Does church have anything meaningful to say for your life?" we asked.

"Are you kidding? The church has no impact on our society at all. It is just something from the past."

Christianity can flourish, and it can wane. It can also disappear. In AD 400, one of the strongholds of Christianity was a northern African city by the name of Hippo. The bishop of that city, Augustine, became well known. St. Augustine wrote two historically influential books, *The City of God* and *Confessions*. Hippo was a flourishing area of Christianity with influence over the entire Mediterranean Christian movement. Today, that area of Africa is almost 100 percent Muslim. Times can change spirituality!

Today, hot spots of spiritual resurgence are occurring in many places around Europe. We focus on England because the culture is somewhat similar to North American culture. They speak a brand of English, like most North Americans. Their churches have flourished, then waned, and now there are a growing number of congregations in a variety of movements experiencing vitality.

North American Christians are experiencing a landslide of secularization. Many churches are spiritually anemic. Entire denominational movements are sounding alarms. God is getting our attention. England is a valuable classroom to get a snapshot of hope and a glimpse of how God works to turn around aging, plateaued, and declining churches.

North America, in the spiritual cycle, often follows behind Europe in general and England in particular. Canada is about ten to fifteen years behind England. The United States is about twenty years behind England in the spiritual trend. Following several indicators of secularization, the symbols of downturn in North America occur in much the same way as in England, but several years later.

The early signs of awakening are visible. We define an *awakening* as a "spiritual wake-up call" among Christians. An awakening in churches often precedes a revival in the land. The ability to forecast how God might be moving gives Christians a window of opportunity to prepare. Every year, since our first visit to England, Church Doctor Ministries has taken Christians to England so they can *experience* a classroom of God's possible future activity here in North America. We believe it is time for churches to get ready for what God may be doing next. Are you ready?

How? How do you get ready? The response is surprising, counterintuitive, and for most, outside their historical worldview. By nature, we human beings want to **do** something. It is, literally, a leap of faith to discover that it is more about **being** and **becoming**. Do you want to be used by God? Would you like to help bring about a spiritual move of God, as God moves through you? It's all about becoming spiritually healthy. Healthy Christians make healthy churches. Healthy churches thrive! Church health comes from recapturing Kingdom culture—the culture of King Jesus. It is not a program. It is a spiritual environment, a way of life. It is the air you breathe.

A UNIQUE COLLABORATION

In 2007, we began to field-test the concept of health and vitality as a key ingredient for effective disciple-making and growth of the church. We connected with Thrivent, a unique Fortune 500 company dealing in financial instruments such as insurance and wealth management. Thrivent is the only Fortune 500 company designed as a fraternal organization.[5] They are a company

> By nature, we human beings want to **do** something. It is, literally, a leap of faith to discover that it is more about **being** and **becoming**.

of Christians, and they give back financially to churches, ministries, and communities.

In 2007, we made a proposal for a grant from the Thrivent Foundation. In the process, Thrivent leaders insisted we develop metrics—measurements of churches making progress toward health and vitality. In the consultation ministry at Church Doctor, we have used diagnostic tools for years. We use anonymous surveys to collect data on the churches we serve. The information we gather includes (1) demographics (who attends, what age, educational background, etc.), (2) attitudes, and (3) activities.[6] The idea of measuring results of our work with churches, however, seemed to be challenging and, at first, to be *unbiblical*. I challenged the leaders of Thrivent: "You can't measure the faith in a person's heart." They continued to press until we realized that there is something measurable—the fruit of faith.

Oswald Chambers wrote in his classic *My Utmost for His Highest*, "The bearing of fruit is always shown in Scripture to be the visible result of an intimate relationship with Jesus."[7] This, for us, was a significant breakthrough. Think about it: How many ministries actually measure the results of what they do? We began to measure the spiritual fruit among those in congregations served by Church Doctor Ministries. We asked everyone in the churches to complete anonymous surveys before our work began. We then measured the same elements six months later. Some of the results will be referenced in this book. A snapshot of "core categories" of spiritual fruit is located in Appendix II.

This challenge by Thrivent resulted in a breakthrough. We field-tested our work with numerous churches located across the United States. They reflected various denominations, as well as several independent churches. They were congregations of all sizes, in a variety of settings—urban, suburban, and rural. This field testing has continued for ten years and will continue in the future. The results demonstrated a reality that challenges most Christians. *Increased mission and ministry results are not attached to a program. Results are tied to individual spiritual growth of Christians in the church.*

It takes time to grow an apple tree. Spiritual fruit comes from spiritual growth. It takes more time than most church leaders invest in the spiritual development of congregants. It takes more time than most individuals invest in themselves. It takes time to develop the culture of Jesus' Kingdom among Christians, and there are no shortcuts. A healthy apple tree must mature before it bears fruit.

IT'S NOT ABOUT GIMMICKS AND GADGETS

Jesus spoke harvest language. Some talk about programs. Others look for a quick fix and slap on a bandage. Many tend to act like the church is an organization. Jesus calls it a living organism. It is quite complex.

My friend Walt Kallestad recently shared with me a parable that describes this challenge:

> Organisms are to organizations what a horse is to the cart. Many churches "put the cart before the horse," building facilities and programs....It's not the cart that will get things moving—it's the horse that provides the power to move the cart. We need to feed and care for the horse, but instead our energy goes into the cart, so the horse ends up too weak to pull the cart....Even a healthy horse will weaken and die if it is not properly cared for and nourished. Granted, a cart is much easier to take care of. We can paint it, decorate it in any way we want, show it off to our friends. Horses sometimes wander off on their own and don't always respond like we want. So that's why so many leaders in the church choose to build carts and ignore the horses. Maybe the question we need to ask ourselves is, "What good is the cart when the horse is dead?"

Is your church a cart before the horse, a cart that is becoming an empty, or almost empty, storage container? Is it useless? Christian leaders focus on getting people involved. This reflects a bias toward doing something, not being someone. This is a radical game-changer for the local church. It takes faith to believe that if Christians become more like citizens of the Kingdom, it will further the cause of Christ more than all the other efforts and all the programs.

Think about it. Many of those involved in churches are on the brink of burnout, and many of those churches are declining. Many have little spiritual impact on their communities. What is the response? Get more people busy in the work of the church. It is a huge leap of faith to say, "Stop most of the doing. Let's focus on spiritual growth and spiritual health. Let's identify where our church has drifted into secular values, nonbiblical beliefs, worldly attitudes, human priorities, and detrimental worldviews. Let's focus on realigning with the culture of the King and the Kingdom culture of Jesus."

In his book *Winning on Purpose*, John Edmund Kaiser writes, "Faithfulness is not complete without fruitfulness."[8] Growth in faithfulness produces growth in fruit—results. "But," you say, "I... we in our church...*are* faithful to Jesus. We believe in Jesus wholeheartedly for salvation. He is the only way to heaven." Yes, that is an important part of faithfulness. What about fruitfulness? Can you grow that? The answer is "Yes, you can!" How? By growing in faithfulness to Kingdom culture!

In the following chapters, you will discover just how far most churches and most Christians have drifted from Kingdom culture. You will learn how, through Kingdom culture, God produces Kingdom results. He does this by working through people like you. Making disciples is an inside job, long before it becomes an outside reality. The growth of your church begins with Kingdom growth on the inside of each member, inside of you. This is the climate, the atmosphere, for an abundant harvest. This is how churches thrive.

KINGDOM DNA

Look at Scripture from the perspective of spiritual health. Focus on the teaching of Jesus. See how often His teaching begins with, "The Kingdom of God is like..." Most Christians have read this. It is frequently taught and preached. However, few churches live it, as you will discover. When they do, it makes all the difference. That is why Jesus focused on Kingdom culture. That was His investment in His disciples. That was the power behind the beginning of the Christian movement. It is the air you breathe. It shapes everything you do because it directs and reflects who you are.

This may be a new focus for you. It was for me, too. I was attracted to the Church Growth Movement early in my career. It has been my passion to reach lost people for Jesus Christ. I became the pastor of a church struggling to reach those who were not yet Christ-followers in our community. I resonated with Church Growth leaders. Why? They were focused on making disciples!

Church Growth principles—principles of mission strategy— empowered those in the churches I served in Detroit and later in northeast Indiana. How did Church Growth thinking help? It was not through programs. Church growth is not about gimmicks and gadgets. Both of these churches grew substantially. However, they grew through the slow, patient, consistent building of Kingdom culture. They grew by breathing Kingdom atmosphere.

The value of church health is a breakthrough revolution. The concept of building Kingdom culture into the lives of others is a transformational experience. It changes everything. It changes people. It changes churches. Those churches influence their communities and change society. Kingdom culture will change you. You will then be used by God to change the world. Doesn't that make sense?

> The concept of building Kingdom culture into the lives of others is a transformational experience. It changes everything.

Do you remember? The Scripture calls the community of believers (the church) the body of Christ. It is a living organism, like your human body. Think of your church, and consider some of the realities of medicine. My friend Paul Stratton reminded me that some issues could be on the outside, or topical. However, life-threatening issues, like cancer, must be treated on the inside, or systemically. If you can grasp that many churches, as well as some whole societies, are "life-threatened," you will benefit more from this book. Jesus said His Kingdom brings life, and you may "have it abundantly."[9] This is a life-or-death matter, in the spiritual sense.

The genius leader Jesus started this movement. There is no question about it; Jesus is the Son of God. Jesus is the Savior of the world. Most Christians get that. What many don't appreciate enough is that Jesus was a genius about developing a movement. How would you start a movement like Christianity?

As we read the Gospels, we recognize familiar stories. Some of us have heard them from childhood. Yet, many have missed the movement meaning. How do you move the Christian movement? How did Jesus move the movement? Jesus invested most of His ministry effort into cultivating Kingdom culture. He did this through teaching, "The Kingdom of God is like…" This meant, repeatedly, "The Kingdom of God is not like the world around you." Jesus taught it, but He also demonstrated it. Further, He empowered His followers to practice it. They got it. They did it. The New Testament church exploded with growth. Today, many have forgotten it. Paul Pierson in his book *The Dynamics of Christian Mission* states: "We never see significant mission breakthroughs, new mission movements, without renewal."[10]

When people get it, the movement moves, still today. The result is the greatest, longest-lasting movement on the planet. According to David Bryant in his book *The Hope at Hand*, the church today is eighty-three million times larger than when it first began.[11] The outward movement of the gospel is the largest continually sustained endeavor in the history of humankind. This Kingdom DNA works miracles through people who get it.

In the human body, DNA uniquely shapes the organism. John Medina is a genetic engineer at the University of Washington. He reports that 1.8 meters of DNA are folded into each cell nucleus. It is like putting thirty miles of fishing line into a cherry pit! To write out the information in one cell would take 300 volumes, each 500 pages thick. The DNA in one person, if stretched out, would circle the sun 260 times.

This is the incredible power of DNA. If an adult rides a bike for one hour at ten miles per hour, it uses the amount of energy contained in three ounces of carbohydrate. If a car were this efficient with gasoline, it would get nine hundred miles to the gallon! This is the power of Kingdom DNA in the Christian movement and in the local church. Kingdom DNA fuels the Christian movement. This is why Jesus poured His life into a few for so long. He focused on Kingdom culture, expecting enormous results. We should do the same. This is the key to the Christian movement in your church. Do I have your attention? Can Jesus get your attention?

It is not about another program. It is about a holy infusion, an other-worldly operating system. It produces a holy infection that begins a Jesus epidemic. The teaching of epidemiology should be required for every Christian. Christianity does not spread through sermons, Bible classes, programs, and activities. It spreads relationally, through contagious Christians—carriers of Kingdom DNA. It determines who they are and when they interact with everyone else. The sermons, Bible classes, programs, and activities for spiritual growth nurture the journey. Nevertheless, the growth of the movement is when one follower of Jesus with holy infection infects another. It happens through relationships. It occurs when you are up close and personal with other people. This is the way the movement moves.

> It is not about another program. It is about a holy infusion, an otherworldly operating system.

Jesus, the Savior of the world and genius of the movement mentality, designed an approach that, literally, could touch everyone in the world. That's the point about "making disciples of all nations"[12] and being witnesses "to the ends of the earth."[13] What did you think, that Jesus would promote an impossible cause? The centerpiece of Jesus' movement is the dynamic of geometric progression. Think of this explosive growth as the dynamic of compound interest.

When Kingdom DNA is unleashed, a church begins to experience exponential explosion. This is not growth by addition. The Kingdom emphasis is on geometric progression—a movement to reach the world. When geometric progression occurs, it is called a revival. If you have never experienced a revival, I understand. This exponential growth may be foreign to you. If you have experienced a revival, as I have, this will begin to make sense.

> When Kingdom DNA is unleashed, a church begins to experience exponential explosion....The Kingdom emphasis is on geometric progression—a movement to reach the world.

This type of growth moves through a transformational stage.

Malcolm Gladwell calls it a "tipping point." Gladwell provides a graphic example. This ought to get your mission juices going: "I give you a large piece of paper, and I ask you to fold it over once, and then take that folded paper and fold it over again, and then again, and again, until you have refolded the original paper fifty times. How tall do you think the final stack is going to be?...As thick as a phone book or...as tall as a refrigerator? The real answer is that the height of the stack would approximate the distance to the sun. And if you folded it over one more time, the stack would be as high as the distance to the sun and back."[14]

Think about your own church. Think about so many churches. We are fixated on bringing someone to church. This attractional model makes the organization the agent of impact. That may be the culture of the local movie theater or your favorite restaurant. It is not the intended culture of your church.

The local church is a holy infectious center. Christians get spiritually reinfected every seven days. It is also the source for strategy: Every seven days, you learn how to get better at infecting others. It is the environment to catch Kingdom culture. You are equipped to grow infectious DNA in those you are discipling.

Christians in a church are not merely students of the Bible. They are not simply an audience for the preacher. They are not just a fund-raising team for the institution. Christians are carriers of the holy infection to their social networks. This is how geometric progression increases, not by adding more staff.

How do you define the primary mission field of your church? The boundaries of your city? A geographic circle of five miles around your church facility on a map? Kingdom culture redefines your primary mission field. It is the sum total of the unchurched people in the social networks of everyone in your church. Ask those in your church to list them, and then count them. You will be surprised and amazed at the size of this huge mission field. It is only one relationship away. This is your *primary harvest* field. It is where you find the "low-hanging fruit," the closest harvest. This works in a church with Kingdom DNA. Healthy churches thrive!

KINGDOM CULTURE DRIFT

Why does this seem so radically different from the culture of so many Christians? It is not a deliberate, massive shift. Kingdom culture drift is a condition challenging every believer from the very beginning. It is not as if Christ-followers say, "We will ignore the culture of the Kingdom." It is more subtle. It is like being in a boat and the current slowly moves you toward the rocks. We live in a secular stream. The current is strong. Guess what? It has always been strong. Look at what the apostle wrote in 1 Peter 4:1: "Since Jesus went through everything you're going through and more, *learn to think like Him*. Think of your sufferings as a weaning from that old sinful habit of always expecting to get your own way. Then you'll be able to live out your days free to pursue what God wants instead of being tyrannized by what you want."[15] Have you ever visited Animal Kingdom at Walt Disney World? One of the central features is the Tree of Life. It is beautiful from a distance. When you get up close, you discover it is lifeless. It is a fake! There is no way that tree could produce fruit. How ironic that it is called the "Tree of Life"!

How ironic that we call our gatherings "the church" but there is so little fruit. Many churches are unproductive at making disciples. Scripture reads, "Every tree that does not produce good fruit will be cut down and thrown into the fire."[16]

Robert Heidler, contributing to the book *Freedom from the Religious Spirit* by C. Peter Wagner, writes: "The Pharisees looked good. Their lives were the outward picture of perfection, but Jesus saw them as whitewashed tombs—beautiful on the outside, but dead on the inside (see Matthew 23:27)....There are two ways to get an apple tree: One comes from human effort. The other grows from an inner principle of life. But only one is real."[17]

You can be spiritual, or you can be religious. Being religious is like saying you can build your own apple tree. It's all about doing—doing the right things, saying the right words, following the right rituals, and having the right look. These are what might be called the smart elements of Christianity. They are programmatic: They can be programmed. Health—spiritual health—is a very different matter. Spiritual health develops from Kingdom culture and is driven by spiritual DNA. This is the centerpiece of the movement started by Jesus Christ.

Kingdom culture is countercultural to secular culture. Jesus made it clear, "My Kingdom is not from this world."[18] In John 8, some Jewish authorities were confused about Jesus' teaching. He was speaking about His connection with His Father and the upcoming crucifixion. Jesus responded in verse 23: "He said to them, 'You are from below; I am from above. You are of this world; I am not of this world.' "[19] The Message version reads: "You're tied down to the mundane; I'm in touch with what is beyond your horizons. You live in terms of what you see and touch. I'm living on other terms. I told you that you were missing God in all this. You're at a dead end."[20] This was hard for religious people to hear. It still is!

As church consultants, we see this in many congregations. Some try to operate from a worldly culture. They seem unclear about this very different Kingdom culture. They try to operate the church *religiously*. They are believers, but they use worldly strategies. The church becomes ineffective, especially in the dimension of mission. It is miraculous that He who is not of this world leads the church. It is disastrous that many are not following. As you align with Him and His Kingdom culture, you become unhindered by worldly approaches that roadblock spiritual health and diminish impact on our world.

Are you caught in a religious rut, in a church that unknowingly operates contrary to Scripture? Many churches nominate and elect anyone willing to serve to a position of leadership. They also look for volunteers, which is a completely secular notion. Consequently, some are spiritually unqualified for a position of influence. This causes havoc in many churches. (You will read more about this in chapters six and eleven.)

Titus was a young leader serving those in Crete, a people group known for their rowdy behavior. In his letter to Titus, Paul instructs him to choose the right people for leadership. Paul's instructions represent a guide to choose people who reflect Kingdom culture—the values, beliefs, attitudes, priorities, and worldviews Jesus taught and modeled. When Jesus declared, "My Kingdom is not of this world," this was not intended to be casual information. This is transformational. As a Christian, you operate differently. As a church, you are a community far different than this world. Does that sound like your church?

Secular culture constantly seeps into the church. Every church, every day, experiences Kingdom culture leak. Every Christian, every day, is bombarded by secular values, beliefs, attitudes, priorities, and worldviews. You are in a cosmic battle of eternal proportions. This makes or breaks your effectiveness for mission. This propels or stalls your church.

In the New Testament, several letters are written to different Christian communities. Read them closely and you will discover that these Christians, even in the early days of the movement, were challenged by Kingdom drift. Read these letters through this lens, and you will see the apostles doing what apostles are called to do: Bring believers back from secular drift so their churches return to effective disciple-making.

SMART AND HEALTHY

As we have worked to develop ways to help churches thrive, we have identified a unique approach, which is: What matters most is spiritual health.[21] If Christians are spiritually healthy, they will figure out whatever other challenges they face. By 2012, we already had put this effort into practice in several churches and began seeing results. In that same year, business consultant Patrick Lencioni published the best-selling book *The Advantage: Why Organizational Health Trumps Everything Else in Business.*[22]

Though Lencioni is a great Christian thinker, his book, as the title reflects, is primarily focused on the business world. However, *The Advantage* independently affirmed what we were rediscovering about the church. Lencioni is right—*health beats smart*. Jesus is right—equipping His disciples in Kingdom culture works. It still works. Most church leaders are fixated on symptom solving with programs. It is a spiritual leap to move to the causative level. Honestly? If you aren't convinced, don't even try.

> It takes a spiritual leap to move to the causative level. Honestly? If you aren't convinced, don't even try.

Your church can have great preaching, excellent leadership, a good location, wonderful facilities, and a knock-your-socks-off worship service, and it still can fall short of the potential for spiritual impact. Your church can have the newest, latest, and greatest programs and still never experience the transformational change that makes disciples for Jesus Christ. A great move of God—one that significantly affects people, communities, and nations—is not a quick fix. It is foundationally spiritual. If God cannot fundamentally change you, He will not change your church.

One pastor recently shared with me, "We've had twenty new programs, one every year for the last twenty years. I'm known as 'the program pastor.' However, our church is essentially no different than it was twenty years ago." What happens when Christians, like you, work so hard but your church does not improve or experience transformation? It drains the hope right out of you!

As a Christian, what is your vision? Are you praying for a move of God? Are you praying for a revival? Are you praying that God will move and change the nation, starting with your community? Are you focused on spiritual transformation? These are Kingdom-sized questions, and they lead to Kingdom-sized visions. It is not about being power-driven or success-hungry. This is about being Kingdom-driven. This is about being impact-hungry.

If you are focused on programs—what you do—you will never experience a healthy, thriving faith. If you are focused on Kingdom culture health—on who you are, and who you become—you will eventually figure out the rest.

This book is dedicated to the resolve that churches can, by God's grace, in God's way, be turned around. *Turnaround*, in

Scripture and in Kingdom culture, is translated as *repentance*. As a turnaround Christian, you recognize it is not about turning your church around. It is all about you and others turning toward God. It is about your church becoming the atmosphere of the Kingdom. You can, by God's power, grow in the values, beliefs, attitudes, priorities, and worldviews of the Kingdom. God can use you and your church to change this world, one life at a time. It is the air you breathe. Healthy churches thrive!

CHAPTER THREE

Outreach—An Inside Job

If the church does not disciple the nation, the nation will disciple the church.

—Darrow Miller[1]

"Can I ask you something?" Linda asked, as they pulled out of the parking lot.

"Of course," Terry replied. "What's on your mind?"

"Well, I was wondering…how does this church…I don't know…why does it feel so alive?"

In her mind, Linda was comparing North Bridge Community to their church at home. Terry and Linda had been visiting their daughter and son-in-law in the northern suburb of Indianapolis.

"I don't know," answered Terry, as he began the comparison with their church in Amherst. "It does…I mean, it really feels different, doesn't it?"

The silence continued for a while as both wondered how a worship experience could be so different in two Christian churches.

Terry is on the church council at his home church. He has been active in the congregation for years. Some years ago, he was congregational president. First Church of Amherst is the only church experience he'd ever known until their daughter Grace married Ed and moved to Indianapolis.

Linda broke the silence. "There are so many young people. Did you notice all the kids?"

"Yeah," Terry returned. "I'm impressed by...I don't know...how can I say it...people seem to be so enthusiastic."

"Joyful?" Linda added.

"Yeah, joyful...happy. You know, excited to be a part of the church," responded Terry.

Linda thought aloud: "Do you think it's because they are growing? I mean, the kids say that it's a growing area. I wonder if they're collecting Christians moving into that part of Indianapolis because..."

Terry jumped in. "But did you see in the worship folder, the number of people baptized last week? They must be reaching those who aren't Christians as well."

The silence continued for several minutes, but the comparison with their home church remained.

Terry finally broke the silence, asking the question neither one wanted to mention aloud: "Why is our church not like that?"

Peggy and Don were married at the church in Bakersfield. Their children attended the grade school sponsored by the church. During their fifteen years at the church, they'd had some serious frustrations. Because of budget cuts, the popular youth pastor was let go. Worship was okay, but generally uneventful. The median age was growing older. Attendance had flatlined. Baptisms were few; funerals were many. It was hard to tell, but it seemed the pastor was caught between frustration and disappointment.

Then, somehow, something began to change. The change was slow, so incremental it was hard to describe. Peggy and Don talked about it almost every week. They couldn't figure it out. As educated people, they felt odd saying worship "felt different." They couldn't put their finger on it. It's like the atmosphere began to change. It seemed contagious, with more joy and more excitement.

New people were coming to church. Where did they come from? How did they get there? Younger people were showing up, and some were bringing friends. How did that happen? Some adults were baptized. Their enthusiasm for faith was like fuel kindling fire, offering warmth and a glow in the church. These new Christians were enthusiastically sharing their faith with their friends, most of whom were not Christ-followers.

Some young adults joined the worship team. Many remarked how encouraging it was to see young people leading worship. Others in their small city noticed the church like never before. The word on the street spread: "That church seems to be where things are happening."

Prayer efforts increased. A few retired men started prayer walking through the community. Members prayed for some with sicknesses, and they were miraculously healed. Dr. Tom, a respected physician and active member, believed they were healed by God's power.

Peggy and Don wondered, "Where is this coming from? How is this happening?"

THE SPIRITUAL CYCLE

In the Old Testament, 1 and 2 Kings and 1 and 2 Chronicles record centuries of Israel's history. Honestly, reading through these books is not exciting. You've heard the phrase "History repeats itself." That is the spiritual history of Israel. It is a repetitive cycle of faithfulness, unfaithfulness, commitment to God, drift from God, better times, and worse times.

Spirituality tends to cycle. In brief, the cycle is faithfulness → drift → ignored prophets → civilization deteriorates → hopelessness → receptivity → repentance → faithfulness. The cycle begins with spiritual decline. A generation faithful to God is followed by a generation of drift from faith. People get busy doing life, raising kids, and working hard to obtain material possessions. Their worship wavers, and the downward spiral begins. The drift from God continues, and the relationship of spiritual influence becomes a distant memory. Faith becomes a tradition of lost value and an exercise with lost meaning.

The fabric of society begins to unravel. Crime increases. Family units disintegrate. The spiritual dimensions of life become distant. More laws are required. The internal compass of morality is in disrepair. The prophets of God call for a turnaround. "Repent! Turn back to God," they say. Many object to the intrusion of these "religious fanatics." They run the prophets out of town.

The quality of life continues to deteriorate. Morality weakens, and lawlessness flourishes. The level of lying, cheating, and stealing continues to grow. Life in general is corrupted and troubled. Civilization reaches the low point of spirituality. Secularization wins the day and imprints the culture. People become hopeless. Hopelessness signals the end of the downward cycle. This hopelessness is not the beginning of the end. It is the end of a new beginning—an opportunity for God's people.

The Spiritual Cycle

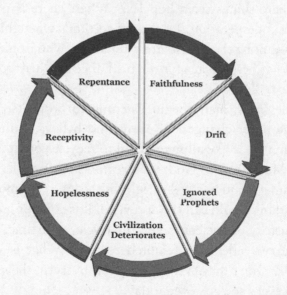

Does this sound familiar? Shift your mind from ancient Israel to today, where you live. Christians sense faith is losing ground. An objective snapshot of society reflects violence, civil unrest, corruption, and internal dry rot of society's institutions. These signposts declare the disintegration of civilization. Accurate or not, it feels like the world is filled with evil. Parents warn children about immoral people. They see neighbors whose lives are riddled with addiction, divorce, and disorder. Churches are empty; prisons are full. Hope is gone; the future looks bleak. Do you want to diagnose the people in your area? Ask those in your social network who are not believers, "What do you think life will be like for your grandchildren?" You will discover that most are chronically hopeless. Researchers call this an "age of pessimism."

The cycle continues. In desperation and hopelessness, many become spiritually receptive. Jim Cymbala notes,

> Charles Spurgeon once said that when a jeweler shows his best diamonds, he sets them against a black velvet backdrop. The contrast of the jewels against the dark velvet brings out the luster. In the same way, God does his most stunning work where things seem hopeless. Where there is pain, suffering, and desperation, Jesus is. And that's where his people belong—among those who are vulnerable, who think nobody cares. What better place for the brilliance of Christ to shine?[2]

In hopelessness, many begin listening to prophets. The prophets' message never changes: "Repent and believe,"[3] and return to God. Repentance is like allowing God to recycle you. It is a spiritual makeover. Many look to God. God restores His people. A common phrase in Israel could be, "All is right in the land." In modern times, some Christians would call this a revival. It is a major move of God.

In the history of ancient Israel, this cycle, over time, is repeated. Contemporary readers are tempted to say, "What is wrong with these people? Don't they ever get it?" Yet, in truth, the same cycle is repeated in every society, even today.

Think about Europe. At one time, it was the center of flourishing Christianity. From Europe came the Roman Catholic Church. Europe is the birthplace of the Protestant Reformation. Great cathedrals were built, representing a flourish of worship. Spirituality was at the heartbeat of culture. Much of the art and music were inspired by faith. Today, Christianity has little impact on many living in Europe. For much of the population, the faith is a distant cultural ritual.

Yet, today, there are rays of spiritual light in Europe. Here and there, in growing numbers, segments of society are experiencing a refreshing of faith. Some churches are experiencing an awakening—a spiritual wake-up call. This is not the first time since the Reformation the cycle has moved into spiritual daylight.

In the 1700s, God used John and Charles Wesley (and others) to lead an awakening in England. God used their instrumental work, along with others', in the American colonies as well. That time is the only time in American history called the Great Awakening.

This awakening occurred in many churches in colonial America and led to a revival—a resurrection of Christianity. An awakening occurs among Christians. They *wake up* to an activation of faith at new levels, recapturing the mission to make disciples. A revival occurs when God uses Christians for a major movement toward the faith. It grows so rapidly that it is humanly unexplainable. Someone said, "Revival is when God gets tired of being misrepresented and shows up to represent Himself."

John Wesley had a common theme for the Christian wake-up call. His message to Christians was to "get back to primitive Christianity." By this, he meant to get back to the basics of the faith and life of a Christian. In our journey at Church Doctor Ministries, before we learned about this dimension of Wesley's teaching, we began to call Christians to return to Kingdom culture. As we began teaching this, our friend Scott Pattison had just finished his breakthrough doctoral dissertation on Wesley's impact. When I read Scott's work, I was amazed to see the affirmation and the similarity to what we had been teaching church leaders. Wesley confirms that the return to biblical culture is the platform for Christian awakening. Revival follows.[4] We believe this could come to North America today.

We have observed a similar pattern in Europe, as I mentioned earlier. Many churches are experiencing an awakening. These churches had been declining for years. They are no longer sleeping; they are awake. God is moving!

It was a typical London day, cloudy and gray with light sprinkles. My wife Janet and I were on our way to the "Family Worship Service" at Holy Trinity Brompton, or as they call it, HTB. We made our way across London on the "tube" and walked the several blocks from the station to the church. We were early, but the mammoth, historic building was already nearly full of young people, many with children. By the time the service began, it was "standing room only." That huge church was packed! The large wraparound balcony was filled. In those days, a screen was awkwardly hung in a front corner, and the organ pipes stood silent. After a welcome and a video clip, the worship band led the service. When you see, touch, and feel God's awakening, it is an exhilarating experience. You can't help but wonder, "Could God do this in my church?"

What you see in worship at HTB is only a snapshot of their ministry. They have now planted numerous extension congregations. Check their website,[5] and you will find ten worship services each Sunday in different locations. In addition, this church has developed a music and worship school called Worship Central.[6] The songs being produced are increasingly used around the world.

HTB has developed a specialized ministry called "Desperation Church Planting." When a church has dwindled to a small group unable to pay the bills, they can invite a group from Holy Trinity Brompton to come in and "take over." The group, usually more than fifty people, brings the awakened DNA of Kingdom culture. (This is a key strategy and the main point of this book.) God infuses this culture into the remnant of the dying church. Holy Trinity provides leadership and a worship team. They remodel the worship space toward a contemporary feel. The atmosphere changes. The church begins to breathe new life with rekindled outreach to the community. HTB has transported several leaders with Kingdom culture to plant a church in Kuala Lumpur, Malaysia, as mentioned earlier. The outreach strategy, Alpha, is a mechanism birthed at HTB.[7] It is reaching millions around the world for Christ.

We take groups to England each year to experience this movement.

North Americans catch a spiritual breath of what God can do. The cycle has now begun to shift in England. We were told that in London, the percentage of Christians has declined for 150 years, until recently. Through the awakening of British churches, the cycle has reversed. Researcher Peter Brierley notes that the black churches are another major factor for the London turnaround. Immigrants from Africa lead these churches that are touched by awakening and revival cycles. These leaders have exported revived Kingdom culture from Africa.[8]

WHAT ABOUT NORTH AMERICA?

North America, as mentioned above, is about twenty years behind the spiritual cycle in Europe. That could make the timing for spiritual breakthrough sometime soon. Spiritual breakthrough is the work of God, who may or may not follow the same timing. We cannot tell God what to do or when to do it, yet our observations show God is already at work toward a breakthrough on the North American continent.

Most God watchers agree that North America, particularly Canada and the United States, has been on a cycle toward secularization for a while. Most church watchers would agree that the Christian movement is increasingly marginalized. Many North Americans feel distress, and many are disappointed in government, education, finance, and business. This leads to a sense of hopelessness. It has been said that you can survive six months without food. You can survive a few days without water. You can survive a few minutes without air. However, you can't survive a second without hope.

Many pastors feel stalled. They suffer from spiritual entropy. Their energy is sapped by dysfunctional systems. Many churches could be rebooted with biblical Kingdom culture. Sadly, a number of congregations have drifted into partial obsolescence. Some pastors are counting the days to retirement—a decade away! This is a symptom of hopelessness. Where there is no hope for the present, there is no faith in the future. Where there is no faith in the future, there is no power in the

- Where there is no hope for the present, there is no faith in the future.
- Where there is no faith in the future, there is no power in the present.

present. Churches try programs and remain stalled. The systemic issues will be addressed in the chapters that follow. Programs are not going to change churches. The issue is one of atmosphere— a return to Kingdom culture.

Breakthrough is closer than you think. When you "walk through the valley of the shadow of death,"[9] God gets your attention. Why? Because there is nothing else left to distract you. At a new level, you become receptive to getting reacquainted with the One who is head of His church. When things are at their worst, Christians are at their best. Alan Roxburgh and Fred Romanuk reflect on congregations reaching the bottom in their book *The Missional Leader: Equipping Your Church to Reach a Changing World*:

> The most important currency a congregation has to spend is hope. If it gets spent down, there isn't much of anything else left....People have tried programs and worked through schemes over and over again but have seen little substantive change. *This drains their hope*. Like their pastor, a congregation can lose hope and cease to believe that the Spirit of God is among them.[10]

Spiritual reconstruction becomes possible when you discover nothing else works. There is nothing left. This is when God acts and renews your hope. Your hope is in Christ. Swiss theologian Emil Brunner believed, "What oxygen is to the lungs, such is hope to the meaning of life."[11] Your hope in Christ brings power to rise above the disintegration of civilization as we know it.

This hope in Christ, if it is to carry you into an awakening in the future, is not a theological construct or a compartmentalized belief. If you take Christ at His word, you, by definition, accept Him as the head of His body, the church. If you accept Him as the head of the church, you subordinate the entire culture of your church to King-dom culture. You become open to every part of the culture of the King: values, beliefs, attitudes, priorities, and worldviews. This is likely more radical than you can imagine. The culture of Jesus is so radical it is transformational.

Now you are open to what God is doing. Now you have hope that matters. St. Augustine said, "Hope has two beautiful daughters. Their names are Anger and Courage—Anger at the way things are and Courage to see they do not remain that way."[12] This is hope that awakens. Now you are ready for the direction of the apostle Peter to "give an answer to everyone who asks you to give the reason for the hope that you have."[13] You can't share what you don't have. No Christian can.

Today there are flashpoints of awakening and revival in North America. These are likely the early signs of revival breaking out. They may not be apparent to most Christians, because most Christians have never been in the eye of the beautiful yet powerful storm of revival. You weren't alive for the Great Awakening and the revival that followed in the 1700s. Unless you have traveled outside the United States, it is likely you have never experienced God at work at a revival level.

For some Christians, the word *revival* is foreign. Sometimes it brings the mental picture of a wild tent meeting with a manipulative preacher twisting minds to produce converts. However, revival does not have to be a foreign concept. It doesn't necessarily reflect your uncomfortable feelings about misuses. I did not grow up with the word in my vocabulary, and I didn't have it introduced to me, not even once, at seminary. To "revive" is to "breathe life into." God can and does do this all the time. Call it what you like. Don't get caught up in semantics. God wants to refresh the atmosphere for you and your church. God wants to breathe new life into you and your church. God wants you to spiritually thrive.

At Church Doctor Ministries, we have, for years, trained pastors and church leaders caught in the exhilarating atmosphere of revival. Whatever you want to call it, in a great movement toward God, you

see the supernatural, spontaneous work of God. God produces exponential growth among those who are becoming Christians, at levels
and in ways humanly unexplain-
able. We have witnessed this in
several areas of Africa, in South
America, and in Europe. Today,
perhaps the largest and fastest-
growing expansion of Christianity
in history could be taking place in
the "underground" movement in
China. While the data is hard to obtain from a Communist country, phenomenal reports stream from China every month. If you ever
experience a revival, a major move of God, you will discover that faith
sees the invisible, believes the incredible, and receives the impossible.

> God wants to refresh the atmosphere for you and your church. God wants to breathe new life into you and your church. God wants you to spiritually thrive.

God is moving in North America. Are you ready? Are you in a
breakthrough environment? A breakthrough environment, according to John Maxwell, has three parts:

1. When you hurt enough, you have to change.
2. When you learn enough, you want to change.
3. When you receive enough, you are able to change.[14]

For several years as God watchers, we at Church Doctor Ministries have been eager to identify where God is moving in extraordinary ways. We have identified recent flashpoints of breakthrough
that are unique and not limited by geography or mode. We believe
these are the early signs of breakthrough for a major move of God in
North America. Here are a few:

1. Widespread hopelessness among those who are not yet
   Christ-followers
2. The growing number of Christian films, books, and television shows, representing a high level of interest among
   the general population in issues of faith from the Christian
   perspective

3. The explosion of Christian radio stations over the last few decades

4. The rise and proliferation of multisite churches using technology to multiply teaching, balanced with the personal touch of discipling

5. The increase of churches intentionally located in marketplace venues to intersect with the everyday life of those who are not yet believers

6. The growing number of churches effectively reaching young adults, and young adult discipling boot camps equipping young adults to reach their own generation[15]

7. The characteristics of the millennial generation representing millions who are primed for challenge, demand authenticity, are passionate to make a difference, and live as natural networkers

8. The "baby boomerang": spiritually lapsed baby boomers returning to church with a commitment to leave a meaningful legacy

9. New training alternatives, particularly the use of online learning, to prepare men and women for ministry, beyond the costly, long-term seminary and Bible school education programs

10. Congregations leaving bureaucratic denominations to affiliate with uncluttered networks focused on mission

11. Increasing outreach to nominal Muslim immigrants

12. The revolution in Christian contemporary music and Bibles translated into the heart language of target people groups

THE ROLE OF HOLY DISCONTENT

As mentioned above, before revival breaks out in the land, awakening occurs in churches. It will not become visible in every church, even though some awakeners are likely present. Awakening will be blocked in some congregations. The roadblocks are usually leaders who are unaware of the opportunity. Many churches sleep right through an awakening; others awaken suddenly. Leith Anderson tells this story: "One evening I was on the highway, very tired. I fell asleep, just for an instant. I woke up, and right before me was the front of a semi within ten feet. Startled, I swerved to the right, only to realize the semi was being pulled by a wrecker going uphill. I didn't have any trouble staying awake after that!"[16] You cannot sleep and drive. The church cannot ignore the action of God and go forward.

Denominational voices, other pastors, and leaders in your church may become critics out of ignorance, spiritual blindness, or jealousy. Some have never personally experienced an awakening. Perhaps you are one of them. Make sure you are *not* one of them. Become open to what God is doing—even if it feels like new and unfamiliar territory.

Several years ago, we consulted Kriengsak Chareonwongsak, the pastor of Hope of Bangkok Church in Thailand. Kriengsak is a brilliant leader who started an indigenous church. Musical instruments and songs reflected biblical content contextualized in the Thai culture. His church grew rapidly. It became a movement. They started planting extension churches throughout Thailand. Kriengsak came under severe attack. It didn't come from the government, the Buddhists, or the secularists. It came from evangelical missionaries who had transported a Western style of Christian practice to Thailand! The Hope of Bangkok has flourished in spite of some criticizing Christians. You can, too!

It is likely that seeds of awakening have already been planted in your church. These seeds are not programs or activities. They are people with holy discontent. We say they have spiritual restlessness. You may be one of them. (If you haven't yet taken the survey in Appendix I, do it now.) Those seeds may include friends you have known a long time. Those with holy discontent are Christians changed by the Holy Spirit. They know something is different. They don't always know what or why. How do we know about this? We discovered this in our consultation ministry. When our Church Doctors help a church, we learn a lot about the issues in the church before arriving on-site. Information is gathered through anonymous surveys and questionnaires. When we arrive, we interview individuals one-on-one for several days. These interviews are private and confidential. It is amazing what people will tell a professional outsider who promises anonymity!

In 2006, our Church Doctors began discovering something new and unusual. While we didn't know it then, we later realized that it was an important ingredient of the coming awakening and revival we had been predicting. We encountered those who were feeling restless for positive change. Before describing the profile of these "seeds," these unique people, let me clarify who they are *not*.

As you can guess, we often interview those we might call "malcontents." For trained consultants, they are easy to spot. They sometimes request an interview. They are not happy people. In so many words, malcontents often say, "If the church doesn't do it my way, I'm going to another church down the road." Many of these Christians have belonged to half a dozen churches during their lifespan. Every church has a few of these people. If you are a church leader, you would likely know them by name.

In 2006, we began meeting some people with a different version of discontent. They have a positive attitude about their church, and they love the pastor. They are loyal; they aren't leaving for another congregation. They generously support the church, and they are involved in ministries. Remember, before 2006, we didn't encounter these types of Christians. Those with holy discontent, or spiritual restlessness, desperately want their church to be more effective in reaching lost people. We began to realize God was up to something new. At first, there were only a few. Over the years, the numbers are growing in every church we serve. What do they look like?

Their reflections and interests are the same wherever you find them, in whatever church. Here is a typical conversation in a confidential interview:

"This is confidential, right? Okay. Well, I wouldn't want anyone to hear this. I love my church. I don't want to sound negative. My husband and I have just talked about this at home. We have not told anyone else. We both have this gnawing feeling we can't get rid of. Our pastor is great. Our church does so many things well. However, we have this ongoing frustration: Why doesn't our church reach more people? Why aren't we growing? Why isn't our worship service bursting at the seams? Why don't more young people come? It just doesn't make sense, and it frustrates the heck out of us. And we can't shake the feeling. However, like I said, we haven't told anyone. We are not complainers."

Our conclusion is that these Christians are the seeds of an awakening. The number of these believers is growing each year. They fear being misinterpreted. They don't want to be viewed as complainers. Consequently, no one knows who they are. They have no idea there are others just like them in their church.

The Stream of Revival

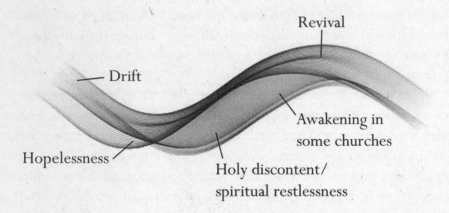

The movement toward revival begins with the work of the Holy Spirit among those with holy discontent, observed as spiritual restlessness. These are the early adopters or pioneers. If they are discovered, nurtured, and equipped to relationally influence others (when they are ready, allowing receptivity to rise), a church, by God's power, can experience an awakening—a wake-up call. In God's timing, this is followed by revival. God will use churches with critical mass, resulting in an awakening, for revival. Others will sleep through it, wondering why a neighboring church has "come alive," sometimes expressing jealousy or suspicion. In this scenario, awakened churches will grow more rapidly, and sleeping churches will decline with increased momentum. Why? Those with holy discontent will move to churches where they are encouraged and supported. The sleeping churches lose some of their most active members first, increasing the momentum of decline.

> The movement toward becoming a thriving church begins among those with holy discontent and spiritual restlessness.

As mentioned earlier, we believe that Christians with holy discontent are spiritual early adopters or pioneers. They can become the core, the beginning of a movement, raised by the Holy Spirit, to bring an awakening into their church. The movement toward becoming a thriving church begins among those with holy discontent and spiritual restlessness. They are gathered together and nurtured in Kingdom culture. They are encouraged to invite others who show receptivity. Those who respond join the movement. Christians with holy discontent and spiritual restlessness are God's greatest sign that an awakening could be coming to your church.

Are you a person with holy discontent? If you are reading this book because you *want* to, you may be one of God's seeds for your church. If you are reading this because you *have* to, or someone with holy discontent asked you, you *may become* a person of holy discontent! God may use you to change the atmosphere of your church toward Kingdom culture. You have in your hands powerful DNA based on the Word of God!

CORRECTING DRIFT

God uses pioneers and early adopters to make spiritual course corrections. Those with holy discontent and spiritual restlessness encourage realignment toward Kingdom culture. This concept is not new. Long before the New Testament era, secular leaders were challenged by drift. Emperors would conquer new lands and place the inhabitants under their rule. These rulers would set up their kingdom by establishing their own culture—their values, beliefs, attitudes, priorities, and worldviews. The challenge they faced is similar everywhere: New people drift from the king's culture.

From antiquity, kings have had ambassadors. These ambassadors were appointed to live among the people in various areas of the kingdom. In the New Testament, Pilate represented Rome as an ambassador.[17] Ambassadors were to represent the king who couldn't be everywhere at once. This has been an important part of civilization forever. Throughout history there have been those who were "special ambassadors" uniquely equipped in one specialty area: the king's culture. They were trained to know the values, beliefs, attitudes, priorities, and worldviews of the king. These special ambassadors were very important. The people in the kingdom would drift back into the culture that was prevalent before the new king, and the special ambassadors would focus on correcting this drift. These special ambassadors, long before the New Testament, were often called "apostles."

In the early church, those who knew the culture of King Jesus were also called "apostles." When you read the letters the apostles wrote to the churches in the New Testament, you will see they were constantly correcting Christians from Kingdom culture drift.

Why? *Kingdom drift diminishes Kingdom results.* Christians are always subject to drift; they always have been. In Jesus' Kingdom, cultural drift undermines the power and impact of Kingdom work. The effectiveness of your purpose, your mission as a Christian, is directly related to the culture of the Kingdom. This Kingdom culture is not like the culture of this world. However, you live in this world. As a Christian, you constantly need apostolic correction from Kingdom culture drift. We all do.

When you recapture Kingdom culture, God will use you as a vehicle to transform lives by His power. When you operate with Kingdom culture, your effectiveness for the Great Commission increases. When you influence those in your church for realignment of Kingdom culture, God uses you to change the atmosphere. Your church becomes healthy.

Kingdom culture increases Kingdom results.

Your church thrives. *Kingdom culture increases Kingdom results*. Ultimately, it begins with you and me. It is an inside job.

The following chapters describe the greatest challenges—and opportunities—for God to use you and those in your church to thrive, to prosper, and to produce a harvest. Warning: This is not an easy road to travel; it is just the best one. Jesus laid out the journey. The road map is the culture of King Jesus. The symbol is the cross. On the journey, Jesus calls you to carry only one thing: "Take up your cross, and follow me."[18] Follow the road map and you will never be the same. Encourage others to follow it and your church will never be the same. As you and other Christians follow it, this world will never be the same. It begins with you, but it never ends there.

CHAPTER FOUR

The Culture of the King

The...best way forward for most stagnant churches is to
reconstitute their understanding of their main business
and become "apostolic" (or "missional") congregations.
—George G. Hunter III[1]

Jesus really has not one but two interrelated missions. The first is to
take the judgment and penalty for the sins of everyone in the world.
He is uniquely qualified as the perfect God/Man. In Old Testament
fashion, He is the sacrificial Lamb whose blood seals forgiveness for
everyone. Whoever believes in Him will be saved.[2] The mission has
implications for eternity, and it also speaks to everyday life. This
Kingdom makes a better world: "Peace to all men and women on
earth who please him."[3] Jesus' second mission is to set in motion
a movement—the most impactful, longest-lasting, greatest life-
changing movement in history. This movement endures through
time, from one century to another, from one epoch to another. This
movement spans cultures: from the Tswana people of Southern
Africa to the Mayan people of Central America, the Maori people of
New Zealand and the Pacific Islands, converted Muslims in Indianapolis, and thousands more.

This movement perpetuates the spread of His Kingdom, in a world
where other kingdoms come and go, no matter how great. The Otto-
man Empire? The Roman Empire? Gone! The Kingdom of Jesus?
Alive and growing! This Kingdom not only survives persecution, it

thrives on persecution, in Communist China, Buddhist Myanmar, Hindu and Muslim India, and secularized Los Angeles.

WHAT WOULD YOU DO?

If you were chosen to engineer the greatest movement on the planet, what would you do? Where would you start? Would you raise funds through electronic crowd sourcing, or offer an IPO and sell stock? Would you build an organization with bylaws, boards, a hierarchical structure, annual meetings, and *Robert's Rules of Order*? Would you have an organizational chart on the wall? Would you follow a constitution or a bill of rights? Would it be for-profit to provide cash flow to sustain it? Would you use chili suppers to make money from outside customers, like a restaurant?

Since this movement is spiritual, would you begin by building a seminary, Bible college, or monastery? Would you launch your movement with a church building? Would you recruit an army? Train a sales force? Develop a marketing division? Start a publishing arm? Form a denomination? Get corporate?

Why does the human approach seem foreign to what Jesus developed? We like structure. We gravitate toward things. Human intuition for a movement is to go big and move fast. We judge success by size. A big crowd gets our attention. Size matters!

Recently, we were invited to teach a conference for church leaders in the Central American country of Belize. The topic was "discipleship." The local organizers decided the conference should be held on a Friday and Saturday. They knew most of the pastors in the country are bi-vocational. They thought most of them would be able to take Friday off work, but they were wrong. The venue was set for three hundred, but the crowd was closer to fifty. After a presentation by Steve, the missionary who organized the event, I was supposed to give the keynote teaching on discipleship. When I was finished, my clothes were soaking wet from exertion. Alex, a Hispanic pastor from Chicago, was there to interpret for those who spoke no English. After my session, Alex came to me privately and said, "Kent, how can you be so passionate and enthusiastic with such a small crowd?"

I confessed, "Alex, honestly, I used to be influenced by the size of the crowd, and my adrenaline would show it. But the more I've studied Kingdom culture, the less important the size of the audience has become. You never know the long-term impact. Of course, we always want greater impact. But God is in charge."

As it turned out, a pastor at the conference operates a Hispanic radio station in northern Belize. His station reaches a good portion of southern Mexico. He asked for a copy of my notes: "Can I have your permission to translate this and teach it on the radio?" "Absolutely," I said. The impact of the effort was growing already!

Three months later, Kenzie, who works on our staff and leads SEND North America, received an e-mail from Steve, the conference organizer. Steve said, "There is a young man, Jean, from Belize. He wants to participate in the SEND training in northeast Indiana. He is a gifted leader, very sharp. He wants to learn through SEND and return to Belize to reach many for Christ."

This is the nature of Kingdom culture. The impact is always more, not less. Why? Because God is behind it. God is at work. Jesus' approach for birthing His movement is not to go big and move fast. It is to move slow and go deep. To human beings, this approach does not come naturally. It comes supernaturally. It is counterintuitive that Jesus would invest most of His time and energy with a handful of disciples. This is so contrary to the world's way. Perhaps that is why so few Christians disciple others. "Focus on one or two people, for months...maybe years? I'd rather advertise widely and gather a crowd," my own human nature used to say.

Think about it. Most Christian parents don't consciously disciple their own children. Most pastors don't intentionally spend time discipling a small group of leaders. In larger churches, with both senior and associate pastors, rarely does one disciple the next to lead the church in the transition after the senior's retirement. Most ministry interns report their supervising pastor spends little or no time in the one-on-one, slow and deep process of discipling. Most seminary professors don't disciple students.

Jesus set the pattern: Focus on a few. He developed them way beyond training to do the job. He imprinted them with Kingdom culture. He infused divine DNA with the crowning power of Pentecost, the Holy Spirit. As Howard Hendricks said, "You can impress people from a distance but you can impact them only up close."[4]

> Jesus' approach for birthing His movement is not to go big and move fast. It is to move slow and go deep. To human beings, this approach does not come naturally. It comes supernaturally.

The miracle of the movement is not limited to one big crowd listening to one great speaker. This movement is every believer imprinting others, one person at a time. The disciples caught the Kingdom imprint. It wasn't simply what they were *trained* to do. It was who they *became*. Jesus didn't just train them in tasks. He changed the atmosphere. Once they became Kingdom healthy, they were ready for the challenges and opportunities life brings. Once they were Kingdom healthy, they would figure out the strategic stuff of life. With Kingdom focus, they could thrive in changing times, in various cultures, forever.

Consider this complex issue: The Gentiles wanted to be followers of Jesus the Messiah. They had a big challenge. From the Gentile perspective, the movement was primarily Jewish. Should the Gentile men be circumcised? Should the women learn to operate a kosher kitchen? "No, this is just programmatic stuff," the leaders decided in Acts 15.[5] How could they be so brilliant? They caught Kingdom culture. They had Kingdom health. They could differentiate between style and substance. They could change style and preserve substance. This Kingdom mission was not a program. Their DNA wasn't following a manual or a hymnal. It was who they were and who they became.

Think about that when you review the history of some well-meaning missionaries who spread out around the world in the colonial period. Consider how they carried their own cultural baggage: language, dress code, and ministry approach. Many of them inadvertently made their target group jump through cultural hoops to become Christians. This approach greatly restricts the movement and roadblocks progress. Think of all the foolishness involved in clinging to certain worship styles. Do you ever wonder why congregations have lost so many young people? Consider how some Christians cling to meaningless words, like *thou* and *thy*. You see, without Kingdom culture, you can easily confuse the packaging with the content. It is not what you do, but who you are and who you become.

The human tendency is a quick-fix program that "worked" somewhere else. Thom Rainer and Eric Geiger in their great book, *Simple Church*, make the distinction between programmers and designers:

> Simple church leaders are designers. They design opportunities for spiritual growth. Complex church leaders are programmers. They run ministry programs.
>
> Church leaders who are programmers focus on one program at a time. Their goal, though never stated, is to make each program the best. Church leaders who are designers are focused on the end result, the overall picture....
>
> The simple church leaders we surveyed were expert designers. They were not the producers of spiritual growth and church vitality. Only God is the producer of the growth.... These church leaders are expert builders (see 1 Cor. 3:10). They have skillfully designed an *environment* where life change is likely to occur. They have designed a simple process that moves people through the stages of spiritual growth.
>
> To have a simple church, you must design a simple discipleship process.[6]

Jesus didn't begin a program. He changed the environment. The atmosphere changes everything. Jesus started a movement. Does your life reflect this movement? Does your church resemble a movement, or a program, organization, or institution? Spiritual health and vitality begin by catching the movement. The movement begins to take over your human culture as you become a citizen of a different culture, the Kingdom of God. As you catch this Kingdom culture—which is not of this world[7]—you become more effective as a movement carrier. This is how Christianity grows in geometric progression. This is how churches grow. As strange as it feels, it really isn't what you do. It is who you are and who you become. Yes, you're going to hear that over and again. Why? This is what Jesus did. This is how He started the most impactful movement in world history.

Consider the impact of the Christian movement: twenty-one centuries and growing, with billions of followers encompassing hundreds of different cultures. It is truly an amazing experience to rub shoulders with Christians in various cultures. I think about the opportunities I have had to teach, preach, and worship with fellow Christians in an inner-city African American neighborhood in Detroit, a Hispanic church in Chicago, an Iranian congregation in Los Angeles, and the Church of All Nations (consisting of former Muslims) in Troy, Michigan. I think about the churches around the world where I have taught—in Russia, Japan, Thailand, the Philippines, the Amazon jungle of Brazil, South Korea, Myanmar, Honduras, the Zulu church in South Africa, the Kalahari Desert in Botswana, Kenya, Nigeria, Malaysia, England, India, Kazakhstan, New Zealand, and the Aborigine church in the outback of Australia. This Kingdom of God is like no other. When you hang out with Christians of various cultures, you are spiritually infected with a sense of family: a transcending connection that defies description. This is Kingdom culture, the Kingdom of God.

> This Kingdom is like no other. When you spend time with Christians of various cultures, you are infected with a sense of family: a transcending connection that defies description.

Consider the various ways the Kingdom impacts our world: orphanages, universities, hospitals, feeding the hungry, educating the masses, and improving the quality of life. Think of the millions of people who respond to the call to full-time service, with minimum earthly rewards. The King of this Kingdom has empowered hundreds of thousands of career missionaries to leave their own culture, to live in uncomfortable conditions and die thousands of miles away from their families. Think of the massive number of martyrs who endured unimaginable pain and suffering and gladly died for the King of this movement. This movement has penetrated entire countries, establishing a code of conduct that has influenced laws and systems of government. This movement has overthrown empires through the peaceful and powerful change of culture. The weapon of this movement is love! What Jesus said is powerful and true: "My Kingdom is not of this world."[8] That is for sure!

When Jesus left His followers, He said to those who were gathered, "As the Father has sent me, so I send you."[9] He implied, "In the same way I have lived the Kingdom culture, you now go and live the Kingdom culture. I also have a little job for you: Go out and win the whole world." Impossible? One hundred and fifty years later, the early church father Tertullian wrote, "Christians are everywhere."[10] In a dozen or so decades, this movement had infiltrated much of the Roman Empire.

RECAPTURING THE MOVEMENT

Most Christians realize that America has entered a deep chasm of secularization. The evidence is on every newscast, in our schools, among many of our neighbors. For decades, our team at Church Doctor Ministries has communicated that the United States is the third-largest mission field in the world. Only two countries have more self-declared non-Christians: China and India.

We are on a mission field, but we've never been trained to be missionaries. And the results show it. In a survey, we asked 75,000 people, "Did you become a Christian before you started attending this church or after?" This question reveals the effectiveness of their churches in reaching the largest group of people in the country: unbelievers. We also measured this over time, asking *when* they joined their present church.

Did You Become a Christian Before You Started Attending This Church or After?

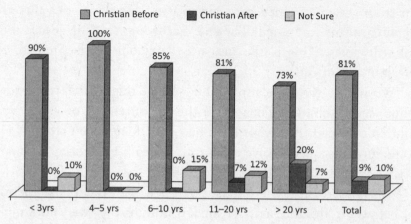

Notice that, as the country became more secular, the ability of churches to reach the unchurched has diminished. We are incompetent at reaching the lost. Most churches need a transformational change to recapture the movement.

Many church leaders are scrambling for better methods. If you want to be famous, get rich, and write a best-selling book, feed Christian consumers with a nuts-and-bolts strategy or a self-help quick fix. You will be a bright star, but not for long. You will become a shooting star. The quick fix is, well, quick—and then it's over. Popular writers use the latest jargon to introduce better methods. In the context of failing churches, Christians are eager to grasp new methods. God is not looking for better methods. He is looking for better people. God is looking for people who will recapture authentic Kingdom culture. You can't improve on Jesus' model for church health and vital Christianity: making disciples who make disciples. As a Christian, hopefully you understand. Some of this popular but misguided quick-fix stuff is normal. When you're part of a sinking ship, you focus on life "preservers"—we call it maintenance ministry.

All these programs and activities exhaust Christians, yet they are not focused on causative issues. They flirt with symptoms. Here is a parallel: Last year fifty thousand people went out to purchase a quarter-inch drill bit. Not one of them wanted a quarter-inch drill bit. Not really. They wanted a quarter-inch hole. The busyness of Christian activities is never an end in itself. Activities of value are simply a means to an end. The end, according to King Jesus, is to make disciples. This is the measure Kingdom Christians use to determine effectiveness.

"We had a *great* vacation Bible school this year," the leader announced in church. Then came the measurement of *great*: 180 children attended. Really? If Jesus had been focused on crowds, He would have discipled twelve thousand. Instead, He worked primarily with twelve. What did He do with them?

Jesus poured His life into those twelve. We call them His "followers." However, from the lens of Kingdom culture, they were not simply His followers. That was not His final objective. His ultimate mission as a leader was not to develop followers but to multiply leaders.

My son, Jon, began his ministry at St. Thomas Church in Crookes, an area in Sheffield, England. He cut his ministry teeth at one of the epicenters of the movement taking place in the UK. Since I've been trained as a diagnostician who asks questions, I decided to ask Jon a defining question. The answer to my question would help me determine if he was grasping Kingdom culture. We were on Skype from our home in Indiana when I asked, "Jon, what is the one thing a pastor must do every week? No matter how many interruptions. No matter how many funerals or crisis-counseling issues screaming 'urgent,' what is it that a pastor absolutely must do, week in, week out?"

I know what I would have said at his age. I was just out of seminary, and to me it was very clear. What is the one thing, as a pastor, I must accomplish every week? Prepare my sermon! "After all," I thought, "you are publicly accountable every seven days!" However, Jon was discipled in an entirely different culture, I'm happy and envious to admit. With

> If Jesus had been focused on crowds, He would have discipled twelve thousand. Instead, He worked primarily with twelve.

no hesitation, he answered, "That's easy. The one thing every pastor must accomplish every week is to disciple, to raise up leaders, and multiply." Do you see the difference? Do you feel the mission? Can you experience the passion? It sounds like Jesus' priorities, doesn't it? What about you? What is your primary mission as a Christian? What are you passionate about?

Jesus began a movement with twelve normal, uneducated men. Each was invited, "Come, follow Me." He invited them to sacrifice what they were for what they could become. He didn't explain what they were supposed to do. He nurtured them to become citizens of the Kingdom.

It was a few years later when Jesus gave a profound challenge: "All *authority* has been given to Me."[11] Clearly, this assignment was from the King of the Kingdom. He continued, "Go and make disciples."[12] Later, when they received Holy Spirit power, the challenge included a strategic emphasis: "You will be My witnesses...to the ends of the earth."[13]

This is not rocket science! Anyone can get this: invitation and challenge. The invitation is, "Come hang out with me. Catch the Kingdom culture." The challenge is, "Go, multiply yourselves. Just as I imprinted you, imprint others." This approach is so unnatural, so different. Sadly, it is almost entirely lost in the climate, the atmosphere, and the culture of most Christians and their churches.

Jesus multiplied Himself twelve times in three years. Even He lost one, but it turned out to be true that "God works all things together for good of those who love Him."[14] How many have you multiplied in the last three years? Okay, you're not Jesus. What about the last thirty years?

Jesus modeled going deep with a few over a length of time. His theme was, "The Kingdom of God is like..." What He taught was very different from life as they knew it. It still is! Sophisticated or arrogant Christians do not easily assimilate this approach. As someone once said, "Entering God's Kingdom is like going through a door that is exactly as high as you are—when you are on your knees. If, in the pride of ego, you stand up straight, you will not fit." How do you fit? If you are ego-driven, you won't like this book, even if it does sound like the Jesus of the New Testament. Pray for humility—I do!

What Jesus shared with His disciples, He clarified by teaching, modeling, and being Himself. Jesus was *real* to His disciples. They saw Him laugh, cry, pray, feed the crowd, drive out demons, and heal the sick. They saw Him bleed, die, and rise again. What they caught was a significant contrast to what they experienced in their everyday lives before Jesus. They were engaged. Jesus challenged them to *experience*: "Here, you pass out the food to the five thousand."[15] "Sure, you are ready to walk on water, come ahead."[16] "You go into the village and share the Good News of the Kingdom."[17] "You go catch a fish with a coin in its mouth and pay the temple tax."[18] They experienced the Kingdom personally. They caught it. They would never forget it. How are you doing as a Kingdom Christian? Who are you inviting? Who are you challenging? Who are you engaging? Who are you discipling? Who, by name, are you multiplying?

> Jesus was *real* to His disciples.... Jesus challenged them to *experience*.... They caught it. They would never forget it.

As Jesus taught about the Kingdom of God, He often told stories. He used picture language, such as a mustard seed, a man beaten up on the road to Jericho, a king who gave management responsibilities to three guys, a man pounding on a neighbor's door in the middle of the night asking for bread, yeast in bread, and more. He used story after story. Why?

In Matthew 13:10, the disciples asked Jesus, "Why do you use stories?"[19] Jesus implied that this Kingdom culture is beyond the common experience of most people. He told the disciples that because they had been with Him for a while, they understood more of His teaching. At least they were starting to get it, whereas those outside their little group needed help to get it. He said, "I tell stories...to nudge the people toward receptive insight."[20]

One of my favorite historical figures understood how to change culture. His name was William Wilberforce, and he was from Great Britain. He brought about change through a relentless and persistent approach of changing the worldview of the British Empire concerning the slave trade. He used metaphors, stories, and relational alliances to slowly change the parliament, the British Empire, and the entire world in a very significant way. This is the impact of a movement. Think about the impact even on the United States. What if the British Empire still had been involved in the slave trade and had joined the Confederate Army during the Civil War? Certainly, the Confederacy would have won, and the United States would be a very different place. Think of the impact! This is the power of a dedicated man, William Wilberforce, and the energy of a movement that absolutely changed history. This is the power of movement!

This Kingdom of Jesus is so different. It is difficult to grasp. It is transformational. Paul, in his letter to the Philippians, challenges Christians to a transformational life.[21] This Kingdom culture is so radically different. It puts others before ourselves! It takes divine courage to fuel this culture. Courage is not the absence of fear; it is the absence of self. It is beyond consumer culture. It is about being a servant. This is the courage to give ourselves, as Jesus did. Jesus had a cross; we have a cross. Jesus says, "Take up your cross, and follow me."[22]

> It takes divine courage to fuel this culture. Courage is not the absence of fear; it is the absence of self. It is beyond consumer culture. It is about being a servant.

This Kingdom is not at all like this world. Paul wrote to the Christians in the church at Rome. They were surrounded by a pagan culture. They were constantly bombarded and tempted to drift. Paul challenged them, "Don't copy the behavior and customs of this world, but let God transform you into a new person by changing the way you think. Then you will learn to know God's will for you, which is good and pleasing and perfect."[23] You might say Paul was challenging them to experience a Kingdom heart transplant.

Most Christians would be greatly empowered through a spiritual transformation. This is a challenge for Christians. The culture of Rome (the world) knocks at the door of every church, every day. The culture of the church is not supposed to look or feel like the culture of this world. This Kingdom is otherworldly—that is what makes it so attractive, intriguing, and refreshing. Where has the culture of Rome crept into your life? Your church?

THE COMPONENTS OF KINGDOM CULTURE

Kingdom culture comes from the lips of Jesus. The disciples got it. After Pentecost, they discipled others, who then discipled others. This culture drives behavior. In the early days of Christianity, the movement was called "the Way."[24] It was the way of Jesus. Contagious, on-fire believers spread Kingdom culture across the Mediterranean world like a holy infection.

The Kingdom culture has five parts. They were described, briefly, earlier. Now it's time to unpack this spiritual DNA.

(1) **Values:** Values are what you consider important. Jesus said the Kingdom is the most important component. He said, "But seek first his kingdom and his righteousness, and all these things [you worked so hard at] will be given to you as well."[25] That takes a leap of faith! As someone once said, "Make sure what you're living for is worth dying for." What would you die for? Who would you die for?

(2) **Beliefs:** Beliefs are what you demonstrate you believe is true. These are not theoretical or simply academic beliefs. Jesus said, "You will know the truth and the truth will make you free."[26] This isn't limited to the freedom from punishment for sin. You are free to be. You are free to be God's person. You are free to be an ambassador for Christ.[27] You are free to grow spiritually. You are free to rearrange your life and remove the clutter. This is conviction-level belief. Rick Warren quotes Howard Hendricks: "A belief is something you will argue about. A conviction is something you will die for."[28] What do you believe? Does it show?

(3) **Attitudes:** The apostle Paul wrote in Philippians 2:5, "Have the same attitude that Christ Jesus had."[29] Your attitude is your posture before God. If you fly in commercial airplanes, you may have noticed there are at least two pilots in the cockpit. They both have several important duties. One has responsibility for constantly adjusting the angle of the nose

of the airplane in flight. Airplanes don't fly flat. The angle is constantly changing due to outside forces, such as wind speed, altitude, fuel consumption (which makes the airplane lighter), and barometric pressure. One pilot is constantly "trimming" the nose of the airplane to obtain optimum angle. The angle of the airplane affects the performance in ground speed and fuel consumption. Pilots call this angle of the nose of the airplane the "attitude" of the airplane. What is your attitude?

Perhaps you have seen this on a sweatshirt: ATTITUDE IS EVERYTHING. Attitude is not everything in Kingdom culture, but it is an important ingredient for spiritual DNA. You may know people in your church with negative attitudes. Maybe you are one of them. Those with consistently negative attitudes have a spiritual health issue. They do more harm to their church than they realize. It is one thing to disagree; it is entirely different to be disagreeable. How is your attitude?

(4) **Priorities:** Priorities are what you will always do first. Every day, you make hundreds of choices. Priorities are signposts of importance to help you decide what you will do and when you will say no. The apostle Paul wrote in 1 Corinthians 15:3–4, "For I delivered to you as of *first importance* what I also received: that Christ died for our sins in accordance with the Scriptures, that he was buried, that he was raised on the third day in accordance with the Scriptures."[30] One of the Pharisees, a lawyer, questioned Jesus, "What is the greatest commandment?" Jesus replied, "You shall love the Lord your God with all your heart and with all your soul and with all your mind. This is the great and first commandment."[31] Everyone has priorities. They demonstrate them every day.

Think about your priorities:

> A person lost in sin—or a scratch on your new car?
> Missing the worship service—or missing a day's work?
> Your church not growing—or your garden not growing?

Your Bible unopened—or your Instagram account unchecked?

Your contributions decreasing—or your income decreasing?

Your children late for Sunday school—or late for public school?

Church work neglected—or your housework neglected?

You miss a Bible class—or a ball game of your favorite team on TV?

(5) **Worldviews:** Worldviews are how you understand the world, how you understand the world of the church, and the way Jesus expects the church to work. Jesus constantly rearranged the worldviews of His followers. In Matthew 20:20, a dispute broke out among the disciples. The mother of the Zebedee brothers asked Jesus for a Kingdom upgrade for her two kids. Jesus focused on worldviews: "You know that the rulers of the Gentiles lord it over them, and their great ones exercise authority over them. It shall not be so among you. But whoever would be great among you must be your servant, and whoever would be first among you must be your slave."[32] How do you understand the world? Is your world Jesus' world? Does the Kingdom teaching of Jesus operate the world of your church?

These five elements of Kingdom culture can be compared to a spiritual DNA helix: complex, intertwined, and overlapping. *This DNA is the platform God uses to grow His Kingdom.* Why? Because Kingdom culture drives behavior. This is not natural, human behavior. This is Kingdom DNA. This is not the kingdom *of* this world. It is, however, the Kingdom *for* this world. Ezra Taft Benson said:

The Lord works from the inside out. The world works from the outside in. The world would take people out of the slums. Christ takes the slums out of people, and then they take themselves out of the slums. The world would mold men by changing their environment. Christ changes men, who then change their environment. The world would shape human behavior, but Christ can change human behavior.[33]

You don't claim Christianity is true because it works. Christianity works because it is true. *Who we are* determines how we *do* church.

You don't claim Christianity is true because it works. Christianity works because it is true. *Who we are* determines how we *do* church.

The more you look at Kingdom culture, the more you will see drift in yourself and in your church. This is not an exercise in despair; it is the dawning of a new day. This is a wake-up call. This is the Holy Spirit birthing your future. The more you let God correct Kingdom culture drift, the more effectively you and your church will make disciples.

CHURCH HEALTH

Church health is not an institutional makeover. You might wish it were as easy as restructuring. Church health is about spiritual vitality in you and in those in your church. Church health looks like the Kingdom Jesus described. We are called to be *unlike* this world, yet we are called to be *in* this world. This is where it gets tricky. Jesus is not the manager of a divine organization. He is the leader of a spiritual movement. What is the difference? Stephen Covey in his book *The 7 Habits of Highly Effective People* said it well: "Management is efficiency in climbing the ladder of success. Leadership determines whether the ladder is against the right wall."[34] Management is about programs. Leadership is about movements. Kingdom leaders lead Kingdom culture. Yes, it begins with you. And it begins with me.

When a church is unhealthy, it looks a lot like the world. In the chapters that follow, we will observe what Kingdom culture looks like and why a transformational change would revitalize so many Christians and their churches. Kingdom culture is so shocking and so revolutionary because so many Christians are convinced that what they do, they do so well. The difference needed in the movement today is the difference between being efficient and being effective. You work very hard at being efficient—doing things right. Perhaps you have not put enough energy into being effective—doing the right things. Rick Warren says, "Efficiency is like rearranging the deck chairs on the Titanic. Everything is in order, but the ship is going down."[35] Honestly, this could describe many churches. However, you can be part of the solution.

When the church is unhealthy, from the Kingdom perspective, it is less effective. The following is a true story: In a relatively small town in the upper Midwest, a tragic car accident took the lives of four high school students, two boys and two girls. When one family arrived at the funeral home to view the body of their daughter, they discovered something that astonished them. The girl wearing the dress they had given the funeral director wasn't *their* daughter but the other girl. Simultaneously, at another funeral home across town, the same horrible experience was happening to the family of the other girl. The hospital, morgue, or funeral homes had mixed up the bodies. Apparently, no one along the line had checked the identities to make certain they had the right body. The confusion was followed by lawsuits and bad publicity for the funeral homes.

This is a horrible story but a great example of ineffectiveness. Each of the funeral homes had done its job (at least minimally) by making sure they properly embalmed and prepared the bodies. After all, that's what funeral homes do. In this case, they were very efficient, but they were not effective. They had prepared the wrong bodies. This happens too often in the body of Christ. Christians are very efficient with all the religious activities, yet they are not effective. "We do so many programs so well," said the pastor, "but we are a dying congregation." You can do things right, but it may not always be the right things. The result is devastating for the Kingdom of God.

On Easter morning 2015, CNN reported results based on research conducted by the Pew Research Center.[36] For the first time, Islam was outpacing the growth of Christianity. Happy Easter!

Don't blame the Muslims. Don't blame CNN. Don't blame the Pew Research Center. Don't blame "those secular people who are just not interested in church." Look into a mirror. On the morning of November 4, 2015, CNN reported that further research by the Pew Research Center showed church attendance in the United States dramatically declining.[37] For most of us, when it comes to the mission of the church, we are greatly efficient and extraordinarily ineffective. And there are significant consequences. These research findings should sound a four-alarm fire in every Christian, in every church. If this disturbs you, great. It disturbs me. It's time for a wake-up call, and it's time to get back to basics.

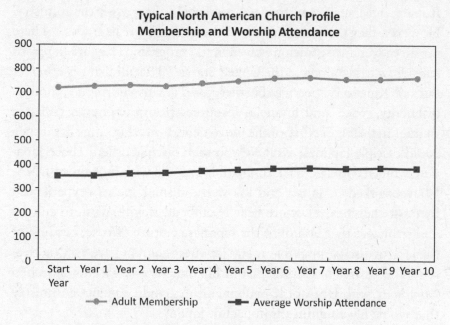

Typical North American Church Profile
Membership and Worship Attendance

A picture is worth a thousand words. Here is an average ten-year profile of membership and worship attendance of churches prior to our consultation. This general pattern is all too familiar.

A few years ago, my colleague Rupert Loyd and I consulted a large church near Detroit, Michigan. As usual, we made several recommendations. One recommendation was directed toward an outreach to Japanese women. This ministry had been pioneered by the church years earlier. It focuses on the wives of Japanese engineers employed by Detroit automakers. Most of these engineers spend two years or more in the United States. Many bring their wives, who know nothing about American culture, such as how to shop, where to find health care, and how to get a driver's license. This is an *efficient* ministry to hundreds of Japanese women. The women make friends with one another as well as with the women from the church who help them assimilate into American culture. However, we discovered that very few of these Japanese women and their husbands are discipled as Christ-followers. Almost none of them become members or active worshippers of any church.

The American women who lead this ministry include prayers and Bible study, but Kingdom results are negligible for disciple-making. Rupert and I suggested that we could help them with the ministry. However, they never took us up on the offer. The reason was, "There are already many women involved in the program. They are happy to learn how to get along in the United States." This ministry is *efficient* but not Kingdom *effective*. Furthermore, it saps enormous amounts of energy, space, and financial resources from the church. What a shame! In the big picture of the movement, I was thinking that if they could disciple Japanese women who then disciple others, those Japanese women could go back to Japan imprinted with movement DNA. I have worked in Japan and know the dismal success experienced by most churches. They are heavily embedded with Western culture and strategies that do not fit the Japanese culture. Worse, because of the lack of disciple-making, many Japanese churches are very ineffective. The growth of Christianity in Japan is very slow. This church in Michigan, with DNA of Kingdom culture, could conduct a ministry that would have significant impact in Japan.

Contrast the Japanese ministry with another group on the other side of Detroit. POBLO (People of the Book Ministries) is reaching Muslims for Christ throughout the United States.[38] We have worked with them for more than ten years, constantly pressing them to develop strategies that make disciples. Some of the dynamics of the Japanese ministry are the same for POBLO. Muslim immigrants from the Middle East, North Africa, Malaysia, and Indonesia respond well to POBLO's International Friendship Centers, located in churches throughout the United States. The initial approach is similar, to help new arrivals assimilate into the United States. However, they have also learned to disciple leaders who have become Christians. They equip them to become "missionaries" to their own people groups. They birth Christian churches comprised of and led by former Muslims who reach people in their own culture. POBLO is *efficient* and *effective*. They practice Kingdom culture. The harvest fruit is in conversions, baptisms, and new cultural churches comprised of former Muslims who have discovered that the God of love is Jesus Christ.

John Maxwell in his audio teaching series the *INJOY Life Club* made this distinction:

> Efficiency is doing things right.
> Effectiveness is doing the right things.
> Excellence is getting the job (mission) done right.[39]

My friend Mike Ruhl says it another way: "We Christians need to change our minds and our attitudes. We need an attitude adjustment if churches are going to be effective. We must change in the following ways:

1. The church exists for those who don't yet belong.
2. The church exists to train Christians to make disciples.
3. The church must discover the real source of joy: 'There will be more joy in heaven over one sinner who repents than over ninety-nine righteous ones who do not need to repent.' "[40]

For many Christians, this is a radical change in atmosphere. What does it mean for you? There is a direct correlation between Kingdom health and *effective* Christians who change this world. Recommending change to Christians and their churches is not an easy sell. Change is hard. Ask any cardiologist who advises patients to change their habits or die. Five out of six die. Many churches die. This is why an awakening, orchestrated by the Holy Spirit, is so exciting and has such great potential.

Christians with holy discontent and spiritual restlessness are seeds of change. God has planted them in every church. They are in your church. They are eager to see your congregation become more effective for making disciples. They are open to looking at Kingdom culture to determine what it means for your church. Kingdom culture is a spiritually healthy atmosphere for followers of Jesus to produce fruit. Kingdom culture is the software

> Change is hard. Ask any cardiologist who advises patients to change their habits or die. Five out of six die. Many churches die.

that drives the movement. This is not about a different program. It's about becoming different people. Behavior—what you do—does not drive Kingdom culture. Kingdom culture drives your behavior. It is not about what you do; it is who you are. The secret is not a new program. It is the air you breathe. It is the spiritually charged air in the atmosphere.

As a Christian, you are in this world for a purpose. It is the same purpose, the same mission, as Jesus' mission: "to seek and to save the lost."[41] George Peters in his book *A Biblical Theology of Missions* writes, "The church that makes God's business her business will soon discover that God is in her midst to make her concerns His business."[42] When you recapture the mission of the Kingdom, Jesus elevates you to the rank of an ambassador.[43] It is like the janitor I spoke with at NASA. He was cleaning the toilet in the men's room. At first, I didn't see the toilet brush in his hand. I asked him, "What do you do here at NASA?" He said, "I'm helping put a rover on Mars."

In his book *Go: The Church's Main Purpose*, George Hunter summarizes the insights of George S. Odiorne in his classic book *Management and the Activity Trap*. He writes:

An organization typically begins with a clear mission and goals, and they devise programs and activities to achieve the goals and fulfill the mission. But over time, the ends are forgotten and the programs and activities become ends in themselves. The people now focus on "the way we've always done things around here." The programs and activities become impotent and less meaningful, and the organization bogs down in "the activity trap."[44]

Does that sound like you? Your church? Most churches we have worked with during the last forty years fit this profile—not 100 percent, but about 80 to 90 percent. The lack of results shows it! Look at this devastating profile. It is similar to many churches we have analyzed.

Membership Gains and Losses Typical of Many North American Churches

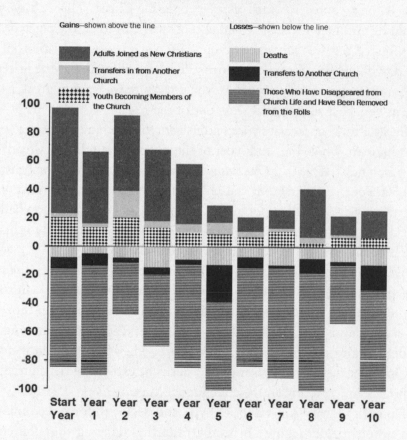

It is a hard question: Have you subconsciously fallen into an ineffective mission culture? The Kingdom culture of Jesus is in direct contrast to the subtle and destructive worldviews that drive secular behavior. Eddie Gibbs pinpoints the cause of this in a way that every Christian should contemplate. In his book *ChurchNext: Quantum Changes in How We Do Ministry*, Eddie says, "The church needs to move from the *Constantinian* model—which presumed a church culture—to an *apostolic* model designed to penetrate the vast unchurched segments of society."[45]

Constantine, the emperor of Roman rule, declared the empire "Christian." This concept assumes everyone is already a Christian. This relocates a Christian from mission to maintenance. I've seen this attitude myself. Years ago, I was invited to consider the role of pastor at a church in northeast Indiana. I asked the leaders to carefully consider if they wanted to reach many people for Christ. Their answer would determine whether I would accept their call to be their pastor. They said, "Yes, we want to reach out." Of course, most Christians, if asked, will say this. Yet subconsciously, few are willing to pay the price of change. Some of them probably thought, "Sure we want to grow, as long as you, pastor, do it all." Don, one of these leaders, said to me privately, "Pastor, I appreciate your enthusiasm for reaching out. But I've lived here my whole life, and most of the people around here already have a church." This is a *Constantinian* worldview toward northeast Indiana. Four years later, our church was five times larger, and most of its growth was from those who were previously unchurched. Don had already adapted to the *apostolic* worldview when he apologized for his earlier comment. People can change! You can change.

What happened at that church in northeast Indiana? As their new pastor, did I start an evangelism program? Did I lead them to consider a more contemporary form of worship? Yes, I did, but those *programs* came later. I spent *years* preaching, teaching, mentoring, modeling, and coaching Kingdom culture. The church did not *do* mission. The people *became* missionaries. The growth of the church, and much more, followed the changing culture.

Don't think this is just a lot of hype and decide to force-feed mission culture to your fellow Christians, radically changing your church by this time next month. The objective is not to kill Christians, or to get killed. Jesus already died for the church. Even if you did get killed, don't expect to rise on the third day. Even if you did, it wouldn't have the same impact. It may be that your first move is to bring relief to worn-out Christians fixated on inefficient programs. In the next seven chapters, we will look at proven strategies for renewal and revival.

BREAKTHROUGH STRATEGIES FOR THE SEVEN CEILINGS

CHAPTER FIVE

Turn Your Church Right-Side Up—Breakthrough Strategy #1

Ceiling #1: Corporate Confusion

> Churches must be prepared to dismantle many of their hierarchical structures. These hierarchies...have become too inflexible and unresponsive.
>
> —Eddie Gibbs[1]

One day, Jesus was talking to His disciples, using one of His classic methods of discipling: asking questions. Listen in on the conversation. "Who do people say the Son of Man is?" Jesus asks. The disciples shared the speculations of others. Jesus got personal: "But who do *you* say I am?"

Peter responds, "You are the Messiah, the Son of the living God."

Jesus returns, "Now I say to you that you are Peter (which means 'rock'), and upon this rock I will build my church."[2]

Jesus went on to say, "and all the powers of hell will not conquer it."[3]

Think about that. As a Christian, who or what can stop you? Who or what can stop your church? Not secularization. Not another religion. Not a government. Not the enemy, Satan. Not an ideology. Nothing can stop the Christian movement, except Christians. That is a scary thought! When a local congregation closes, Christians have given up, died off, or both. *Most often, Christians have drifted far from Kingdom culture.* The death of a church does not come from outside. A church becomes impotent. It doesn't grow. People age. "As your church dies, would the last person please turn out the lights?" The demise of a church is *always* an inside job.

It is also clear that you and I don't build the church. Jesus said He builds the church. Another issue is equally clear: Jesus, the head of His body, uses the members of His body to build His church as He works in and through them. The power is in Jesus, the Word [who] became flesh.[4] You and I are the conduit God uses. God doesn't reach people in a vacuum.

> Nothing can stop the Christian movement, except Christians.

Salvation occurs by grace, through faith.[5] Grace means salvation is a gift from God. Just because it's a free gift to you does not mean it has no cost. It cost Jesus His life. Remember this? *Justice* happens when you get what you deserve. *Mercy* occurs when you don't get what you deserve. *Grace* is getting what you don't deserve. You don't do things to become a Christian. Yet, when you become a Christian, you do things that *become* a Christian. This is where your mission gets complicated. It is where Christians get off track and drift from Kingdom culture.

Christians confess that we don't *do* anything to receive salvation. It is God's work. When it comes to the salvation of others, though, we persistently work at it. The way many churches approach it, it looks like it depends on us. This is the mission side of salvation by works. The book of Acts is called the *Acts of the Apostles*. Actually, it should be called the Acts of the Holy Spirit. The Holy Spirit works through apostles and all Christians. This is Kingdom culture. Ironically, most churches look for a great program to build the Kingdom. God is looking for renewed Kingdom people to build a great movement. God is looking for Christians with Kingdom DNA. Is that you?

At a leadership meeting, my friend Barry Kolb told me, "A great commitment to the Great Commission makes a great Christian who makes a great church that makes a great community that makes a great world."[6] The question is, what does a great Christian look like?

A KINGDOM CHRISTIAN?

Try diligently to put aside the concepts that you "belong to a church," "go to church," or "grew up in a church." The seed of Kingdom DNA creates the miraculous embryo of potential: You *are* church.

No one chapter in the Bible explains the church. Instead, Scripture uses a variety of metaphors. Why so many? The church is like a diamond. It is as multifaceted and complex as it is precious. These metaphors help you get a handle on the most unique body (the body of Christ) in the entire universe. Nothing is like it, and you are a vital part of it.

Churches count members. God counts believers in relationship with Christ. This is evident from the following metaphors: (1) the sheep and the shepherd, (2) the flock of God, (3) the vine and the branches, (4) the bride and the bridegroom, (5) the living temple with living stones, (6) the priesthood of all believers, and (7) the body of Christ.[7]

What can you learn from these metaphors? The church is a living organism. It is not a building. It is not just a place. It is a family of believers, equipped and deployed to penetrate their social networks, infecting Kingdom DNA and affecting joy, peace, and hope through the power and presence of Jesus Christ. Someone once said, "Church is what you have left when the building burns down." Church is not really something you go to. It is who you are. When people ask, "Where do you go to church?" you could respond, "I don't have to go anywhere. I am the church. Do you mean, 'Where do I attend church?'" When someone asks, "What kind of church do you belong to?" you could answer, "Actually, none. I *belong* to Jesus Christ." This is the centerpiece of Kingdom DNA. It is not denominational. It is not institutional. It is relational.

What lens do you use for church? If your lens is theology, you are "conservative" or "liberal." If your lens is trend, you are "traditional" or "contemporary." If your lens is organization, you may be "Baptist" or "Catholic" or "Lutheran," and so forth. From the perspective of Kingdom culture, you see church as a *movement*. Your categories are "in or out," "alive or dead," "growing or declining," "impactful or irrelevant," "fruitful or ineffective," "healthy or sick," or "religious or spiritual."

THE LENS OF KINGDOM CULTURE

When you look through the lens of Kingdom culture, you focus on church health. Most churches will never achieve health until they leave the highly structured form of church-as-organization. *The organizational structure of most churches is a major roadblock for thriving Christianity*. The bureaucratic approach is the result of secular drift. Rick Warren wrote, in the foreword to *An Unstoppable Force* by Erwin McManus:

> For twenty-five years I've taught pastors that "the church is a Body, not a business. It is an organism, not an organization! It is a family to be loved, not a machine to be engineered, and not a company to be managed." Pastoring is an art. It has nothing to do with being a CEO. It's all about servanthood and authenticity and taking risks in faith.[8]

A few years ago, I was working with a Presbyterian church in Tennessee. During the consultation, I interviewed a man who is a vice president of FedEx. He is in charge of all their building projects. When his Presbyterian church added a small wing to their building, the pastor felt he would be the ideal person to lead the project. He told me he was used to working with billion-dollar projects for FedEx. He said,

> When you look through the lens of Kingdom culture, you focus on church health.... *The organizational structure of most churches is a major roadblock for thriving Christianity.*

"They were challenging, hard work, but they do not compare to the building project at church. Everyone had an opinion. Everyone was my boss. It was the hardest building project I ever had!" Church is tough, especially the way it is usually organized.

The living organism called "church" has suffered so much drift! Most churches resemble a hierarchical bureaucracy. This reflects several secular, unspiritual trends. They undermine the vitality of Kingdom culture to work through people like you.

1. *Disrespect for Authority.* The fifth commandment teaches respect for those in authority, beginning with parents.[9] Some people in every church refuse to be subordinate to God's order of authority. They disrespect their pastor and leaders. They do not serve in the decision-making group. They want authority without responsibility. Authority without responsibility is one indication of insanity. It is a direct contradiction of Kingdom culture. This is the result of subconscious drift. It is the non-Christian notion of entitlement. It's killing secularized society, and it kills churches.

Disrespect is often directed toward the pastor. Some treat their pastor as a hired hand instead of one who has a divine appointment— a call from God. How cruel to second-guess and undermine a pastor who is well trained for the role and who knows the Scripture. Try that with a medical doctor, dentist, or an officer who pulls you over for speeding. "Pastors aren't perfect," you say. That's not the point. Many pastors spend every waking moment focused on the church. They have thought through and prayed about issues more than anyone else. Why? Pastors are accountable to God for what happens in their churches. Most pastors take this responsibility seriously.

To make matters worse, many churches allow a public forum, open to everyone in the congregation. This concept is baptized as holy, so no one challenges it. However, those who are spiritually mature should handle sensitive and challenging issues. This approach excludes spiritual children, new Christians. In Kingdom culture, Christians are called the "children of God." Some are more spiritually mature than others. Many churches treat everyone equally as long as they are members. Often, infants in Christ have no biblical basis for decision making. How could they? Nevertheless, they are

> Authority without responsibility is one indication of insanity.

allowed to speak and vote. What family would meet about whether or not to pay the mortgage and invite input from the twelve-year-old? Congregational or republic forms of government result from secular influence. They represent Kingdom drift.

How does it look in Kingdom culture? Scripture says some in the body have the gift of leadership. Those in spiritual leadership face many decisions. Leaders lead. Leaders should be chosen based on their public demonstration of a commitment to and the practice of Bible study. Those with deep faith are chosen and discipled into a leadership role. That is Kingdom culture. In Kingdom culture, leaders are identified by biblical wisdom, chosen by gifts, and discipled by another leader. How different is that? Again, Jesus said, "My Kingdom is not of this world."[10]

2. *Consumer Mentality.* The Kingdom approach is focused on what God wants. In many churches, Christians say the Lord's Prayer regularly. The prayer includes the phrase, "Your will be done, on earth as it is in heaven."[11] This means, "Lord, in my life, I want what You want, just as it is in heaven." It signals, "In my church, I want what You want, just like in heaven." Jesus taught this Kingdom culture for decision making. Do you want your church to thrive? Do what the Father is doing; go where God is blessing. Seek His will, and do that.

If you seek God's will, all other issues are subordinated. These issues include: "We can't afford that." "We've never done it that way before." "I'm uncomfortable with that." "I don't like change." Read the letters to the churches in the New Testament. The apostles urged the Christians away from consumer mentality.

During a consultation at a church in San Diego, I attended worship. The service ended with the Lord's Prayer. Everyone prayed, "Your will be done." Immediately following worship was a short meeting for a proposed construction project. As an observer, I was amazed to watch so many argue about what they wanted. What happened to the Lord's Prayer? What happened to Kingdom culture?

In this world, every commercial approaches you as a consumer. In the Kingdom of Jesus, you consume in a different dimension. Jesus told His disciples, "My food is to do the will of the one who sent me."[12] Kingdom drift is fueled by secular consumerism. Leaders make a proposal, then the issue is open for discussion. People speak *their* minds. What happened to the mind of Christ?[13]

> In the Kingdom of Jesus, you consume in a different dimension. Jesus told His disciples, "My food is to do the will of the one who sent me."

The Kingdom culture approach is simple but profound. What does God want us to do? What are the compelling reasons God would want us to do that? The consumer drift is evident when Christians focus on what *they* want. When there is division in the group, most Christians consider it an issue of preference. However, most often, the issue is conflict between Kingdom culture and Kingdom drift. Think about this: Every ad, commercial, and billboard is engineered to ignite your consumer appetite. Scripture says you receive when you give; you are rich when you are poor.[14] The Kingdom of Jesus is more about taking up a cross than stepping into a hot tub.

3. *Entitlement Mentality.* Entitlement is a serious contribution to the disintegration of civilization. "I don't want to work, but I'm entitled to a paycheck." "I haven't studied the issue, but I'm entitled to a vote." "I didn't do my homework, but I'm entitled to have a better grade." "I know the speed limit is forty, but if there's no cop around, I'll do sixty."

In the church, entitlement goes like this: "I come to the church once in a while. I should be entitled to have a say." "I don't have a theological degree, but I should be entitled to talk with others about how I disagree with the pastor." "I'm withholding my offering because I don't like the new building program." These behaviors kill churches, divide Christians, and age pastors. Entitlement thinking cuts the body of Christ off at the knees. If you want to reclaim Kingdom culture, it will include a serious overhaul in the way your church operates. Kingdom culture will turn your church right-side up.

TOP-DOWN DISASTER

Pastor Jack is an energetic and gifted senior leader. He has a passion for reaching the lost. The church Jack leads in Ohio has many tangible assets, including six hundred who worship regularly, great facilities, and a Christian school with an excellent reputation. Most important, Jack loves Jesus, and it shows.

Jack has been troubled for some time. His church is not effectively making disciples. A church assessment confirmed what Jack suspected. In spite of all the blessings, the church is not seeing much fruit. Jack is frustrated.

When Jack read about a conference in a nearby city, it caught his attention. A popular Christian leader who wrote a book on making the church "missional" was going to lead the conference. He thought, "This conference is for me."

The conference was inspiring. Jack returned and declared from the pulpit, "This church is going to become a mission." In the coming months, he led the charge. He wasn't going to let anything or anyone get in the way. "After all, this is what church is all about," he said.

Today, Jack's church is half the size. "I grew my church down to three hundred," he said, with the look of a deer in the headlights. What happened? Pastor Jack meant well. He had the right cause. But, as some of his people said, "He crammed it down our throats."

President Dwight Eisenhower said, "You do not lead by hitting people over the head—that's assault, not leadership."[15] This is a serious challenge for church leaders. Ironically, those who are most enthusiastic for Kingdom growth are often most susceptible to this danger. I've heard John Maxwell say, "If you're one step ahead of your people, you are a leader. If you're ten steps ahead of your people, you're a martyr." That's true, and it reflects Jack's pain. What went wrong with Jack's leadership? The answer lies in the nature of culture influence.

Jack never had training from the Kingdom perspective. He didn't know how to move a movement. Do you? Jack suffered implementation backlash. Those who left described it well: "If you weren't on board and excited about outreach, you felt like a second-class Christian."

THE YEAST STRATEGY

Jesus gave you the mission to make disciples. You are surrounded by those who have not experienced the new life only Jesus Christ can deliver. You have good news to share with a struggling world. Why wouldn't a pastor like Jack get excited about the hype to become more missional? Jack had the right *idea*. But he had the wrong *strategy*.

Most lofty goals die at the feet of strategy. It is relatively easy to cast vision for a goal. It is more difficult to develop the right strategy to get there. Where does the confusion originate? It starts with the differentiation between outreach and disciple-making. Jack rushed to outreach. Outreach, in Kingdom culture, occurs *through* those who have been discipled.

The Kingdom cause is not first about quantity. It is about quality: making disciples. Growing Christians to spiritual health is always the first and most important step for an outreach strategy. Think about the model of Jesus. As much as He wants to save every-

> Most lofty goals die at the feet of strategy.

one in the world, He began discipling the few. That must have taken some discipline! That is possibly why the word *disciple* is related to the word *discipline*. Jesus' approach is to go slow and deep. That is the difference between a movement and a program. Pastor Jack meant well, but he was caught in the program mentality. Where are you? Where is your church?

The first strategic step, according to Jesus, is to "die to self."[16] That is not an event but a process. Robert Schuller once said, "We must die as a church and be reborn as a mission."[17] This, however, is the slow, yeast-into-bread work of the Holy Spirit.

When Jesus spoke about yeast, the lesson was not about baking. He warned His disciples about the "yeast of the Pharisees."[18] They weren't bakers either. Jesus was talking about the *culture* of the Pharisees. He was referring to the atmosphere, the tone, climate, assumptions, and objectives of the Pharisees. He was talking about their values, beliefs, attitudes, priorities, and worldviews. He was describing the DNA of the Pharisees. Jesus was contrasting the culture of religion with the culture of the Kingdom. Pastor Jack— whoever you are—do you get this?

Think about yeast in bread. Have you ever watched a loaf of bread rise? If you have, you learned two important lessons about the Kingdom: (1) it's a slow process, and (2) it changes everything. Evangelism often becomes a program of an institution. Making disciples is a lifestyle of a movement. Can you see the dramatic difference? Upside-down churches are like the man who planted an acorn and expected it to emerge the following spring as an oak two-by-four.

Jack chose the quick-fix strategy. In his enthusiasm, he failed to follow the yeast strategy and develop Kingdom culture among his people. He tried to plant mission seeds in soil that was not prepared. Come on, Jack! How many times does Jesus describe the Kingdom of God and refer to seeds, hard ground, rocks, weeds, and fertile soil? It's great to want to make unbelievers into new disciples. Jesus is all for it. But if you want your church involved, cultivate the soil of the Kingdom. This was only one of Jack's biblical errors.

The other Kingdom culture mutation was the way Jack approached it. His attitude (posture before God) was wrong. He acted like the CEO of a company handing down orders. Guess what, Jack? These people you call "church" are not on your payroll. They are the children of God. Is this the way you raise your own children? Is Mrs. Zebedee your mother?

The mother of the Zebedee brothers had power on her mind when she came to Jesus and asked for plum jobs for her sons.[19] This gave Jesus another opportunity to teach the culture of the Kingdom. Jesus said leaders in His Kingdom are not like the kings of the Gentiles, who "lord it over their people." Jesus explained that if you want to be great in the Kingdom of God, be like a servant of others.[20] This teaching sets up the structural issue of Kingdom culture in your church.

Church structure begins with the Kingdom approach to leadership. Jesus modeled this leadership. Like everything else, it is not like this world. Jesus is a servant Savior.[21] This raises some questions. How can you lead people as a servant, as a slave to people? How does a servant gain influence? How does that work? Jesus led by relationships. In Kingdom culture, influence travels from one person to another as they relate to each other.

This leads to the Kingdom perspective of how Kingdom Christians make decisions. Some call this issue church government or church governance. It's how church is organized. The key is to organize without becoming an organization.

> In Kingdom culture, influence travels from one person to another, not from a CEO or board to the masses. This is the difference between a movement and a government, culture and a program, transformation and conformity, grace and the rule of law, spiritual formation and bylaws.

CEILING #1: CORPORATE CONFUSION

Most organizations are hierarchical: top-down direction. Movements are the opposite: bottom-up influence. What is the structure of your church? How does it square with Kingdom culture, according to Jesus, the head of the church? Loren Mead, in his classic *The Once and Future Church*, reflected: "I am reminded of an apocryphal church board whose members all died in a church fire because they could not figure out the proper way to use *Robert's Rules of Order* to adjourn the meeting."[22]

Churches are organized with church councils, sessions, consistories, or boards of directors. Sometimes they are called elders or deacons, names that often disguise a board of directors. Most operate in a top-down approach. Sadly, many Christians never question this approach. "That's the way we've always done it," they say. Many denominations reflect the epitome of top-down, hierarchical operations.

It is mind stretching to consider turning a hierarchical ministry upside down to right-side up. Of course, Jesus is good at stretching your brain. That is why Christianity is called *transformational*, not only in theory but also in practice. Perhaps a real-life story (parable) will help.

Some years ago, Church Doctor Ministries was chosen to consult a denomination called the Church of the Lutheran Brethren. This relatively small group has about 115 churches in the United States and Canada. They are soundly biblical yet delightfully progressive. They hired Church Doctor Ministries to take a close look at their structure and make suggestions.

Instead of limiting our approach to their leadership, we chose to model Kingdom culture by seeking input from the grassroots. We asked everyone in all their churches to complete a survey. This is the Kingdom approach: bottom-up. The medium of assessment shadowed the desired potential outcome. Like most denominations, they were organized as a hierarchy. We encouraged them to become more like a movement.

The three-year project built ownership from every level of the denomination. Remember, their structure was quite hierarchical when we began. To make changes would require a "step of approval" from the leadership staff and board, followed by a vote of delegates from all the churches at their convention. This is the Achilles heel of Ceiling #1 transformation: You must start where you are.

The Church of the Lutheran Brethren was structured like many denominations. The denominational office housed several department heads, under the leadership of elected president of the denomination Joel Egge. As we interviewed the denominational staff, it became clear they were courageous leaders with a "whatever it takes" attitude. This was also true of the transition task force, under the outstanding leadership of layman John Heie. For years, the denomination had been organized into several districts. A president, who operated as the top-down leader of the congregations, led each district.

In the end, convention delegates voted to turn the denomination from upside down to right-side up. They reduced staff, deleted the district presidents, and added regional support personnel who would regularly interact *relationally* with pastors and church leaders. They now operate more closely to the way the New Testament church functioned.

The early church didn't use the words, but I would call this an *Apostolic Theocracy. Theocracy* indicates that the guiding principle for all decisions is consistently seeking God's will. They want what God wants; they look to the Scriptures for guidance. *Apostolic* reflects the bottom-up, relational approach of the apostles in the New Testament.

In Kingdom culture, the church is a flat organism. It operates relationally, supernaturally arranged by spiritual gifts. One of the gifts is leadership, but the culture is servant driven. This dramatically changes the atmosphere and the climate. This reflects Kingdom culture as Jesus taught it.

Most churches operate in a culture of high control / low accountability. This is a serious reflection of drift. If you want a healthy, productive church, it will be necessary to turn your church rightside up. High control handcuffs the body of Christ. Once you catch the DNA of structure according to Kingdom culture, you will feel liberated. Kingdom culture is low control / high accountability. The bottom-up approach makes an enormous difference.

HIGH CONTROL

How does high control impact life in your church? Consider the story of Jane. Jane visited her cousin's church while on vacation in Palm Desert, California. As a visitor, she gravitated to the welcome center, where she met Mark and Sharon, a friendly couple enthusiastic about their church. "They are a lovely couple," she thought. Jane began thinking, "Wouldn't it be great to have a welcome center at my church?"

Jane returned to her home in Corvallis, Oregon, and spoke to her pastor about it. He thought it was a great idea and suggested she share a proposal with the church council. She asked for time on the agenda. Tom, the council chairman, said the agenda was already full. He suggested she send in a written proposal. A month later, Jane had not heard from Tom. She sent him an e-mail. He got back to her, saying there was some discussion. A few of the council members had questions, so it was tabled. "We will discuss it again next month," he promised.

At the meeting the following month, Jim, one of the trustees, commented, "Since a welcome center has implications for the church building, it should be an issue for the trustees." The council then deferred to the trustees. Jim said they would take up the matter the following month.

After the trustees' meeting, Jane did not get any feedback for three weeks. So she asked the pastor about it. He said he wasn't at the meeting. "I'll check with Jim," he told Jane. A week later, the pastor e-mailed Jane, "Jim said the trustees formed a committee to look into it." He continued, "I'm sure the committee will be in touch to get your input. The committee is led by Bill."

After a month, Jane phoned Bill. "Hi, Jane," said Bill. "Yeah, we met a couple of times. We thought we could easily build a welcome center. Do you know Fred Ritchie? Fred is supposed to get a cost estimate for the meeting next month."

After six weeks, Jane left a note in Bill's mailbox at church. "Bill, any update on the welcome center?" she wrote. Six days later, Bill called Jane. "Sorry I didn't get back to you right away, Jane. I had to get your phone number from the church office. Fred got an estimate for the materials. At next month's trustee meeting, we'll review it. Our meeting is on the third Thursday of—oh—no, that's not right. That's Holy Week. We won't meet next month. It'll be the month after that. Anyway, I'll let you know."

Eight weeks later, Bill phoned Jane. "Just wanted to let you know that we are going ahead with the welcome center," he said. Jane asked, "When will it be finished?"

"Oh, that's hard to say at this point. The money is not in the budget, so we have to take it to the finance committee. They'll tell us if the church can afford it right now. Things have been pretty tight lately."

"How much is it? I'll write the check," said Jane.

"That's really generous of you, Jane," responded Bill, "but it still has to go through the finance committee. Then it will go to the council for approval."

Are you smiling? You shouldn't be. You should be hopping mad! Jane was! Please understand. The Christians in this story are not "bad." They are caught in an inefficient, high-control system.

Are you trapped in a culture of high control? In 1 Corinthians 14:40, the Bible says that everything should be done decently and in order. However, high control is not Kingdom culture. It is tyranny. What happened? Kingdom drift happened. Church leaders have confused discipline with control. Think about your church.

The church decision-making system is supposed to be a permission-giving mechanism for order in the church. In many congregations, it becomes a permission-denying system at worst and a bureaucratic maze of frustration at best. Think about Kingdom culture. God's covenant is "I will be your God, and you will be my people."[23] The blood of Jesus Christ seals that covenant. The covenant of God is like a child's car seat. It is loving protection for the child of God. Out of love, this relationship holds the child close to the heart of God for protection. The spirit of religion promotes rules, regulations, politics, votes, committees, and control. It turns the child's car seat into a straitjacket.

The New Testament church was a rapidly growing movement. It was out of control, humanly speaking. Think of any movement, such as the American Revolution, the Civil Rights movement, or the abolishment of apartheid in South Africa. Movements can't move when they are under tight control. When churches develop systems of control, they become stalled. Many denominational structures are extreme examples of this dynamic.

Revivals, great moves of God, are characterized by lack of human control. Think of the incredible growth of the underground church in China. When China became a Communist country, Chairman Mao ran off all the missionaries. Without pastors, Christians had no alternative: They had to operate like the priesthood of all believers.[24] Today, the Communists can't control the Christian movement in China. Every time they try, even with persecution, the movement grows. This is a Kingdom culture dynamic. Kingdom culture doesn't feel normal to this world.

The New Testament church was not under human control; it was under the control of the Holy Spirit. This reflects that Christ is, indeed, the head of the church. This scares many Christians, and rightly so. It takes a leap of faith to let go of human control and trust that God is in charge. We humans like life in the church to be neat and tidy, but by definition, mission is messy.

> By definition, mission is messy. If you want everything neat and tidy in your church, you will settle for mediocrity. Spiritual order does not mean high control. It means, in the order of things, Jesus, the head of the church, rules. Everything and everyone else is subordinated.

A great move of God is often chaotic! I preached at a small church in a remote outpost in the Amazon jungle. The people had cleared a patch of the jungle to create a place for worship. They put a fence around the area where they built the little church. Cows were grazing inside the fence to keep the area clear. Otherwise, the vegetation would quickly smother the church building. On the way to worship, I had to step carefully!

To reach the church building, people could enter through a gate in the fence. The building was raised three feet above the ground to keep the termites from eating the floor. The walls were simply studs to let the air through, to compensate for the intense heat and humidity. The roof was solid. It is a rain forest!

Forty people were sitting on rough-sawn wooden benches. The woman in the front row was nursing her child. A cow walked by during my sermon, giving a loud bellow. No one looked at the cow except me. A dog wandered up the middle aisle, begging me to pet him, which I did, as I preached. A little boy was lying on the floor asleep, next to the woman nursing her child. The boy, still asleep, wet his pants. A yellow river was creeping toward my left foot. I glanced to the right. A spider the size of a tennis ball was crawling toward my right foot. I thought, "This is church. This is mission." Out of human control, the Holy Spirit was all over those people and all over me. I thought about some high-control churches back home. If you're fixated on neat, you'll have a challenge to do real mission.

Your church will not thrive if it is ruled by high-control decision making. If you absolutely have to be neat, then clean houses. Don't lead a church. Most churches are so antiseptic, so overcontrolled, there isn't room for the God of surprises. Your church cannot effectively reach lost people and make disciples as a hyperorganized institution. Unintentionally, you cripple the body of Christ.

LOW ACCOUNTABILITY

Oddly, while many churches operate with high control, most are also low in accountability. In Kingdom culture, the balance is always between control and accountability. Accountability is the idea of holding *one another* accountable. This is a way of life in healthy churches. Low control balanced by high accountability is the atmosphere of Kingdom culture.

Accountability is not the role of a board. Kingdom culture is influenced by relationships, not votes. Talk about Kingdom drift! Some churches have a staff-parish committee to handle complaints about staff. They are structured to *promote* gossip and discourage relational accountability! This approach undermines Jesus' teaching about relational accountability. It's more evidence of Kingdom culture drift. Some denominational leaders have drifted into high control balanced by low accountability. This spark starts the disintegration of many denominations. These so-called leaders are actually managers—and poor managers at that. They are poor role models suffering from Kingdom culture drift.

> In Kingdom culture, the balance is always between control and accountability.... Low control balanced by high accountability is the atmosphere of Kingdom culture.

Jesus anticipated Christians would occasionally get sideways with one another. He explained Kingdom culture behavior. He said, "Love your neighbor as you love yourself."[25] Jesus taught that if someone offends you, go to that person, one-on-one, privately. If that doesn't resolve the conflict, take someone with you, as a witness, and do it again. If that still doesn't work, get someone in leadership of the church involved, and repeat the process.[26]

The apostle Paul wrote to the Ephesians, "Speak the truth in love."[27] Think about how this would change the atmosphere of your church. Paul says we should speak the truth. That means you base your comments on facts. You do your homework. You don't subjectively communicate from emotions, hypotheses, generalizations, or biases. You don't speak from ignorance or arrogance. It means you want to be as clear as possible in your understanding before you say anything. This is especially important when the issues are sensitive. Kingdom culture says you should not only be smart, but also be wise. Wisdom is more than head knowledge. The psalmist says wisdom begins with the knowledge of God. It means you let God inform what you understand.[28] This is the culture of King Jesus.

Two areas where Kingdom culture of low control / high accountability is abused are in gossip and in church bullies. These two areas are like cancer to a healthy church. Both are symptoms of Kingdom drift.

Gossip occurs when you say something—anything—that disrespects, dishonors, or undermines a person, and you say it to anyone except that person. If you have a negative criticism or someone has offended you, Kingdom culture says, "Say it to them, and them only." Your words must be based on fact and spoken in love. There is only one purpose for this approach: to help the person become a better citizen of the Kingdom. In the Kingdom culture, God's people confront one another. The Scripture implies strongly that the confrontation is to be face-to-face, not by letter, e-mail, text, or even by phone. Why? Because Kingdom culture is relational. It is the spiritual air you breathe.

Some Christians will say, "I can't do that. I'm not comfortable. I don't like confronting another person. I can't stand conflict." No one likes conflict. If you do like it, you need to see a therapist! Some people believe that because the Bible says, "God is love,"[29] it must be a top priority for God to make you comfortable. Nothing could be further from the truth!

There is no evidence in Scripture that God has exceptional concern for your comfort. In fact, the Bible demonstrates the opposite. Sometimes God allows you to be uncomfortable. Christian growth often occurs in times of extreme discomfort. Anyone who knows about Good Friday should understand that God is more interested in the fulfillment of His mission to save people than the comfort of His own Son. Your comfort is not a high priority on God's agenda.

The church bully is the second main issue where low accountability defines the culture. After consulting hundreds of churches, I can assure you that there are bullies in most every congregation. In recent years, society has finally put a foot down on bullies on the playground. Yet, in many churches, bullies are allowed on the "playing field" of church life. How ironic!

The profile of a church bully has several elements. Bullies turn gossip into a fine art, which is not at all "fine." In most cases, church bullies mean well. They are generally upset with some aspect of the church: the pastor, the music, a youth worker, or any type of change. Bullies often suffer from a consumer mentality, saying, "I want my way." They usually have a severe case of entitlement. They often want privileges (like the power to make decisions) but avoid responsibility. They are likely spiritually immature but not involved in Bible study. They tend to be negative and controlling. They don't realize it, but they cast a dark cloud in the atmosphere.

A few bullies can hinder an entire church from moving forward for years. In many forms of church governance, there are open meetings that provide a platform for bullies to speak. When they do, they discourage others. In a biological family, immature children do not have a voice or a vote. However, in some church families, there is no differentiation for spiritually young or new children of God. Some baby Christians come disguised as sixty-year-old men and women.

Jesus says, "Come unto me, all you that labor and are heavy laden."[30] The Christian church is one of the few communities with this public invitation: GOT TROUBLES? COME HERE. Some troubled people actually come! That pleases God. However, you need to recognize that hurting people hurt people. This is why a Kingdom culture of high accountability is so important. Congregations with a culture of low accountability allow hurting people to cripple the vitality of the church. An atmosphere of low accountability does not discipline bad behavior. It actually encourages it!

The numbers vary, but in most churches, at one time or another, there are two to six bully "cheerleaders." Guess what? Almost everyone knows who they are! These bully cheerleaders influence the vulnerable who can number, in larger churches, up to fifty or sixty people. Those who are vulnerable would not exist without the influence of the bully cheerleaders. The challenge is not those who are vulnerable. In fact, the challenge isn't the bullies. The real cause is the culture of low accountability, which fails to help bully cheerleaders improve their behavior. In most cases, if they were admonished by someone speaking the truth in a spirit of love, those who are bullies would be more cheerful Christians. Without cheerleaders, the "party spirit" dissolves. The power of Kingdom culture is that low control balanced by high accountability turns your church right-side up. It is the antidote to corporate confusion.

There are four options for your church:

- High control / high accountability, which is imperialism.
- Low control / low accountability, which is chaotic anarchy.
- High control / low accountability, which is organizational bureaucracy.
- Low control / high accountability, which is Kingdom culture.

Ironically, as our research shows, when the issues are clarified, more than two-thirds of church leaders identify low control / high accountability as the most effective approach. What is their response when they see survey results? "Why in the world do we operate the way we do?"

Inevitably there are those in every church who fear total rebellion against strategies that lift the ceiling of secularized, top-down corporate boards and bylaw-driven church structures. In fact, churches are more prepared for Breakthrough Strategy #1 than many would think. When they do break through this ceiling, the most frequent comments we have heard are, "We feel liberated. The joy is back!"

Church Leaders Identifying Their Preferences
for Church Governance[31]

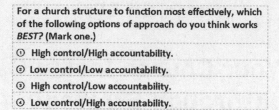

For a church structure to function most effectively, which
of the following options of approach do you think works
BEST? (Mark one.)
① High control/High accountability.
② Low control/Low accountability.
③ High control/Low accountability.
④ Low control/High accountability.

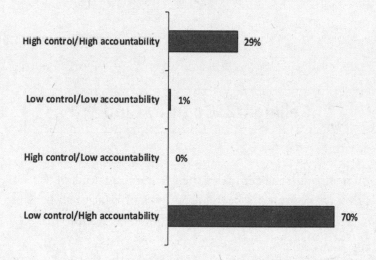

We are now ready to turn our attention to Ceiling #2: Country
Club. The breakthrough strategy is to turn your church inside out.

CHAPTER SIX

Turn Your Church Inside Out— Breakthrough Strategy #2

Ceiling #2: Country Club

> Down through the centuries the great expansions of the
> Faith have commonly been along lines of relationship.
> —Donald A. McGavran[1]

In *The Christian's Calling*, Donald Heiges tells the story of a gang of laborers drilling holes five feet deep in a street. Their boss did not tell them the purpose. In fact, he looked in each hole and then said, "Okay, fill 'er up." At noon, the men announced, "We quit. Pay us off." When the boss asked why, they replied, "Digging holes and filling them up only makes fools of us." The boss then told them why the drilling was done—to find the location of a "lost" water main. Deep down, human beings want to see some point in what they are doing, even if what they are doing makes no great demands upon their mind or body.[2]

What is the primary purpose of the church? "What a dumb question," you might think. "Everybody knows that." I wish that were true. Our research may shock you. It may even depress you. However, if God is going to get the church back to the Kingdom culture Jesus initiated, we must start with this fundamental question.

A church cannot be healthy and thrive if it is stuck in maintenance mode or if it is turned inward. This is Ceiling #2: Country Club. Sadly, that's where many Christians live. You can help lead them on a journey to the Kingdom of Jesus, but first, where are you?

The questions about the purpose of the church can be asked in different ways:

• What does Jesus consider the most important effort of your church? On what would Jesus want you to focus the most?

• According to the Bible, why does your church exist? Why does any church exist? Among all your answers, which do you think is most important?

• Why did Jesus come into the world? Does that have any bearing on the top priority of your church?

• Why did Jesus die on the cross? What is the main reason He would do that? Does that have anything to do with you? How does that direct your life and the life of your church?

• What is the mission of your church? For what reason does your church exist? In what business is your church?

• What does the mission statement of your church say? Do you know it? How much do your church activities reflect that mission statement?

• What does the New Testament church demonstrate about the purpose of the church? By their actions, what do you learn about those early Christians? What was their understanding of God's purpose for their church? How does that translate into your church?

You might want to ask these questions in your church—and keep on asking them. Think with me about the role of asking questions and their power for developing Kingdom culture. Asking questions, as mentioned earlier, is one of the ways to develop Kingdom culture. Technically, it is called "interrogative influence." In his book

Influencer, Joseph Grenny shows how influencers can guide others by asking questions when issues are difficult and subjects are sensitive or hard to comprehend.[3]

Jesus, the Master of movement mentality, modeled the power of developing Kingdom culture by asking many questions. In Luke 10:25–37, for instance, Jesus shared the story known as the Good Samaritan. The culture-teaching question is: "Which of these three would you say was a neighbor to the man who was attacked by bandits?"[4]

In Matthew 16:13, Jesus asked His disciples (and everyone else who has read this for centuries), "Who do people say the Son of Man is?" He asks, "What about you? Who do you say I am?"[5] Who do you say Jesus is? Savior? Of course. Mission developer, sender of missionaries like you and me? Not so much, as you will see by our research. This is a key issue and a challenge if you want a thriving church. You will likely agree that you need to turn your church inside out.

The Pharisees challenged Jesus about the Sabbath laws. Jesus asked them, "Have you never read what David did when he and his companions were hungry and in need of food?"[6] This question carries a little drama, because the Pharisees had, of course, read this many times, along with the rest of the law and the prophets. They were so-called experts. The power of Jesus' question is way beyond the appropriate answer!

When we consult churches, we use surveys to ask questions. The data is valuable, but so is the dynamic of asking questions. It gets people thinking about their church in the framework of Kingdom culture. We encourage church leaders to ask many questions. We suggest, for example, that you approach restaurant servers by saying, "We're going to pray for our meal. Can we pray for you? Is there anything we can include for you?" This helps Christians practice Kingdom culture. They will also learn that most people are more receptive than they ever dreamed. We train church leaders to ask, "Anybody want to share what God has done in your life lately?" We suggest asking this any time a group meets at church for ministry or Bible study, except for worship. It is an approach to help Christians develop a culture of sharing their "God stories." We ask those in the church, "Who are the people in your social network who show no signs of being a Christ-follower? Would you make a list of them and pray for them every day?" This helps Christians develop a prayer life for those who are unchurched. If they keep praying, God may answer their prayer, and likely use them to get the job done.

Why don't church leaders use questions more often to build Kingdom culture? Why didn't I learn this at the seminary? If you want to build Kingdom culture, start asking questions.

Without a doubt, one of the most fundamental questions is, "What is the primary purpose of the church?" It is like asking, "What are we here for? What has God called the church to do?" This is the heartbeat of Kingdom culture.

In our research among churches, we recognize that turning your church inside out at the most basic level begins with clarity about the purpose of the church.

Even though most churches have the Great Commission, or "making disciples," stated as their main purpose, those who choose "To make disciples" as the primary purpose of the church represent only 34 percent of those surveyed. This is how we posed the question:

> Choose one statement that best describes the main purpose of the church:
>
> ○ To teach people how to live the golden rule
> ○ To be the moral backbone of society
> ○ To make disciples
> ○ To provide a place of fellowship, to share God's love with one another.

In our survey results, the first two choices result in 3 percent or less of the responses in most congregations.

The answer "To provide a place of fellowship, to share God's love with one another" has a national response rate average of 57 percent. This is a consumer mentality that has taken over the Kingdom culture. It is what some have called the "country club" worldview of the church. (There is a 4 percent margin of error, based on respondents who read this item as mission outreach.)

After six months of Kingdom culture focus, clarity concerning the purpose of the church grows, on average, to 68 percent, influencing a critical mass of more than two-thirds of the congregation. This is the beginning of breakthrough toward Kingdom culture focus.

The Primary Purpose of the Church

Choose the *one* statement which *BEST* describes the main purpose of the church. (Mark one.)

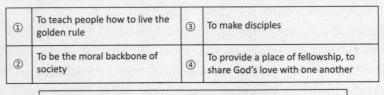

①	To teach people how to live the golden rule	③	To make disciples
②	To be the moral backbone of society	④	To provide a place of fellowship, to share God's love with one another

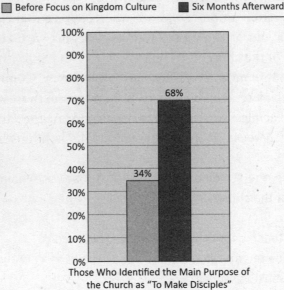

Those Who Identified the Main Purpose of the Church as "To Make Disciples"

Jesus demonstrated the purpose of the Christian movement in many ways, including His willingness to suffer and die on the cross. He spoke in various ways about the mission of the Kingdom. Perhaps the best-known marching order for the church is the Great Commission in Matthew 28:18–20. It begins with one of the few times Jesus declares His authority: "All authority in heaven and on earth has been given to me."[7] This announcement signals, "This is a big deal." It is a *great* commission, to make disciples.

It is a commission, not a commandment. This is more important than many realize. It shapes the motive and the motivation. It describes the strategic approach of Kingdom culture. The Great Commission is not a law to obey, nor is it a duty. It is not a way to test your faith or commitment to Jesus. It is an honor and a privilege, like being an ambassador for Christ.[8] The motivation is not, "You'd better do this!" The cultural perspective is, "I get to do this!" This signals an important motivational approach for leaders to use in Kingdom culture. Even in this, the Kingdom of God is not anything like the kingdom of this world. This culture is unique. This is a completely different atmosphere.

This commission is a co-mission: "I get to join hands with the Ruler of the universe every time, at every step, whenever I participate in making disciples. Are you kidding me? How special is that?" This co-mission is an amazing confession of faith by the Son of God, who has all the authority in the universe. Jesus says, "I believe in you more than you believe in Me. You can't believe in Me more than I believe in you. I'm perfect." In addition, He gives His power through the Holy Spirit.[9] He says, "The one who believes in Me will also do the works that I do and, in fact, will do greater works than these."[10] How is that for a dose of Kingdom encouragement? Could that culture fire up your church? Does it fire you up? If not, check your heartbeat. You may need spiritual resuscitation! Many Christians will, if their churches are to thrive!

The commission implies that the head of the body is in this mission. We are not in this alone. Not ever. It implies that Jesus did it, and we get to do it, too. This commission begins with the "authority clause" and ends with a personal promise: "I am with you always."[11] Technically, that means "in all your

> Without a doubt, one of the most fundamental questions is, "What is the primary purpose of the church?...What are we here for?"

ways"—when it seems to be going well and when you feel the mission is a struggle. It also means "in all your days." That includes your smooth days and your rough days.

Think about how great this Great Commission is. It is not just "great" that Jesus would call you to participate. It is also "great" because you are part of something that changes the eternal destiny of people. It is "great" because it changes communities and nations. It is also "great" because it is a daunting task. The whole world? Wow! When it's over, everything is over.

Jesus was asked about when everything would end. He talked about several events that are not the end, such as wars, earthquakes, tsunamis, 9/11, ISIS, and Ebola. Then He said, "And this good news of the kingdom will be proclaimed throughout the world, as a testimony to all the nations; and then the end will come."[12] The door of history is hinged on this commission. Yes, that's great. As a Christian, you are a vital part of the hinge on which the door of history swings. How could you or your church ever, ever feel unimportant?

> The door of history is hinged on this commission. . . . How could you or your church ever, ever feel unimportant?

I know my failures, my weaknesses, and my shortcomings. So does my wife! So does God. What did the missionary Paul say? "When I am weak, then I am strong."[13] What was that other detail I tend to overlook? Paul said this as well: "It is no longer I who live, but it is Christ who lives in me."[14] Yes, that's great.

GO!

What is the measurement of progress in your church? Is it membership figures? The year-end average worship attendance? Achieving the annual budget? The number of baptisms? All of these are important statistics to track and monitor. But the key measurement, according to Kingdom culture, is "How many people have been discipled?" According to the Scripture, measuring discipleship is the most important element of effectiveness.

Does your church measure the number of people who are discipled each year? What about the number of those who are in the process of being discipled? That would include those who are at any stage of being discipled. It is the most important measurement of effectiveness for the Kingdom, yet most churches do not measure or report those being discipled. Most denominations do not ask for this information. Talk about Kingdom drift! Most churches only measure organizational statistics. Very few measure movement statistics.

Have you ever heard the phrase, "What gets measured gets done?" What if you asked church members every year how many people they are in the process of discipling? Do you think that would change the culture of your church? Remember, interrogative influence means asking questions. Asking questions is a Kingdom strategy to influence culture!

The apostle Paul was speaking to the issue of Kingdom drift among the Ephesians. In Ephesians 5:15–17, he says, "So be careful how you live. Don't live like fools, but like those who are wise. Make the most of every opportunity in these evil days. Don't act thoughtlessly, but understand *what the Lord wants you to do*."[15] What does that mean for you?

The commission of the Kingdom begins with the words "*Go and make disciples.*" The first word is *go*, but it is not the end. The result of the Great Commission is to make disciples. The words *go*, *teach*, and *baptize* are means to a greater end. The commission is not achieved when you go. It isn't over when you teach. It doesn't end when you baptize.

The word *go* could be translated "as you go" or "as you are going." The idea in the Great Commission is: *As you go about your daily lives, make disciples.* This is huge! It has several major Kingdom culture implications to reorient drift in your church. (1) The privilege of disciple-making is not limited to Sunday morning, Wednesday night, or activities at the building. (2) It is an everyday lifestyle, not a program. (3) The movement includes everyone. It is not restricted to a pastor, staff, or some outreach committee. (4) The mission field of your church is not five miles around your church. It is wherever Christians go. It is the unchurched, non-Christian people in the social networks of all those who are part of your church. Get this, and it will turn your church inside out. This is the breakthrough for the country club, Ceiling #2.

Most pastors and church leaders spend too much time on the squeaky wheel and not enough time on the steering wheel of the church. *The steering wheel of Kingdom culture is to equip God's people to go into their social networks and make disciples.* If you counted the number of those far from God who are already known by those in your church and with whom they have a relationship, you would be shocked to discover the size of your church's primary mission field. When it comes to the harvest, those who are already in relationships with the Christians in the church represent the "low-hanging fruit." They are the easiest to reach. They already exist within the relational influence sphere of your congregation. Change your worldview about this, and you will open the Kingdom dimension for outreach. Why is this so foreign to so many?

As you reach new people, they bring new social networks into the picture. If they are non-Christians, it is likely their social network includes many non-Christians. If they are discipled to disciple others, if they "get" the commission, and if they see it as their privilege, then your church is on a roll. Your church transforms from an institution to a movement. Get it?

Kingdom culture is to *go* make disciples, yet the posture (attitude) of most Christians is "you all come." This is a major factor of Kingdom culture drift. It cripples the potential mission (purpose) of so many Christians. It undercuts the potential mission and purpose of many churches. The Kingdom culture says *you need to turn your church inside out.* It is not so much about programs, committees, or even staff. It is about every Christian, every day, in every way, reaching out to those who are non-Christians in their social networks. This isn't an institutional effort. It is a personal lifestyle. This is the explosive movement genius of Jesus. Why don't we get this?

The "you all come" strategy focuses on preaching pizzazz, fancy facilities, and worship that wows. None of that is bad. Worship God the best way you can; just don't make it your only outreach strategy and expect to reach people for Christ in great numbers. You will always attract some lapsed Christians and those who leave their home church for whatever reason. A few of your members have been discipling and bringing newcomers when they're ready—to worship. But don't hold your breath for revival-level breakthrough until you turn your culture inside out. Why?

The largest fishing pool of unchurched people in North America is secular, second-generation non-Christians. For some, their parents left the church, and they grew up in a non-practicing home. The next largest group is Muslims and other non-Christian religions. (Many of them are lapsed in faith.) For these types of people, walking onto a Christian campus is like a lifelong Christian visiting a mosque for the first time on his own. It's traumatic, scary, and spiritually foreign. Revival will never take off in churches primarily focused on the "you all come" culture. You need to turn it around. Instead of taking people to church, you need to take church to people. What does that look like?

> Kingdom culture is to *go* make disciples, yet the posture (attitude) of most Christians is "you all come."

Let's say Laura is your friend at the school where you teach. You develop a relationship, and Laura shows receptivity. Instead of inviting her to church, it is more effective to invite her to coffee. There is no spiritual culture shock in that strategy. Start by sharing with Laura how God has worked in your life. Plant seeds, gently. If the spiritual conversation continues, then share more over time. When the time is right, invite some of your Christian friends to your house, to a restaurant, or to a picnic in the park, and invite Laura. She will meet other Christians and discover you are not alone in this faith. Then offer a low-level, enquirers' Bible study, which is a little deeper introduction to Christianity. Many churches across the world use Alpha, an outreach mechanism developed by Holy Trinity Brompton in England.[16] Ask your friends to share their stories about what God has done in their lives. As Laura hears their stories, she will begin to see that you are not the only person who is a believer and who finds Christianity a great value for life. When Laura is ready, bring (don't invite) Laura with you to church, and sit together with your friends, who are now her friends, too. Afterward, go out to a restaurant or a coffee shop and give Laura the space to debrief her experience in the safety of her new Christian friends.

Then what? Invite Laura to a membership class at your church? Not if you're in the Kingdom culture! If you are one who disciples, then *you* disciple Laura. The join-the-church thing can come later.

Do you see what we do? We rush people into the institutional system—the membership class. We actually contribute to Laura becoming a Christian with an organizational worldview rather than modeling the Kingdom worldview. (We will look at the strategic importance of multiplication in chapter nine.)

Multiply personal discipling by everyone in your church—then you're in accord with Jesus. The Kingdom culture in your church is ripe and ready for God to bring His great movement—a revival, an explosion of growth, and a breakthrough! This is Kingdom culture. It is an exponential multiplication atmosphere. It is a Jesus epidemic.

CEILING #2: COUNTRY CLUB

In the Old Testament, Israel was to be a "light to the nations."[17] How did that work? It worked like the light on your front porch in the summer, which attracts bugs. In the Old Testament, God resided in the temple, on the Temple Mount, in Jerusalem. God was a destination. If you wanted to check out God, you went to Him. People would take pilgrimages to Jerusalem. Jesus and His parents, as good Jews, made the pilgrimage to Jerusalem when Jesus was a small boy.[18] The Old Covenant was a pilgrimage approach. It was centripetal, like water going down the drain.

People came from other countries to check out the God of Israel. They would talk to the priest in the temple. However, only the priest could go into the Holy of Holies, which was the center of the centripetal Old Testament movement. Isaiah 60:1–3 says, "Arise, shine, for your light has come, and the glory of the LORD has risen upon you. For behold, darkness shall cover the earth, and thick darkness the peoples; but the LORD will arise upon you, and his glory will be seen upon you. And nations shall come to your light, and kings to the brightness of your rising."[19]

Jesus turned this inside out. He was the bridge from the centripetal faith to a centrifugal movement. Centrifugal force occurs when a heavy object swings at the end of a rope. Swing it around and around, harder and harder, then let go, and it flies outward. Jesus said, "I am the light of the world."[20] He told the Pharisees that the temple was now Him: "Destroy this temple, and in three days I will raise it up."[21] Many of the believing Jews got excited about what Jesus said. They had anticipated the coming of the Messiah. The Pharisees were indignant. They felt Jesus was using language reserved only for God. Jesus declared, "And I, when I am lifted up from the earth, will draw all people to myself."[22] Jesus turned the salvation approach inside out. When did it become a movement? Precisely when He said to those who followed Him, "You are the light of the world."[23] He stated, "As the Father has sent me, so I send you."[24] Jesus also said, "Therefore go and make disciples."[25] He affirmed, "You will be My witnesses...to the ends of the earth."[26] The movement became centrifugal, all the way to the ends of the earth. Jesus turned the movement inside out!

Today, many churches are New Testament in faith but Old Testament in outreach! This is a major element of Kingdom drift. The church building, for most Christians, is a destination, not a launch pad. The church becomes a mutual admiration society rather than a marching army. It's crazy! Some churches still sing "Stand Up, Stand Up for Jesus" while they're sitting down. They sing "Onward, Christian Soldiers" and then go home to chicken dinner and roast preacher.

> Today, many churches are New Testament in faith but Old Testament in outreach.

The temple of the Old Testament was fixed in one location. However, Jesus said, "Your bodies are temples of the Holy Spirit."[27] He declared, "You are the body of Christ."[28] That means wherever you go, Jesus goes. That is a fact. The challenge is that so many Christians aren't *going* anywhere. They are fixated on an Old Testament form of outreach of bringing people to church. If that's the primary strategy, you won't see exponential growth. You can grow a church, but you won't experience the Jesus epidemic.

In our research, we ask Christians in worship, "Which definition best describes the word *mission*?"

The Definition of Mission

The word *mission* is best described as: (Mark one.)
① The task which God has sent *every* Christian to do in every place, namely to proclaim Christ as Savior so that people become responsible members of the church.
② Efforts to share the Gospel of Jesus overseas.
③ A church needing financial help from other churches.
④ The work of the New Testament apostles, demonstrated today whenever Christians share the love and forgiveness of Jesus Christ with one another.
⑤ Anytime we offer "a cup of cold water to a thirsty person" and we are motivated by God's love.

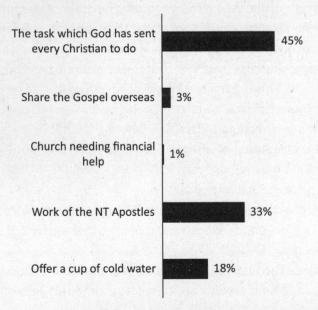

The bar graph above indicates the total respondents.

- The task which God has sent every Christian to do — 45%
- Share the Gospel overseas — 3%
- Church needing financial help — 1%
- Work of the NT Apostles — 33%
- Offer a cup of cold water — 18%

The Kingdom of Jesus grows most effectively by people going. I visited the sanctuary of Trinity Baptist Church in San Antonio,

Texas. The senior pastor at the time, Buckner Fanning, pointed to the walls around the sanctuary. They are painted with scenes of the city of San Antonio. He explained that the paintings are to show that the Lord never told the world to go to the church. He told the church to go to the world. How ironic! Many Christians consider their church building the destination of mission. You drive by a church building and your friend says, "That's where I go to church." Jesus might ask, "Where does the church go with you?"

LOOKING INSIDE OUT

The inside-out Kingdom culture looks a lot different. There are many implications:

1. Worship is primarily for believers, not unbelievers. Why would anyone who doesn't believe in God want to worship Him? This is not a wholesale rejection of "seeker-sensitive" worship services. There are many lapsed Christians, wandering believers, and mobile churchgoers who just moved into the area. You should make worship as sensitive and welcoming for new or lapsed Christians as you can. Just don't make that your primary mission strategy. You will never reach optimal New Testament outreach breakthrough.

2. Another implication has to do with your worldview. Your primary mission is "out there." Christians should be helped to identify their network of relationships as their personal mission field. Jesus called disciples to be "fishers of men [and women]."[29] The disciples fished with nets. Today, you should be equipped to work your nets, which are your networks. This is your primary mission field. Christian outreach is all about relationships. The movement moves through relationships. Breakthrough occurs through relationships. Every revival spreads through relationships. Remember, the movement is a Jesus epidemic. People catch it by being up close and personal with those who are spiritually contagious.

3. The church (the facility) is for two purposes: worship and equipping. This is where worship can be deep and wide—deep in Christian teaching and wide with mission implications. Equipping

should be for reaching out. *The most valuable equipping takes place when you catch Kingdom culture.* When you become a Kingdom culture person, everything you hope for mission will occur. It will be your DNA and your lifestyle. It is not what you do but who you are and who you become. A trip to Walmart or Starbucks becomes a short-term mission trip. The server at Applebee's becomes a person for whom Christ died—and you may be the ambassador He has in mind for her.

4. It is more productive to hold activities in the community than at the church whenever possible. It is more important for the church to be in the world than in the building. For example, many churches provide vacation Bible school at their church building. It is more productive to use a vacant store in a shopping center, a park pavilion, or a public elementary school. The cost of rental should come out of your mission budget rather than your education budget. The neutral turf will increase the likelihood children will invite their unchurched friends, and their friends will more likely respond.

5. Bible studies work much better at a coffee shop or restaurant than at the church building. For example, suppose your men's Bible study met at Joe's Bar. Your unchurched neighbor named Fred might stop in for lunch. He sees you and says, "Hi, Dave, what are you guys doing?" This is not an interruption! It is a divine appointment. You tell Fred you regularly attend this Bible study. This may lead to a future opportunity for you to share with Fred why you study the Bible and what God has done in your life. If the men's Bible study is held in the church basement, the chances of Fred coming by and "bumping into you" are likely nonexistent.

6. Your church office is best located in a strip mall or a shopping center. It ought to have a spacious lobby, and the sign in the window should offer help through a variety of services. The "go" culture puts the church in the marketplace of life. As Church Doctors, we have consulted several growing churches that were out of room. On numerous occasions, we have recommended they purchase a box store in a shopping mall. This has worked very well for these churches. The "go" element of the Great Commission challenges you to go public.

7. Your church building may not need to be as large as you thought. If your church were considering a building project, it would be a good time to think about the centrifugal implications of Kingdom culture. Your challenge for space may give you added opportunity to turn your church inside out.

KNOW A MISSIONARY?

Try this experiment at your church. It will help everyone *think* inside out. Ask, "Does anyone know a missionary, personally?" If anyone raises their hand, ask them to write down the name. Then ask, "Did anyone write down his or her own name?" Whatever the response, you will start turning the mental wheel about Kingdom culture inside out.

As a Christian, the missionary you know best is the one you see in the mirror. Think about Kingdom drift. The word *missionary* comes from the Latin word *missio*, which translates as *sent*. When Jesus says in John 20:21, "As the Father has sent me, I send you," it means you have been sent with authority on behalf of Him who has sent you, to perform a special duty. Every Christian is a missionary. When Jesus gives the Great Commission, He says, "Go." As a Christ-follower, you become a "sent person." Rick Warren says, "We believe being a missionary is not crossing the sea, but seeing the cross."[30] When you turn your church inside out, Kingdom culture calls you a missionary. Do you know any church that calls their people "missionaries" instead of "members"? Neither do I. I have consulted churches from the Missionary Church denomination. I love their name! However, even they usually call their people "members."

We think of missionaries as those who go to faraway places to reach "heathen" people in strange lands. There are many missionaries like that, but they are not the only missionaries. You are a missionary because you live on a mission field and because you are sent to that mission field by the King of the universe.

> As a Christian, the missionary you know best is the one you see in the mirror.

I worked with a Presbyterian church that consisted of upper- and upper-middle-class white-collar people who live in an all-white bedroom community. Like prim and proper Presbyterians, they were careful to follow the Presbyterian liturgy and practices, what they call the "Presbyterian Way."

Before they invited me to consult their church, some of their members, as the story goes, were studying and reading a book about being more mission-minded. They continued their conversation over several months, developing a vision for being a missionary-minded church. However, they soon discovered not everyone in the congregation agreed with their point of view. It was too much change. Many were not comfortable with the desire to turn the church inside out. The conversation continued, and the tension increased. Ultimately, the church divided. Those who resisted change remained in the church building. The missionary-minded group left and eventually rented a room in a former junior high school.

At this point, the new group wrote to their denomination and said they were mission-minded. They wanted a pastor who was a missionary. At the same time, a Presbyterian pastor in Jamaica was feeling the call to be a missionary to America. This tall, black, Jamaican pastor wanted to serve on the mission field America had become. The timing was perfect. The denominational executive who received both letters at about the same time decided to send the new missionary pastor from Jamaica to the mission-minded breakaway group. When he arrived with his family, the people were shocked. This is when I was asked to consult the church. The pastor spoke English with a heavy Jamaican accent. His family represented the only people of color in the whole city. He influenced the church to begin worship with a little Jamaican beat, and even a little dance. Remember, these people are Presbyterians! After they recovered from culture shock, the people quickly fell in love with their new pastor. God has a sense of humor!

Unfortunately, most churches in the United States are sleeping through a sweeping change. What it takes to reach unchurched Americans today are missionary pastors and missionary people. If we do not do the job, God will continue to bring missionaries from

South Korea, Africa, Jamaica, and many other places. They will get the job done. God wants lost people reached, and He will do whatever it takes.

How could we have drifted so far from the Kingdom culture of being a sent people? No wonder it seems like a huge challenge to turn the church inside out. In my perception, the drift in the United States began in the early days of colonialism. The United States was colonized by many who were Christians fleeing from the abuses of state churches in Europe. They came to America to live in religious freedom.

Somehow, over time, America became subconsciously perceived by many to be a "Christian" nation. At different times in history, many European countries, Canada, and others have experienced a similar trend. Years ago, many in America had come to accept this worldview of a Christian country. Today, most everyone is aware this is not the case. However, since the United States was previously considered to be a Christian nation, the mission field became known as someplace "over there," far away. When churches wanted to become involved in missions, they would raise money to help support missionaries "over there." Missions became synonymous with writing a check.

Meanwhile, many seminaries and Bible colleges put little or no emphasis on missionary training for pastors. Mission strategies were not part of the curriculum. I have met thousands of US pastors who would agree that their training has been primarily toward maintaining churches. In his book *Thinking for a Change*, John Maxwell writes:

- Unsuccessful people focus their thinking on survival
- Average people focus their thinking on maintenance
- Successful people focus their thinking on *progress*[31]

The first-century Christians were focused on *progress*, to win the world for Jesus Christ. This is Kingdom thinking. Today, many churches are plateaued or declining. Several decades ago, denominational and seminary leaders woke up to the growing number of non-Christians in the United States. With demands from churches, some training institutions began offering one or two courses in evangelism, witnessing, and/or church growth.

Years ago, Frank Page and John Perry interviewed Dr. Donald McGavran, the founder of the modern Church Growth Movement. In that interview, he said, "Remember that at the heart of the Church Growth Movement here or anywhere in the world is the Great Commission. We must never lose sight of this perspective, which encompasses the whole world, every human being." This reflects the priority of Kingdom culture.[32]

> Somehow, over time, America became subconsciously perceived by many to be a "Christian" nation.... The mission field became known as someplace "over there," far away. Missions became synonymous with writing a check.

In contrast, the worldview of most pastors is that of a caretaker. It is a shepherd concept. Some pastors may gather a few willing people to form an evangelism committee, which occasionally ends up mostly talking about how outsiders can learn about their church. Many churches organize an annual "Bring-a-Friend Sunday." In past decades, many churches had an evangelism program, like Evangelism Explosion. Today, most pastors and church leaders have little or no training in the strategic elements of missions. Consequently, it is impossible for them to equip those in their churches in mission strategy.

Over the years, there have been pastors who felt called to be missionaries. For most, this meant the call to go overseas. After completing Bible college or seminary, they would attend a special missions school to learn mission strategies to use on the mission field in a foreign land.

My own calling to ministry was fueled by a strong desire to reach people for Jesus Christ. I followed the preparation route of my denomination: four years of college followed by four years of seminary. In my last year of seminary, the only outreach training I received was an elective on evangelism. Under the conviction that there had to be more outreach training in my denomination's system,

I applied for graduate school. After completing the work for a PhD in Theology, I reached two conclusions: (1) I received an excellent education in theology, and (2) there was practically no mission training, at any level, for a pastor in my denomination. No wonder my denomination has been in decline for almost fifty years!

After graduate school, my placement in ministry sent me to a church in urban Detroit, as I shared earlier. Worship attendance was about 1,200. In the previous ten years, the church had declined by 67 percent. It was an old Anglo congregation in a predominantly young African American neighborhood. The median age of those in attendance at church was approximately sixty-four years old. Most of our neighbors were unchurched. My passion for outreach was still strong. The church leadership board was willing to pay for me to get evangelism training in the Evangelism Explosion program.[33] I spent time learning from Dr. D. James Kennedy in Fort Lauderdale, Florida. I took two men from the church with me, and it was a great experience.

The reason I share this in more detail is because we had a program, but my church did not have Kingdom culture. We faithfully implemented Evangelism Explosion. I found about twenty people who were willing to make evangelism calls in our cross-cultural setting. I had learned that the program works best when you are reaching a person who has visited your church, but we didn't have any visitors from the neighborhood. Honestly, many of us were afraid of "them," and many of them were afraid of "us." We made numerous calls, for two years. We met some great people. Our evangelism team trained others, and over time, the effort grew to about twenty-six people. However, seldom did anyone that we visited come to church.

I was depressed. I refer to that year as my "desert time." I called my denomination's regional office in Ann Arbor, Michigan. I told the person who answered, "Look, whatever we try doesn't work." The answer was not what I wanted to hear: "We don't know what works to reach blacks in Detroit. Our denomination has already closed twenty churches in the metropolitan area." Then I called my denominational headquarters in St. Louis. My phone call was routed to the North American Missions office. I was told, "We're not very good at that." I said, "Give me the name of a church, any of our churches, reaching out cross-culturally to African Americans." The response was, "We don't have any." I replied, "Okay, give me the name of any church, any denomination." The man said, "We don't talk to them." Really?

In my frustration, I prayed for some help. One day, I picked up a piece of third-class mail that came to our church office. It was promoting the Doctor of Ministry program at Fuller Theological Seminary in Pasadena, California. I had never heard of the school. What caught my eye was their claim to have one of the largest missions schools in the world. I decided to try it. I went two weeks at a time for three years, basically training in missionary strategy. I will be forever grateful to my mentors (Peter Wagner, Chuck Kraft, Donald McGavran, and many others), former missionaries from the "faraway" mission field, for training me for the American mission field. I will never be the same.

By the grace of God, I did not start a program at my church. Instead, I began methodically, patiently, to develop what I would now call Kingdom culture. Slowly, I communicated a worldview of mission thinking. Most were receptive. The result? Our church grew cross-culturally with no split or turmoil. It was not about a program we did; it was who we became. Many of the long-term members said, "We've been church members all our lives, but this is the most exciting experience we've ever had." What happened? They became Kingdom culture people. You can, too.

Yes, we developed mission strategies. However, they would have never taken hold in our congregation if we hadn't started with the Kingdom culture.

In January of 1998, the magazine *Mission America Monthly* declared, "The United States is now the third-largest mission field in the world. Only China and India have more nonbelievers." Do you see the dilemma of our drift from Kingdom culture? Over time, mission leaks. Mission drifts from making disciples to limited ministries operating programs and doing good deeds. Most pastors can't lead church members to turn the church inside out. They have never been trained. Most Christians cannot identify the purpose of the church as the Great Commission.

Our challenge is basic, and it is systemic. The last thing your church needs is another program. If you want to see your church in terms of Breakthrough Strategy #2 and turn your church inside out, it is an inside job. It is not what you do but who you become. Can you become a citizen of the Kingdom? By God's grace, of course you can! Leave the country club behind. Fellowship is great; it just isn't your primary mission. It never was!

As we turn to chapter seven, we will look at the deeply spiritual issue of taking God at His word.

CHAPTER SEVEN

Turn Your Faith into God-Sized Potential—Breakthrough Strategy #3

Ceiling #3: Baby Food

My God is not just Someone I believe in. He's Someone I know. I've felt His presence. I've seen His activity. I've experienced His deliverance. I've been touched by His healing. I've witnessed answered prayer. I've "heard" Him speak straight to me through His Word. Yes, I believe. But more than that, I know.

—Beth Moore[1]

The apostle Paul wrote these challenging words:

"I'm completely frustrated by your unspiritual dealings with each other and with God. You're acting like infants in relation to Christ, capable of nothing much more than nursing at the breast. Well, then, I'll nurse you since you don't seem capable of anything more. As long as you grab for what makes you feel good or makes you look important, are you really much different than a babe at the breast, content only when everything's going your way?"[2]

During our research in a congregation in New England, we learned of an interesting dispute. The conversation became heated between Pastor Barbara and Jim. Jim was visibly angry about a change Barbara had made in the worship service. Barbara operated on an assumption: The Bible is truth. Jim, in response, provided insight to his perspective: "I don't care what the Bible says. I think…" We have experienced this debate before. Perhaps you have seen it as well. It is usually more subtle.

Do you belong to a church effectively reaching new people? If so, you are constantly interacting with those who have little knowledge of the Bible. They are on the infancy end of spiritual growth. They are new in the lifelong journey of growing in the wisdom of God. Each person is at a different level on the journey described as growing "in the grace and knowledge of our Lord and Savior Jesus Christ."[3]

CEILING #3: BABY FOOD

Thankfully, churches don't give annual exams on Bible knowledge. You don't receive a sticker that designates you at level three, though your spouse is at level eight. It gets even more complicated, as every congregation has one-year-old children of God who have been attending the church for twenty years. They stopped growing at the end of the first year, repeating the cycle twenty times. Plateaued at the level "spiritual infant," they have stayed there ever since.

Nowhere does this surface more dramatically than in the day-to-day living of Kingdom culture. It shows in the five elements of Kingdom DNA: values, beliefs, attitudes, priorities, and worldviews. Kingdom culture drives behavior. Biblical illiteracy is rampant among so many Christians. Many churches operate like an NFL professional football team in which only 36 percent ever learned the playbook. They could never win the Super Bowl, and you know it. Likewise, most churches will never win their neighbors to Christ.

When God created human life, He made babies egocentric and selfish. If a baby is hungry or uncomfortable in a wet diaper, he will cry and holler. The baby doesn't care if it is three a.m. and you are exhausted. This egocentrism is a wonderful mechanism for survival. Babies are created to live selfishly. As babies grow into young children, and children grow into healthy adults, they become increasingly *self-less*. As Christians mature, they care about others. Paul underscores this important element of Kingdom culture in 1 Corinthians 14. It is also a key factor for a healthy church to produce Kingdom fruit.

In Matthew 10, Jesus sends His disciples into a village to announce the Kingdom of God. They visit people in their homes. If people are receptive, the disciples are to spend time with them. If they are not responsive, the disciples are instructed to "shake off the dust from your feet as you leave that house or town."[4] This implies that receptivity is not the disciples' responsibility. It is God's work. God is the One who makes the harvest ripe.

When the disciples are invited into a home where people are receptive, Jesus says, "Eat what is set before you."[5] At first blush, this seems like a strange command. Had Jesus been in some of these homes and discovered they were good cooks? No, this teaching is about being selfless and mature, not selfish. The Kingdom principle is this: *The more mature Christian subordinates his or her preferences to those of the less mature Christian or unbeliever.* For effective mission, mature Christians subordinate their "menu" to that of the less mature Christian or the unbeliever, as long as it doesn't violate Scripture.

This is why, when my wife, Janet, and I were in Zimbabwe, we ate mopani worms. These cooked caterpillars are a delicacy of the Tswana tribe. Since we operate under Kingdom DNA, it means we don't offend people by saying, "No, thanks. Is there a McDonald's somewhere around here?" That's how Kingdom culture works on the mission field. How does it work in your life and in your church? You do know you are on a mission field, right?

A healthy church will be filled with healthy Christians. Healthy Christians are mature in a biblical lifestyle. This is how it works: Roger is the children's pastor at King of Kings Lutheran Church in Omaha. He approached some parents, asking, "Can your children leave worship to attend children's church?" The parents objected. "We want to worship together as a family." Roger made his case for children's church. "The chairs fit their smaller bodies, the messages are geared to their attention-span level, and visuals connect with kids." The parents responded, "We want to worship together." Roger replied, reflecting selfless Kingdom culture, "I agree. Why don't you come with them and sit on the floor. You can adjust to their level, but the children can't adjust to your level."

My colleagues and I have interviewed countless parents whose children are in their thirties and forties. So many lament about how their children have erased Christian practice from their lives. I am convinced that, for many, it was their insistence that their children sit in a worship service that was not age-appropriate. I say this not to pile on guilt. They are in too much pain already. I point this out to underscore the value of knowing the playbook. Generations are at stake!

What would your church be like if most everyone grew to a mature level of spiritual selflessness? How would it affect attitudes about change? How sensitive would Christians be to guests? What would be the sensitivity toward children? How would people treat new, young Christians? How eager would everyone be to engage in Bible study? How compassionate would church members become toward those

> A healthy church is filled with healthy Christians. Healthy Christians are mature in a biblical lifestyle.

who are homeless, incarcerated, or addicted? If you want a healthy church, your people need to grow beyond spiritual baby food.

Biblical maturity toward Kingdom culture makes effective missionaries. What if 70 to 80 percent of those in your church were practicing missionaries to their own social networks? It would likely result in a major move of God, a revival. Your spiritual atmosphere would be transformed. Your congregation could grow and become a contagious example to other churches.

BIBLICAL AUTHORITY

It's strange: Mature faith is childlike faith. Ongoing childlike faith grows into mature faith. This is a Kingdom culture attitude. It is your posture toward God, your Kingdom profile. What is your church's posture about the Bible? Is it childlike, trusting God at His word? If so, you can grow from there. Sadly, not every church has this foundation. At the end of the day, the only foundational guide we have is the Scripture.

Remember Jesus' teaching about little children? The Pharisees were arguing, using biblical gymnastics on the subject of divorce. The objective was not to learn about divorce; it was to trap Jesus. They weren't *childlike* in faith, with hunger for spiritual growth. They played a *childish*, illogical game. It was their goal to prove Jesus an imposter.

The teaching about childlike faith follows right after the sophisticated twisting of Scripture by the religious leaders. Jesus says, "Whoever does not receive the kingdom of God as a little child will never enter it."[6] *Jesus provides a snapshot of the Kingdom culture approach to biblical truth.*

Our research shows only 36 percent of active worshippers in the churches we studied attend a regularly scheduled Bible study. After six months, this grew to 51 percent.

Bible Study Participation on a Regular Basis

Do you attend a regularly scheduled Bible study either at church or elsewhere?

①	Yes	②	No

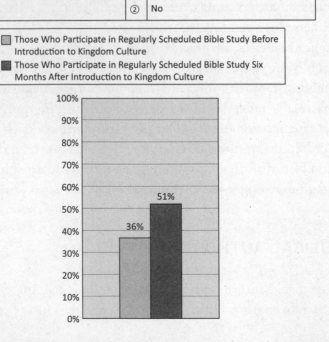

Those Who Participate in Regularly Scheduled Bible Study Before Introduction to Kingdom Culture

Those Who Participate in Regularly Scheduled Bible Study Six Months After Introduction to Kingdom Culture

An increase to 51 percent is moving in the right direction. Consider how God could use your church if it were 90 percent!

Why is this so difficult? If Christians really believe "Your word is a lamp unto my feet, and a light unto my path,"[7] what would that look like? (1) Almost everyone in your church would participate in a Bible study. (2) The number of practicing Christians who are biblically illiterate would greatly diminish. (3) Churches would be healthier. They would operate more like Kingdom culture than a corporate bureaucracy. (4) Churches would flourish and grow. (5) Christians would function according to God's plan, not the latest program or most recent fad. (6) Christians would identify themselves as "missionaries" rather than "members." (7) As you effectively reach more people for Christ, the demand for spiritual growth would increase.

Many Christians give lip service to the importance of Scripture. The percentage of church leaders biblically challenged is astounding. Staff becomes stressed by biblically immature Christians who demand secular direction for the church. This is especially true for the issue of *how to be the church*. Well-meaning yet biblically ignorant leaders unintentionally hijack the church.

Biblical literacy is low for several reasons. (1) The appetite for Kingdom culture is suppressed by demands of busyness. Rather than "Seek first the kingdom of God,"[8] the priority is to get through the agenda. (2) Churches create a system that demands a massive amount of time and energy for maintenance of the "machine." (3) Many congregations elect anyone who is willing to serve. Little attention is given to identifying those who have "the mind of Christ."[9] (4) Few are discipled into positions with sensitivity to their spiritual gifts. (5) Often it is an issue of unintentional arrogance.

John is a successful businessman, so he is considered a good candidate for the church board. No one asks, "What is John's posture toward the Word of God?" Is he *beside* the Word of God? (Is it a part of his life?) Is he *above* the Word of God? (Is he so busy that spiritual growth is not a priority?) Is he *under* the Word of God? (Is he eager to learn, grow, and allow God's Word to guide his life, his decisions, and his church?)

The issue about biblical authority is sometimes arrogance. In Luke 18, Jesus speaks of the Pharisee who enters the temple. In prayer, he apparently brags about being an exemplary believer. Meanwhile, a tax collector (hated by Jews) is humble and asks for mercy. This is arrogance versus humility.[10] St. Augustine said, "If you believe what you like in the gospels, and reject what you don't like, it is not the gospel you believe, but yourself."[11] *It takes humility to grow in Kingdom culture.* Humility is a strange virtue. Like a greased pig, the minute you think you have it, you've lost it!

When you are not clear about the Scripture, you lack a biblical worldview. You don't know God at a mature level. You don't know His passion, priorities, or character. You don't know what He wants. You don't immerse yourself in God's Word and are excessively flattered by your own opinions.

How do you approach the Bible? If you want to catch Kingdom culture, don't mess with Scripture. The truth is the truth. Receive it like a little child. Don't try to twist it to fit your circumstances.

> Clearly, the Kingdom of God is not like this world. That is why Kingdom culture is so valuable.... You are excessively flattered by your own opinions.

You can be physically fit but spiritually anemic. You can have a PhD in whatever and be ignorant of Kingdom culture. What happens? As Christians gather to consider an issue about church, many are not on the same page. Literally, they are not on the same pages of Scripture. Churches are riddled with division. Decision-making groups are all over the map of opinions. John Wesley said, "I allow no other rule, whether of faith or practice, than the Holy Scriptures."[12] No wonder God could use John Wesley to bring an awakening in England and in the colonies of early America.

Ironically, in many corners of Christianity, this issue of scriptural truth is a controversial subject. However, you can't catch Kingdom culture anywhere else. It is fundamental, because Kingdom culture, more than anything else, fuels a healthy church. Healthy churches reach people for Christ and impact the world. The air healthy

Christians breathe is an atmosphere powered by a Word that is God-breathed: inspired![13]

We have worked with many churches struggling with hidden division. Some Christians are vocal, dissenting from the mission focus. They frustrate others. The heart of this challenge is often undetected. Dissenters operate from a worldly worldview rather than a Kingdom culture perspective.

Jerry attends a large church we consulted in Nebraska. He is a retired successful business owner. Jerry was chosen for a leadership position without any thought of his spiritual development. He was not discipled into the position by a mentor with biblical wisdom and a sense of Kingdom culture. Instead, Jerry was nominated for leadership because he had been successful in business. He was the "perfect" candidate because he was retired and available.

Jerry truly loves his church and loves God. However, he is naively ignorant of the world of the church. Jerry knew how to run a business, but he never learned about the way church is supposed to work. Over time, Jerry became an irritant to the pastor and other key leaders. He influenced a minority of others who were unintentionally dragging down the church. See how this works?

As consultants, we often see this. Many pastors miss the issue behind the issue. They encourage members to assume leadership positions. Pastors provide a forum to speak publicly because this method has been successful in secular culture. These Christians are infants in Kingdom culture. The result? So much effort is wasted on symptom solving.

Christians who submit to the Bible are more productive at making disciples. Those who are unchurched respond to an undiluted version of Scripture just fine. Bill Hybels, senior pastor of Willow Creek Community Church in South Barrington, Illinois, says, "I don't think anybody is coming to church anymore for a mild dose of God. We say: 'all killer, no filler.' "[14] You've heard "the truth, the whole truth, and nothing but the truth." Long before this was part of the court system, it was foundational for God's system and for Kingdom culture. Christians who approach Scripture as total truth provide greater potential for their church to grow. Why?

When we interview those who are new Christians in a church, we ask, "How is it you were attracted to this church? Why do you continue to attend?" The common response is, "The message, the teaching." When we unpack their comments, it is clear that people are attracted to a solid biblical message.

Peter Brierley is a respected researcher of the Christian movement. He has also identified this connection through his study of growing churches in England and, specifically, in London. He says there is likely a significant link between outreach effectiveness and firm belief in the "whole of Scripture."[15] One common thread in churches experiencing an awakening is the childlike faith in the authority of Scripture. We have seen this firsthand where Christianity is rapidly growing in areas of Africa, South America, Asia, and "hot spots" of recent movements in Europe and Australia.

THE BACKBONE PHENOMENON

Some think that if you serve Christianity "lite," you will attract more people. Our research shows this is a fallacy. Actually, churches are more attractive to those who are searching when they are clearly "not ashamed of the gospel," which is "God's power for salvation."[16] People respond to Christians who know what they believe and believe what they know. The body of Christ without a spiritual backbone is not attractive to those searching for meaning to life. The body of Christ with a sound biblical backbone is distinguished from all other organizations, including some churches.

One of the early research studies about commitment to Scripture occurred in 1972, when Dean Kelley published *Why Conservative Churches Are Growing*. Kelley demonstrated that people respond more to churches providing a clear sense of life's purpose. Kelley's research shows that where religion fails to do this, a church, while busying itself with a host of programs, inevitably declines and even dies. Kelley summarizes his research, "The religious organization may err, not in being too conservative, but in being not conservative enough."[17] This concept is not new. In our consultation work, we have observed this for decades. Dean Kelley got it right.

Many churches have drifted in a liberal direction. Some believe parts of the Bible, subtly ignoring the more supernatural dimensions that feel foreign to sophisticated worldviews. Others drift to a focus almost entirely on social dimensions of being the hands and feet of Jesus but lose the balance of sharing the faith and making disciples. Still others determine that the strictly academic view of Scripture is appropriate, but the life-changing power of God at work—whether it be Jonah and the whale or the resurrection of Jesus—are allegorical or mythological.

Beyond theological implications, our experience in research shows, from a mission perspective, this drift does not produce healthy churches. Long term, they do not expand the Kingdom or impact their communities in a transformational way. This is an issue of Kingdom culture. The apostle Paul says, "Now to him who is able to do far more abundantly than all that we ask or think, according to the power at work within us, to him be glory in the church and in Christ Jesus throughout all generations, forever and ever. Amen."[18]

The other extreme of liberalization is churches teaching antiseptic faith. This is Bible theory in a vacuum. Christians become "so heavenly minded, they are no earthly good," as Peter Wagner said.[19] The motto might be, "We are right. Dead right." They are missionally dead. These Christians gloat about pure doctrine but act like it's a secret they must keep to themselves. Their mission is to point out where other Christians are wrong. This is spiritual suicide. God's Kingdom is transformed into "my kingdom."

If there is energy in a church, it needs a positive outlet. If there isn't the grand vision to make disciples, which energizes the culture, the energy goes toward each other. The church implodes. However, when those in the church are focused on the mission to make disciples, they have little energy left to criticize others. Charles Van Engen clarifies: "It doesn't say that 'God so loved the church that He gave His only begotten Son' in John 3:16. It

> If there is energy in a church, it needs a positive outlet. If there isn't the grand vision to make disciples, which energizes the culture, the energy goes toward each other. The church implodes.

says that 'God so loved the world that He gave His only begotten Son.' Our mission is the world, not the church."[20] Churches that focus on the Bible and spend all their energy boasting about how they're right (and everyone else is wrong) are often spiritually constipated when it comes to mission.

Landa Cope, in her excellent book *Clearly Communicating Christ*, provides a great warning for balance:

> At some point in history the church...became focused on our message rather than on serving our audience. The burning question wasn't, "Where are people hurting? How can we apply the Gospel to meet those needs?" Instead it became, "Are we being faithful to Scripture? Is that the exact meaning of those words? Are we communicating in balance with the whole of the Bible?" Instead of pouring our hearts into reaching people, our passion became defending the message. If God felt that way, John 3:16 would have read, "For God so loved the *message* that He sent His only Son." ...It's people who are in danger! God so loved the *world*.[21]

There is a mutation in churches where leaders think their mission is to protect pure doctrine. As an extension of that attitude, they believe their role is to become judge, jury, and executioner for everyone else in God's Kingdom. At the extreme, you find the church, or the pastor, that believes the purpose is to criticize other Christians who "don't get it right—like I do." Every strain of Christianity has some elements of distinction when interpreting Christian truth. That is reality. It is another issue to flaunt your views publicly about how other Christians don't get it right. This seems like a modern hobby on social media for some Christians. In truth, this is arrogance. It is especially damaging to those who are not yet Christ-followers. They say, "That is being a Christian? Why would I want to be one of those? All they do is criticize one another." If you have an issue with someone's theology, follow Matthew 18 and deal with it privately—and spare the reputation of Christianity as being a group of people with bad attitudes.

HEALTHY BIBLICAL CULTURE

From the perspective of Scripture, Christians disciple new believers as they "grow in the grace and knowledge of our Lord and Savior Jesus Christ."[22] The church also reaches out to unbelievers. The *mission formula* is not rocket science. The formula is so easy that you might wonder why more Christians don't practice it for outreach.

1. Meet the needs of those who are hungry, hurting, disadvantaged, etc.
2. In the process, develop a relationship of integrity.
3. Watch for signs of receptivity.
4. Witness: Share what God has done in your life.
5. Disciple: Raise the young believer to maturity in Kingdom culture, in faith, and in service.
6. Send: Let go of the disciple to disciple others.
7. Repeat the process until the day you die.

Many Christians couldn't write this formula if their lives depended on it. In truth, the life of the Christian movement does depend on it. Get with the mission!

What we observe in thriving churches may stretch you beyond your comfort level. When churches are healthy, vibrant, and productively reaching out, there is deep acceptance of the supernatural dimensions of Scripture. This is often described as, "The God of the Bible is the God of today. Anything that occurred in the Bible can and does happen today."

I recently had a conversation with a Christian woman named Sally. I mentioned that some Christians had prayed for Joanne to be healed from a stroke that had occurred during knee replacement surgery. The stroke was "miraculously" gone. Even the non-Christian doctor called it a miracle. To my surprise, the report of this event caused a reaction from Sally. "I don't know if I could believe that!" she said. Sally attends church every Sunday.

As Church Doctors, we have the privilege to privately interview thousands of pastors, leaders, and church members. We hear information that is rarely discussed. Many church leaders have experienced what they believe is God's miraculous activity. Often, this includes miraculous healing. Likewise, many have been involved in ministries of deliverance from evil spirits.

These experiences are rarely reported publicly, yet they occur with a frequency that would surprise most Christians. There is also quite a wide acceptance of the so-called "sign gifts," like speaking in tongues, interpretation of tongues, exorcism, healing, and miracles, even among those whose denominations resist any discussion of these gifts from Scripture. (To be theologically clear, all the spiritual gifts are miraculous. The Holy Spirit is at work through all the gifts among Christians.)

Jesus said in Matthew 17:20, "If you have faith as small as a mustard seed...nothing will be impossible for you."[23] If you want your church to thrive and experience the health of a vital congregation, this is a great encouragement. The task before you is never as great as the power behind you. You can do this! From our observation around the world, when an awakening occurs, followed by a move of God and a revival in the land, it isn't that these supernatural activities suddenly appear. More often, these ministries of the Holy Spirit were there all along; they just became more public. Living Kingdom culture provides permission for them to be discussed. Perhaps Christians are more spiritually open.

The "spooky" areas of faith should be real. They are in the Bible! For those who choose to ignore these parts of Scripture, the burden of proof is on them. I share this as one who was stretched in my worldview during my first introduction to a revival, years ago, in Lagos, Nigeria. My wife and I witnessed a girl who was born

> The task before you is never as great as the power behind you.

blind receive her sight. We will never forget the moment she placed her hand on her mother's face, seeing it for the first time. Acts 2:43 describes the supernatural dimension of Kingdom culture: "Everyone around was in awe—all those wonders and signs done through the apostles!"[24]

Think about the early church: "*Every day* the Lord added to them those who were being saved."[25] This is the worldview of Kingdom culture. It is not only possible but also probable in Kingdom culture to see the Lord add to your church every day. This type of growth in the movement of Christianity is not limited to the first century. It is occurring, literally, in many places around the world, even as you read this. This is the experience of thriving Christians and thriving churches. This is normal. The slow growth or decline of Christian churches is abnormal and disharmonious with the Christian movement. In other words, if your church is not experiencing the Lord adding new believers to your group every day, your church is not operating at full potential. That is either true, according to the Bible, or you have to play some gymnastics and excuse it away by tampering with God's Word. You can't have it both ways.

CHURCH POSTURE

Kingdom culture forms your posture toward your church. This is the DNA of attitude. Chuck Swindoll once said, "Words can never adequately convey the incredible impact of our attitude toward life. The longer I live, the more convinced I become that life is 10 percent what happens to us and 90 percent how we respond to it."[26]

Attitude is one of the five elements of Kingdom DNA. Philippians 2:5–11 addresses the attitude you should have. It is the one Christ Jesus had. He was humble, obedient, willing to become like one of us, meet us where we are, and walk the path of obedience, ultimately to His death. That's quite an attitude!

Can you imagine if Jesus would have had a different kind of attitude? Imagine, for a moment, the living room of heaven before

> Can you imagine if Jesus would have had a different kind of attitude?
>
> What if He had responded by saying, "What's wrong with the way we've always done it?"

Jesus' earthly birth. The Father, Son, and Holy Spirit are having a conversation something like this: "Well," said the Father, "the time has come. We have promised people for a long time that we would send a Savior. Son, I've decided you're the one to go."

Imagine if Jesus had a different kind of attitude. What if He had said, "But we've never done it that way." What if He had responded by saying, "What's wrong with the way we've always done it? We did a flood once; it worked pretty well. Why can't we do that again?" What if Jesus had an attitude that went like this? "Go to earth? Die on a cross? That costs too much. I can't afford that. That's just too much to ask." What if Jesus had this kind of attitude? "Well, that kind of plan will work here in heaven, but it certainly won't work on earth. They just won't respond." Imagine if Jesus had said, "They know where we are. Let them come to us if they want to come."

Attitude has a lot to do with how you respond. I once saw an advertisement in *Time* magazine for General Electric. It read, "Sometimes you have to see things differently before you can do things differently." Attitude changes your behavior. When you encounter a person at church who is negative or disagreeable, it may be an issue of attitude. Unfortunately, we in the church sometimes have a disconnect between Kingdom culture, attitude, and bad behavior. We may never connect the spiritual dots. We think it's simply an attitude issue. Attitude is a spiritual issue. It is a Kingdom culture issue.

When our children are little, they occasionally misbehave. We realize these moments—as frustrating as they may be—are teaching moments. We recognize, in the big picture, our role is to speak into our children's lives. "Hopefully," we say, "they'll grow out of it." Our attitude is that the behavior has to do with their age, and our parenting response is chosen accordingly.

Why don't we have this approach with the *children* of God in our churches? One reason is we don't look at each other as children of God. We call people "members" instead. Most often, we are speaking organizationally, as members of the institution. Rarely do we have the concept of members of the body of Christ who are defined by our gifts and on a spiritual journey of growing up into Christ.[27] Rarely do we think about Christians of all ages growing into maturity in Christ, each at a different pace.

In a healthy church, Kingdom DNA imprints attitudes. The more who "get it," the healthier the church. Did you know the people in the church at Philippi had an attitude issue? Of course you did! It is why Paul wrote the letter to the Philippians. Paul was dealing with Kingdom culture drift. It happens to Christians all the time. Consider the attitude issues Paul identifies in Philippians 2. Do they have anything to say to you today? In verse 1, Paul says, in effect, "If being a Christ-follower means anything to you (has shaped your DNA), show love, care, and compassion."

Think about how a deep understanding of Scripture affects your attitude. Think about how your attitude affects your church. Think about how your church affects your community. Your attitude changes your behavior.

One of the most profound books I've read about early Christians and their attitude of compassion is a book by Rodney Stark, *The Rise of Christianity: How the Obscure, Marginal Jesus Movement Became the Dominant Religious Force in the Western World in a Few Centuries.*[28] Stark describes the scene when the dreaded plague hit the Roman Empire.

What was the protocol for the Romans? Leave home, go to the hills, get as far away from the sick as possible, abandoning those infected and contagious, even those in your own family. Leave them to die. Come back when it is safe and the danger has passed. By contrast, the Kingdom culture of Christians (that Kingdom which is not like the world) was much different. The believers had an *attitude* of compassion. They also had faith. They were not afraid of death. They remained in Rome and cared for the moms, dads, sons, and daughters of those who fled. The Christians had a different *worldview*: "To live is Christ and to die is gain."[29]

During the plague, many Christians died, and a great number lived. Many infected unbelievers also lived, through the care of

Christians. They became "infected" by the power of Jesus Christ. Many became believers. When relatives returned, they were astonished by the compassion of the Christians. Many turned their lives over to faith in Jesus Christ. Meanwhile, many of the Christians who showed compassion developed resistance to the plague! Their bodies developed a greater immunity than those who fled. The impression on those from the Roman Empire was significant.

Christianity conquered the mighty Roman Empire by love and compassion. Kingdom culture *is* different from this world. It makes an impression. How does that work in your life? How does that work in your church? How do the Christians in your church affect your community? If they were arrested for Christianity, as the saying goes, would there be enough evidence to convict them?

Remember the 2014 outbreak of Ebola in Western Africa? The secular media reported that the World Health Organization was so tangled in bureaucratic politics that they delayed help while the epidemic spread out of control. The real heroes, according to *Time* magazine, were Doctors Without Borders/Médecins Sans Frontières (MSF) and the medical relief workers of Samaritan's Purse.[30] Samaritan's Purse, an arm of the Christian *movement*, helped rescue the gridlocked *organization* (WHO).

Christians are still at the front, facing danger against all odds, centuries after the Roman plagues. This is the generational staying power of attitudes. Kingdom culture attitudes impact lives. In Philippians 2, the apostle focused on unity. The attitude of Christ is to get along. Paul says, "Agree with each other."[31] Do you ever experience a lack of unity in your church? What about in your family? The more important question is, "How much effort do you direct toward the development of the attitude of Christ?" Your source, again, is Scripture.

Do you know what unites God's people in a church? Vision. Vision is God's preferred future. Vision unites. Think about how this relates to attitude. Jesus' attitude is reflected in His words, "The Son of Man must die."[32] The vision that drove Jesus to the cross was to reach the world with the good news of the gospel. Nothing unites Christians like the vision of mission. Ever notice how a sports team is unified? It is because they have the same vision: victory. For believers, the vision is also victory—to win the world to Jesus Christ. Proverbs 29:18 says, "Where there is no vision, the people perish," in the King James Version. The New International Version reads, "Where there is no revelation, people cast off restraint." Where there is no driving input from God, people give away their ability to say no, so they say yes to everything. In some churches, many are busy but lack focus—they are without direction. Mission clarifies direction, purpose, and primary objective.

In verse 3 of Philippians 2, the apostle moves to the attitude of humility, which is the foundation for service. Humility also provides a hunger to learn from God and from others. Some Christians are driven by the attitude of "my way or the highway." If they don't get their way, they aren't involved. Gary, a former member of Grace Church, reflected, "Carla and I used to attend. They changed the ten thirty a.m. service to eleven a.m. We could no longer beat the crowd to our favorite restaurant. So we changed churches." What is your attitude about change? (We'll look at change in chapter eight.) What is your attitude about convenience? The Scripture provides everything needed to get Kingdom culture right.

The apostle Paul ends his teaching on attitude with a plea to the Philippians. He focuses on selfishness: "Consider others more important than yourself."[33] Then he points to the model of Jesus, who gave His life because He considered you and me more important than Himself. Someone once asked Dr. Karl Menninger, "What would you advise a person to do if he felt a nervous breakdown coming on?" Menninger replied, "Lock up your house, go across the railway tracks, find someone in need, and do something to help that person."[34] It is not an unusual response. It is Kingdom culture. How would this element of Kingdom DNA, this issue of attitude, affect the culture of your church? If you think, "I may be one of those who is far from this atti-

> The Scripture provides everything needed to get Kingdom culture right.

tude," consider how different your church could be if you would focus on Kingdom culture. The only source I know to improve this attitude is Scripture. The only approach that works is one that believes what the Scripture says.

LOOKING OUTWARD

When we interview long-term members of churches, we ask them if their church is friendly. The answer is always a resounding "Yes!" However, when we interview newcomers to the church, they have a different experience. They say, "Friendly? Not so much." Who is right? They are both right. In most churches, people are friendly—*to each other*. They are nice to newcomers on the surface, through the greeters at the door. It is a "Hello!" to an unfamiliar face, but that's about it. In our work, we often visit a church incognito, attending worship services undercover. We are like the mystery shopper. We stand alone in a crowded area near the welcome center, not far from the coffee. Some people will smile and say hello. Most, however, will not engage, even in an entry-level conversation, such as "Are you new to this church? Where are you from? What do you do?"

Some churches recognize this need, so what do they do? They develop an institutional program! They make name tags for all the members, put more greeters at the doors, and try to find "friendly" people to hand out worship bulletins. While there is nothing wrong with these programmatic approaches, they really don't get to the heart of the issue. How do you look at those beyond your relationship base? What is your attitude about guests? This is an issue of Kingdom culture. You can learn this from Scripture, especially the model of Jesus. It is more caught than taught. It requires catching Jesus from the perspective of Kingdom culture.

Look at the organizational approach of most churches. What is the approach toward *belonging*? In many congregations, you start by attending, or you grow up in the congregation. If you decide you want to belong to the church, it's usually called "membership." In most churches, the way to membership includes taking classes of instruction. The sessions are most often focused on knowing biblical teaching—a basic summary of doctrines—that are promoted through the lens of the church's denomination or fellowship. What is rarely taught is Kingdom culture. Kingdom DNA is caught through relational discipleship, not taught in classes.

As you follow the journey toward membership, it may not be

obvious, but your behavior is somewhat scrutinized. In some churches, if you smoked weed during the worship service, such behavior might limit your progress toward "belonging" in membership. In other churches, if you lived with someone and you weren't married, it could influence your attempt at membership. In other churches, if you have an occasional glass of wine at dinner, it might be an issue. However, if your known behavior fits the unwritten parameters of the church, you would qualify to be a member. This is an institutional organizational approach.

The organizational approach for most churches is this: believe → behave → belong. Most church members would agree this somewhat fits the path to officially belonging to their church. This is how, as a young boy, I became a church member. What is the challenge of this approach? It is counterproductive to reaching the masses for Jesus Christ. It is an organizational model that does not help a church thrive. As you might expect, it does not follow the model of Jesus; it is not the model of Kingdom culture. If you want to improve effectiveness using the journey to Kingdom culture, look at Scripture. How did Jesus do it?

This is the Kingdom culture approach: belong → believe → become → behave. Your church will not maximize effectiveness in outreach until you *live* this Kingdom culture. When people met Jesus, they immediately felt like they belonged. He didn't turn away little children. He accepted the woman caught in adultery. He ate with tax collectors. He hung out with Gentiles. Anyone who met Jesus felt the love; they felt like they belonged. Most of the Pharisees were out to get Him, but Jesus welcomed Nicodemus, who was a Pharisee! Jesus welcomed him because Nicodemus was interested *and* because Jesus started with "belong." Jesus accepted Nicodemus because Jesus was and is Jesus. Kingdom culture is not anywhere close to the culture of this world.

Most Christians think of *belong* as membership in the organized church. Their reaction is, "You mean if people are living in public unrepentant sin, they should become members so they belong?" The answer is most certainly no. That laissez-faire biblical attitude would ruin what it means to be the church. The use of the word *belong* in this context is not an *institutional* term. It is *relational* acceptance, with unconditional love for all people. If they don't feel the love of

Organizational Approach

Believe ➡ Behave ➡ Belong

Kingdom Culture Approach

Belong ➡ Believe ➡ Become ➡ Behave

Jesus, they likely will never grow to believe and become. For mission effectiveness, Christians first sort out the importance and place for love (belonging). Institutional belonging (often described as membership) is later in the journey.

Jesus didn't condone everyone's life as if sin didn't matter. He said, "Go and sin no more."[35] As they went away, they knew, without a doubt, they were welcomed, accepted, loved, and affirmed. How do you react to someone who has committed adultery? Murder? Embezzlement? How do you respond to someone who is gay? A registered sex offender? Those living together, not married? A person with a drug addiction? A Muslim? Would they immediately feel like they relationally belong? Would they feel like the poster that says, "Accept me as I am so I may learn what I may become"?

Unless unbelievers feel unconditional love right from the start, you will not reach most of them. Further, if you don't have that love, you can't fake it. No matter what you say, your body language will give you away. My colleague George Hunter says, "I get the impression that most Christians want to be fishers of men, but they want to be fishers of fish that have already

> People need to feel the love and acceptance of their being, not their behavior.

been cleaned."[36] The Kingdom culture of Jesus is to love the sinner, hate the sin. It is a Kingdom DNA discipline. It doesn't come naturally. It has been said, "A person needs to be loved the most when he deserves to be loved the least."[37]

In the world of social media, opinionated Christians sometimes point the finger in a way that looks like hate, without extending the hand of love. When Christians criticize and judge other Christians, it roadblocks the mission further. It diminishes healthy Christian outreach. Be careful about judging other Christians. My friend Jim Manthei shared this insight with me:

> I was sitting in my living room at Christmastime. I was looking at the Christmas tree, which was decorated and gorgeous. Then I looked out the window in the front yard and saw an apple tree which, in December, where I live, looked totally dead. In reality, the Christmas tree was dead and soon would be thrown out. But the apple tree was really alive. In not too many months, it would bear fruit. This resembles some Christians. Some look alive, but they're really dead. Others may look worn out, but they do produce fruit, they are really alive. It's dangerous to judge on the surface!

Biblical authority is the platform for Kingdom culture. It unleashes the strategic potential for effective mission. You have no other manual than Scripture. Unless many in your church become lifelong students of Scripture, you will never see Kingdom culture on a large scale. And you will never experience a thriving church. You may find it hard to believe, but if you cut out most of the programs and focus on the spiritual growth of members, it would revolutionize your congregation. You may never take a greater step of faith. If it doesn't make sense, it is because the Kingdom of Jesus is not like this world, not even close. Nevertheless, it works.

CHAPTER EIGHT

Turn Up Your Fire for Change—
Breakthrough Strategy #4

> ## Ceiling #4: History's Mysteries

In societies that have more memories than dreams, too many people are spending too many days looking backward. They see dignity, affirmation, and self-worth not by mining the present but by chewing on the past.... Such societies focus all their imagination on making that imagined past even more beautiful than it ever was, and then they cling to it like a rosary or a strand of worry beads, rather than imagining a better future and acting on that.

—Thomas L. Friedman[1]

I read a news story once about a man who reached his hundredth birthday. The reporter mentioned to him, "You must have seen a lot of changes." The man replied, "Yeah, and I've been against every one of them." You may know someone in your church like that. Hopefully it isn't the person you see in the mirror!

CEILING #4: HISTORY'S MYSTERIES

Some Christians perpetuate out-of-date forms and styles. They communicate to unbelievers that the faith is old, out of date, and irrelevant. Their form of Christianity is frozen in time. This bad habit is contrary to Kingdom culture. It is the direct opposite emphasis of the incarnation—God shows up as a person, the God-Man Jesus Christ. These bad habits severely weaken the impact of a church.

This issue is perhaps the most sensitive for you. It carries high-level potential for emotional offense. Honestly, this may feel uncomfortable and, perhaps, even accusatory. It is difficult to reflect on issues of selfishness that hinder the effectiveness of the mission to make disciples for Jesus Christ. What follows may challenge your commitment to Christ's mission more than anything else. No one said being a committed Christ-follower was easy. Jesus Himself used the symbol of the cross, not your favorite hymn book. He said, "Take up your cross, and follow me."[2]

We all know what the cross signifies on the comfort/commitment scale—or do we? The apostle Paul, quoting Isaiah, said the gospel is an offense to some.[3] The stone that caused so many Jews to stumble was salvation tangled with ritualistic works. The activities got in the way of the focus on Jesus, the way of salvation.

Some churches can be defined by an unwillingness to change, when change is good, appropriate, necessary, and strategically important for the Great Commission. Nothing strikes fear in the heart of pastors like the emotional, illogical, and unbiblical reactions to change. Most Christians know the joke, "How many Christians does it take to change a light bulb?" The answer is: "Who said anything about change?" The joke brings comic relief, but deep down, most Christians know that the old guard, the loud resisters to change, are the painful few who hijack the power and potential of the Kingdom.

> How many Christians does it take to change a light bulb? Who said anything about change?

The tendency to hang on to worn-out styles and customs is often described as *tradition*—a smoke screen to perpetuate the past. It reflects the Pharisees' challenge to Jesus. Their position was, "What new covenant? What's wrong with the way we've always done it?"

Christ-followers who subconsciously fall into this "feel-good religion" do more harm to the health of the church than they comprehend. It is a form of ecclesiastical mummification. "Let's wrap up the body of Christ like a mummy and preserve it like it was in the good ole days." The challenge is that a mummy doesn't change people's lives. Who wants to attend a church that resembles a tomb?

It seems like an odd example to compare the decline of pubs in England with the deterioration of churches, yet the dynamics are remarkably similar. In an article titled "Last Call for Pubs?" in *National Geographic*, it was reported that the number of pubs in Great Britain has declined from 69,000 in 1980 to 49,433 in 2012. The article summarized, "Each week thirty-one more close."

The pubs in England are a deep reflection of British culture. They are community centers for neighborhood gatherings. Pubs are where people see their neighbors, share what's new, and watch sports together. The substance of pubs hasn't changed. They still provide some of the best food at the best prices and, of course, a variety of beers. The *substance* isn't killing the pubs. It's the *style*. The article closes with this analysis: "If pubs don't mirror the social and economic changes of their community…they're dead."[4] Think about that in relationship to the churches you know.

FROZEN IN TIME

Churches are complex living organisms. We trademarked the name "Church Doctor" out of respect for the intricacies of the local body of Christ and our seriousness about helping them. One of the markers for health is when a church feels, looks, and acts contemporary and relevant to those in the culture around it. Jesus came in the flesh. He wasn't just anybody. He was the Son of God. But His body could be any body. For the time and space, He didn't look like Moses. Nor did He look like Billy Graham.

Declining churches struggle due to a cluster of factors. One factor is when they look, feel, and act like out-of-date relics. Like the UK pubs, they do not mirror the social and economic changes of the people they are trying to reach. The issue is not to change Bible content. What hurts the Bible message is perpetuating *styles* as sacred, clinging to them like a precious antique. Perpetuation of old-school methods is contrary to the incarnation of God in Jesus. It disregards the basic missionary approach of Scripture.

Leo Tolstoy said, "In our world everybody thinks of changing humanity and nobody thinks of changing himself."[5] Christianity's leader declared, "Behold, I make all things new."[6] The missionary Paul told the Corinthians, "If anyone is in Christ, he is a new creation. The old has passed away; behold, the new has come."[7] Jesus tells the Pharisee Nicodemus, "Except one be born anew, he cannot see the kingdom of God."[8] Many Christians do not exercise Kingdom culture with maximum potential because they are frozen in time. Leonard Sweet calls them museums and monument churches. Sweet states, "These churches are living off old memories and entrenched 'traditions' that are best seen as bad habits…people who are relics even when they're still alive."[9]

Human nature resists change. Mark Twain said, "The only person who likes change is a baby with a wet diaper."[10] Think about it. A wet diaper makes a baby uncomfortable. Perhaps Christians who resist change are too comfortable. Could that be you? Resistance to change is natural. However, the Kingdom culture approach to change is supernatural. The passion is to use the best styles, methods, and approaches to communicate God's love without requiring hurdles to jump. When you perpetuate traditions beyond their lifespan, you practice a form of Amish Christianity.

I have high respect for the work ethic and integrity of those of the Amish persuasion. It is strange, however, that they choose a certain time of history and freeze it as ideal. Have you ever been attracted by the idea of becoming Amish? If not, you have experienced a glimpse of how many postmodern young adults feel about church.

Many Christians perpetuate outdated worship styles, pews, language, and architectural forms. This behavior freezes faith in a random period of history. It sends a signal to those who are not

Christ-followers that God is old and out of date, and Christianity is irrelevant. This is in direct opposition to Kingdom culture. The apostle Paul, the missionary, says, "I have become all things to all people, that I might by all means save some."[11]

Many Christians seem to ignore the medium of the message. The medium is the container. The medium includes the building, dress codes, language, music, governance structures, and even the sign in front of the church. The medium sends a message—always! Long before unbelievers hear the powerful message you share about Jesus, the media have already communicated a message, positive or negative.

In Kingdom culture, the medium is not the message. The message is the message, and you do not want the medium to get in the way. The mission of Jesus uses whatever medium works, and that medium changes with every audience, every time, and every place.

Could you be oblivious to the message that the medium sends? Most Christians give little thought to the language they use. Most church bulletins, for example, contain "in-house" language that leaves a first-time guest clueless. Abbreviations are common. Locations of events are assumed. The message is: "This church is for those who already belong. You are new and unimportant." Try this: Ask a non-Christian to look at your church bulletin or read your favorite hymn. Ask her to circle all the meaningless words.

> Long before unbelievers hear the powerful message you share about Jesus, the media have already communicated a message, positive or negative.

The following is a real-life example from a Lutheran church my colleague Tracee consulted in Michigan. Look at it from the perspective of a non-Christian exploring the faith. "This month's meeting of the LWML will be in the Fireside Room. Be sure to bring your Mite Boxes. If you don't yet have one, they are available in the Narthex." Not to be offensive, but do you ever wonder why the LWML (Lutheran Women's Missionary League) chapter at your local Lutheran church has not added any new, younger members for ten years? Where is that Fireside Room? What is a Mite Box? These women save mites? Are they bug collectors? What is a Narthex? So what is the real message? "We are out of touch...and you are not invited."

George Hunter served as the dean of the School of World Mission and Evangelism for Asbury Theological Seminary. A brilliant scholar of church growth and mission, George says, "All churches are 'culturally relevant'; unfortunately, most churches are relevant to some other culture, or some other generation, or both."[12] The media for many churches scream a message no Christian believes: "God is old, out of date, and irrelevant." Really? Is that what you want to say to your neighbors who don't yet know Jesus?

Why is it so many Christians perpetuate ancient forms contradicting the Kingdom culture of the incarnation? Jesus showed up in the flesh so there would be no barriers to stop your neighbor getting the message. Your neighbor has no barriers to salvation except his own stubborn resistance. Why do Christians use out-of-date language, styles, musical instruments, seating choices, signs, communication systems, decision-making styles, and architecture reflecting another century and another continent? These are real and serious barriers to your neighbor. Do you really want to communicate that Jesus is an out-of-date, irrelevant foreigner?

The symptom may be resistance to change. But the issue behind that issue is a selfish attitude. I don't mean this unkindly, but how can you justify making the good news of the gospel hard to hear? Try to change any of these sacred cows, and you will quickly discover who belongs to the resistance movement. In most churches, the amount of energy and emotional dissonance around the issue of change is phenomenal. Church leaders who want to share the good news, uncluttered, discover they are walking through a minefield!

OPENNESS TO CHANGE

When Church Doctor Ministries learned that resistance to change represents a clear roadblock to effective outreach, we decided to measure it. When we consult a church, everyone in worship is invited to complete an anonymous survey. One of the many areas of our research is *openness to innovation and change*. The focus of research is not on the substance or the content of the faith. It is on styles and methodology—the delivery systems. Appropriate, ongoing change of the media is a key issue if a church is to become healthy in Kingdom culture. The research measures openness to innovation and change to discover the level of enthusiasm concerning the immediate future.

Church Members with High Expectations for the Immediate Future

From your perception, what do you think was or will be the greatest era of this church?

①	40–60 years ago	④	The last 10 years
②	20–40 years ago	⑤	The next 10 years
③	10–20 years ago	⑥	Starting 10 years from now

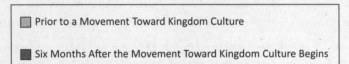

■ Prior to a Movement Toward Kingdom Culture

■ Six Months After the Movement Toward Kingdom Culture Begins

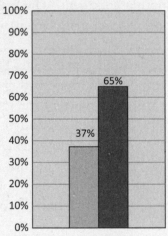

Percentage of those choosing "the next 10 years," representing high expectations for the immediate future and openness to innovation and change.

Obviously, the question, "What do you think was or will be the *greatest era* of this church?" is not a history question. It is a worldview inquiry. This research focuses on two primary interests: (1) What percentage of the congregation responds, "The next 10 years." This answer identifies those who have high expectations for the immediate future. They include the pioneers, or early adopters. They are open to innovation and *change*. For Church Doctors, this is important to know. We make recommendations for Kingdom culture and congregational health. If a church is going to move toward health, it will require change. (2) It is equally important to know how many are stuck in the last ten years, as well as those who remember the good ole days from a period several decades ago.

We worked with a church in Kentucky recently. The research indicated 49 percent of those in worship (at all three services) believed that the greatest era of the church was sometime in the past. Forty-five percent answered "The next 10 years," and 6 percent said "10 to 20 years ago." On the issue of change, this church is clearly divided. Much of the talk about the past is a smoke screen. The real issue is often a worldview that the church is here to serve us, not to reach others. This is resistance to innovation and change. It is contrary to the hope and high expectation embedded in the Kingdom of Jesus, with marching orders to reach the world.

Our world is changing. When some Christians come to church, they psychologically drive a stake in the ground, emotionally thinking, "You can change most of my world, but you are not going to change my church!" If their enthusiasm for not changing were focused on *content*, it would be great. However, it is usually focused on *style*. Tragically, some churches have taken a stand to not change style. They perpetuate sixteenth-century dress codes and worship styles, while *at the same time*, they have changed the content of biblical teaching. This is a supercharged formula for the decline and disappearance of a church.

A church in New Mexico has recently left its denomination to join a network of congregations committed to "the Bible as truth and the Great Commission as the purpose." This church left the strongly hierarchical, high-control structure of the previous denomination. Larry, the pastor, sighs as he shares, "It's so hard to change anything." He continues, "We've been plateaued for fifteen years, even though our community is growing. Obviously, we need to make some changes. If we do what we've always done, we will get what we've always gotten. It takes so long to decide anything…it's always a battle."

Larry's congregation is like many churches locked into irrelevance through resistance to change. The old wooden sign in front of the church shows the wear of forty years. It also represents an oddity to those who live in an electronic, digital world. No matter what the words say, the sign says OUT OF DATE and IRRELEVANT. It speaks on a subconscious level to everyone who travels by the church. The message is powerfully negative. "It's amazing how sacred pews have become," says Larry. How ironic that people arrive in automobiles loaded with electronic devices, drink coffee from Starbucks in the church lobby, and then worship in pews! Erwin McManus makes this powerful comment in his book *An Unstoppable Force*: "Perhaps the greatest tragedy of our time is that we have kept our pews and lost our children."[13] In Larry's church, the median age is sixty-two.

The worship at Larry's church is traditional, sprinkled heavily with words people don't use anymore, such as *thee* and *thou*. The worship is liturgical, linear, and hierarchical, with high emphasis on those who are leaders, dressed distinctively different from anyone in the real world of the twenty-first century. The choir, dressed in robes, appears at the center for an anthem sung before a crowd dressed in jeans and sports shirts.

At one time in history, the pipe organ was, of course, culturally relevant. On one of our trips to London, we stopped to visit the Victoria and Albert Museum. In this museum are two works showing how Christians have frequently tried to teach faith in a contemporary way. One of them is the *Peasant Woman Nursing a Baby*, a terra-cotta sculpture by Jules Dalou (1838–1902). It is an expression of the Virgin Mary with the baby Jesus at her breast. This artist, however, dressed the Virgin as a peasant girl, "which gives this image a new directness," says the plaque in the museum. In the same museum is a wood sculpture called *The Coronation of the Virgin* by Charles Geerts (1807–1855). This was made as a display for a church. In this sculpture, the scene is also typical: the Virgin Mother holding the child on her lap with five angels surrounding her. One of the angels is playing a mandolin, and another is playing a miniature pipe organ! When I saw this, I couldn't help but think about how an artist today would show the Virgin Mother holding the child on her lap, surrounded by angels, with one playing an electric guitar, another on a keyboard, and a third on a drum set! These artists from the nineteenth century had taken the substance of the message and placed it in a relevant style for their day and time.

This is Christianity at its best for that particular era. Some would say, "You have no license to create art that shows angels playing a pipe organ and a mandolin." However, as communication to the contemporary audience in the nineteenth century, this is not an issue of license. This is a mandate: Put the real Jesus in the real world, at your time in history, in your culture. This is what the incarnation is all about. These art pieces were outstanding, engaging communication two hundred years ago. Today they belong in a museum, not a church. What will relevant media look like in a hundred years? That's hard to tell, but one thing is certain: It will be different!

Nancy Pearcey, in her thought-provoking book *Total Truth*, says:

> A Christian church or ministry may be biblical in its *message* and yet fail to be biblical in its *methods*. Hudson Taylor, the great missionary to China, said that the Lord's work must be done in the Lord's way, if it is to have the Lord's blessing. We must express the truth not only in *what* we preach but also in *how* we preach it.[14]

Many Christians assume that the art forms they have accepted are actual depictions of Jesus at the time of the New Testament. One of the most famous is the fresco by Leonardo da Vinci, *The Last Supper*. Jesus is sitting in the Upper Room at a table with His disciples to His right and left. In truth, during the New Testament times, they did not use banquet tables. Jesus likely sat on the floor with a raised platform perhaps a foot off the ground. He and His disciples would have participated in the Last Supper in a reclining position. Some might challenge da Vinci, "By what license do you have a right to do that?" The issue, however, is not about license but mandate! A Christian committed to mission

> This is a mandate: Put the real Jesus in the real world, at your time in history, in your culture. This is what the incarnation is all about.

would not criticize Leonardo da Vinci but applaud his reconfiguration of *style* to make Jesus and the Lord's Supper relevant to those who ate at tables at the time that artwork was developed.

PERPETUATING WHAT FEELS GOOD

In the kingdom of the world is a natural inclination to perpetuate the familiar. Irish Catholics immigrated to the United States and built Irish pubs. They were more than watering holes for Irish stout. They were immigrant safe houses where a minority group could gather as a majority, at least for a few hours, making them feel comfortable. Likewise, European Lutherans who immigrated to North America started their own schools. They called the schools a "commitment to quality, Christian education," which is only part of the story. Many of these schools were cultural "retreat centers" where German or Norwegian was spoken in a land where English was the dominant language.

My grandparents were German Lutherans. They never spoke German around me, except following an occasional sneeze, when Grandpa Adolf would say "Gesundheit" (Good health). Grandma Martha would answer, "Danke schoen. Es ist besser als Krankheit" (Thank you. It's better than sickness). One year, during spring break from high school, I traveled with them by car from Michigan to Florida. I slept on a couch in their motel room. After the lights went out, I heard them pray the Lord's Prayer, as was their daily custom. They said it in German, their spiritual "heart language."

When I travel to countries where English is not the primary language, I am provided a translator for training pastors. I always learn and practice a few key phrases of the local language, phrases like "Hello," "Good morning," "Thank you," and, of course, "Where is the toilet?" Even though my Russian, Swahili, Japanese, Korean, and Portuguese are far from perfect, the fact that I try makes an impression. Why? Any attempt to be incarnational, to meet people where they are and speak their heart language, feels good to them. It also makes them more receptive—which is the point! It is the way the kingdom of this world works.

The Kingdom of God is not of, or like, this world. Nevertheless, Jesus became human, to reach humans. As He did, He taught issues about a Kingdom that is not like this world. Jesus irritated the religious people—the Pharisees, Scribes, and Sadducees. "He doesn't follow the traditions," they would say.[15] Jesus' Kingdom is out-of-this-world different but packaged in the flesh. His Kingdom is a different world, yet He shares it up close and personal. Why is this so hard for many Christians to understand?

Nancy Pearcey, again in her book *Total Truth*, explains: "Christians are not called to be *only* like immigrants, simply preserving a few customs and phrases from the old country. Instead, we are to be like missionaries, actively translating the language of faith into the language of the culture around us."[16]

After interviewing a few thousand Christians during the last forty years, it is clear to me that a major disconnect occurs. Most Christians love Jesus and trust Him for salvation. That part of the Kingdom we understand. However, when we tout "feel-good" worship, we reflect, "It reminds me of when I was a child." This expression reflects several Kingdom culture elements of drift. (1) We miss Jesus' hard teaching, "Deny yourself."[17] (2) We misplace Paul's admonishment to the Philippians to "Consider others more important than yourselves," as Jesus did.[18] (3) There is a disconnect between the mission (being a missionary) and the feel-good forms of being an immigrant.

It was an early Sunday morning. I turned the television on in my hotel room in Rotorua, New Zealand. I watched in awe as the Australian church Hillsong broadcast its service. I love their contemporary, engaging music. As the camera panned the audience, I was thrilled to see people of all ages engaged in worship. When the Hillsong broadcast ended, the next program began with another church service. This was a traditional congregation with a robed choir, organ music, and traditional hymns. The stark contrast hit home when the camera panned that congregation, and I saw almost entirely gray hair! I thought, "Why don't people understand this? It can't be so obvious only to me, can it?"

If you are a fired-up Kingdom culture missionary, you recognize the pain and suffering you must bear. It doesn't come so much from the world as from the church. It comes from those who hold on to worn-out and meaningless elements. Out-of-date forms and styles actually roadblock the mission to reach those who don't yet know Jesus.

Perhaps the most frustrating time of the year for a mission-minded Christian is, of all things, Christmas. In a secular nation, as the United States has become, Christmas is the one time believers can influence some non-Christian friends, neighbors, and relatives to attend church with them. Congregations often involve children in Christmas songs or skits. The crowd is filled with proud grandparents, aunts, uncles, and others who may not be active Christ-followers. The influence of a small child is enormous! Jesus said, "Out of the mouth of babes…"[19]

Think about how most churches present this Christmas prime-time mission opportunity. They drag out old, generationally perpetuated "feel-good" songs. Many of these songs have lost much of their meaning. Consider, for example, "Away in a Manger." (You are likely humming the tune in your head and getting a feel-good adrenaline rush already. I know.) In Sunday school when I was young, they dressed me as a shepherd. Everyone sang it. There is one verse—you know it, hum along: "The cattle are lowing, the baby awakes, but little Lord Jesus no crying He makes." Really? "The cattle are lowing?" Even as a ten-year-old, I wondered, "Why would short cows wake up Jesus?" My research shows that only one in fourteen practicing adult Christians knows that *lowing* is the old English word for *mooing*. So, what does that do for Uncle George who came to see me and who is not a Christ-follower? It is foreign to America—and foreign to Uncle George.

This issue is not new. Feel-good approaches often take precedence over the mission priority. The following are the litmus tests of validity: (1) Does it work to get the good news of Jesus to the unbeliever? (2) Does it grow the faithful in discipleship? Contemporary Christian music is criticized strongly by some of the "old guard." I like to ask them the question, "Did you hear what George Weber said about 'contemporary music'? He called it 'vulgar mischief and void of all religious and Christian feelings.' Oh, you know who George Weber is, don't you? No? He was the music director at Mainz Cathedral. Do you know the music he was criticizing? It was the new 'contemporary' song called 'Silent Night.'"[20]

To insist that all good Christian music was written in Europe two hundred years ago is musical elitism and cultural chauvinism. No music *style* is actually sacred. What makes it sacred is the message! "Christian music" does not exist—only Christian lyrics. The music and the message lose their power when those who hear do not understand, the words are foreign, or the melody does not stir the heart. What was the musical years ago that some religious leaders called "vulgar theater"? It was Handel's *Messiah*! Do you know what they said? "Too much repetition and choruses over and over again. Good heavens, it repeats 'hallelujah' nearly a hundred times!"[21]

Many churches use the Lord's Prayer in worship. I've been to contemporary worship services—music, instruments, dress code, and seating—that still use the Elizabethan word *thy* in the Lord's Prayer. I lovingly challenged a pastor recently to consider using twenty-first-century English for the Lord's Prayer. He responded, "You'll never get me to change that!" This demonstrates two realities: (1) how ingrained "feel-good" perpetuation can get, and (2) how radical it feels to take on the posture of a missionary. German theologian Helmut Thielicke said, "The gospel must be preached afresh and told in new ways to every generation, since every generation has its own unique questions. That is why the gospel must constantly be forwarded to a new address, because the recipient is repeatedly changing his place of residence."[22] This is true of *substance* and *style*. Jesus deserves to be fresh to *every* people group, in every age.

The apostle Paul is the model missionary who says, "For though I am free from all men, I have made myself a slave to all, *so that I may win more.*"[23] Paul describes the clear distinction of nonnegotiable substance and the mission-sensitive flexibility of style: "I didn't take on their way of life. I kept my bearings in Christ—but I entered their world and tried to experience things from their point of view. I've become just about every sort of servant there is in my attempts to lead those I meet into a God-saved life."[24]

Paul's worldview is the radical Kingdom culture of a missionary. This is why missionaries are not stuck in a rut of just one translation of the Bible. The best translation of Scripture is not the one that you read as a child. What is your favorite translation of the Bible? The

Kingdom culture answer is, "The next one!" Christians who perpetuate out-of-date styles are unfaithful to the spirit of the incarnational Christ. They are ineffective in reaching those for whom Jesus died.

KILLING THE POWER OF PURPOSE

It is not easy to deal with selfish perpetuation of feel-good religion. Jesus asked Peter a hard Kingdom culture question: "Do you love me?"[25] It hit a nerve for Peter. He may have thought, "Why do you need to ask that?" Jesus responded, "Feed My lambs."[26]

Sadly, we live in a me-centered culture. We have "I" pads, "I" pods, "I" phones, and "my" space. You can even get a burger and "have it your way." This self-centered approach to life is far from Kingdom culture. The worldview, from the biblical perspective, is to think (and act) like Jesus. Kingdom culture is not about selfishly hanging on to what feels good. So many churches are divided on the me-centered culture of "I want to do church my way."

Kingdom culture is all about putting my way aside; it is thinking like Jesus. It is being interested in what interests God. The Bible says in 1 Peter 4:1–2, "Since Jesus went through everything you're going through and more, learn to think like Him. Think of your sufferings as a weaning from that old sinful habit of always expecting to get your own way. Then you'll be able to live out your days free to pursue what God wants instead of being tyrannized by what you want."[27] Selfishness destroys church health. Self-centered thinking pollutes Kingdom atmosphere.

Healthy churches are those in which Christians focus on reaching unbelievers. They have neither time nor energy to squabble over "monumental" issues like the color of the carpet, the location of the new kitchen, or video screens in the sanctuary. They are sold out to reaching others, whatever it takes. In a world of lost people, trivial issues are like "straining at gnats."[28]

Years ago, I received a call to serve a church in northeast Indiana. We moved from Michigan and arrived at the parsonage late Friday night. It was after midnight by the time our furniture was moved from the truck into our new home. We were so tired that we collapsed on a mattress without putting the bed together. We were sound asleep when the doorbell rang at seven thirty on Saturday morning. I put on my robe, remarking to my wife, "I bet someone died."

It was Dorothy at the door, smiling and wide awake. "Welcome, pastor. I didn't get you up, did I?"

"That's okay," I said, as I rubbed my eyes and tried to wake up.

"I'm here to set up for Communion tomorrow," Dorothy said. "I'm wondering if you could walk next door to the church and tell me how you want it set on the altar."

I replied, asking, "Have you ever set up for Communion?"

"Oh yes," Dorothy replied, "I've been doing this for forty years, but the last pastor got really angry because I didn't set it up exactly the way he wanted. So I thought I had better check with you to see if it is acceptable."

"Oh, that's okay," I responded. "If I have everything there on the altar, it will be fine."

"No," Dorothy insisted, "I won't sleep tonight until I know you approve."

With that, I put on my slippers and walked the thirty yards over to the church to tell Dorothy it was just fine. As we talked, and as I learned more in the coming weeks, it became clear that the previous pastor majored in minors. The church was fixated on internal maintenance. Outreach was limited, and the church was divided over petty preferences. This is what feel-good Christianity looks like.

Majoring in minors was the expertise of the Pharisees. They were focused on traditions, rituals, and "bylaws"—the rules and regulations of religious Jews. Then Jesus came onto the scene. Blinded by their *religion*, many Jewish leaders missed the *spiritual*. Jesus was God incarnate, God in the flesh. John 1:14 says, "The Word became flesh and blood, and moved into the neighborhood."[29] Christianity by rules is catastrophic. It corrupts mission.

"Prince" is a chief of the Maori people, the Polynesians who became the first inhabitants of New Zealand. (His full name is Piriniha Te Whenua Tekotahi Tanga Rewiti. I wonder why they call him "Prince.") Prince told me about the early missionaries who came to reach his people. "When the missionaries first introduced Christianity, most of them focused on the law—the Ten Commandments. They preached about all the things we do wrong, the sins. That was their focus. Most of the people resisted the Christian faith. A few responded and discovered Jesus' love and forgiveness, but not many. Once some Maoris became missionaries, they began by proclaiming God's love and forgiveness. That was when the movement began, and many Maoris became believers." How missionary-minded are you? Does the energy of your church focus primarily on the love and forgiveness of Jesus, or the rules, laws, and rituals of religion?

Jesus represented a new covenant, a new way God was interacting with His people. The religious leaders opposed Jesus, "That's not the way we've always done it." The Pharisees could not handle change. Jesus did not fit into their worldview. He did not look like the model, the way they had always done it. What was their solution? Kill Him.

Many Christians unintentionally kill the power of God's purpose by perpetuating the past. Those who are so loud against change derail entire congregations from incarnating the loving Jesus into our ever-changing world. Make no mistake: To embalm the past is to turn your church into a museum, destroying the future God has for you.

> Many Christians unintentionally kill the power of God's purpose by perpetuating the past.

STYLE AND SUBSTANCE

If you make a golden calf of *style*, you destroy the power of the *substance*. The substance is the meaning and the content of the faith. Rick Warren has pointed out in *The Purpose Driven Church*, "The Columbia Record Company once did a study and discovered that after a song is sung fifty times, people no longer think about the meaning of the lyrics—they just sing it by rote."[30]

An "old guard" member of a church criticized the contemporary worship service. She said, "Dr. Hunter, the hymns in our hymnal have lasted centuries. Do you really think these new songs will be around in several hundred years?" Out of kindness, I didn't respond. What I wanted to say was, "I certainly hope not!" The faith should be as fresh as the morning dew.[31] This may be what the psalmist had in mind: "Sing to the LORD a *new* song."[32]

We visited our son, Jon, and his wife, Esther, while they were Christian missionaries in Malaysia. One day at a hotel swimming pool, I was sharing about some new contemporary songs I had heard. I asked Jon and Esther if they had heard them. Jon, who was just thirty years old at the time, said, "I love those songs, too. But I hope when I'm much older, I won't perpetuate these songs, because there'll be new styles, new expressions, twenty or thirty years from now." Spoken like a missionary!

The packaging (the style) is and should always be changing. It changes from one era and one culture to the next. Think about dress codes. If you really feel old language, out-of-date hymnals, and organ music are sacred and cannot be changed, perhaps you should wear sandals and a tunic to worship. Jesus did! If you did, unbelievers would look at you and say, "You and your God are out of date, irrelevant, and meaningless to my life."

The challenge is this: If you don't change the style, you *will* change the substance—the content. This is what makes traditional churches so ironic. They may hold on to the stylistic patterns of the sixteenth, seventeenth, and eighteenth centuries. The leaders wear religious garb from that era. But what these "conservatives" accomplish is the epitome of theological liberalism! They make the incarnate Jesus appear out of date and irrelevant. They have changed the most important content of the Bible, which is Jesus.

Jesus is as relevant as today's newsfeed. To dress Jesus in old clothes and make Him look ancient is making the living Christ an antique. Jesus becomes a relic to be admired rather than a Savior to be believed. Churches become depositories of ancient history rather than world changers with the power to thrive.

Jesus used the vehicles of His day to communicate the lifesaving message of salvation. He spoke about sheep and shepherds to those who knew all about shepherding. To keep the message (the content of the faith) as powerful as Jesus intends, use meaningful vehicles for the people you are reaching. When we study healthy churches, we find Christians who develop methods relevant to their culture—without changing the content of faith.

A fundamental principle of missionary culture is to share the gospel in a way that allows minimal "noise." The noise reflects distractions from the message. Sharing Christ works best when you speak the heart language of those you are trying to reach. That is the language people use when they dream or make love. Heart language is more than words. It includes music, tempo, instruments, and volume. It includes architecture and spatial relations. It includes dress codes. Increasingly, it represents technology.

> If you don't change the style, you *will* change the substance—the content....Jesus becomes a relic to be admired rather than a Savior to be believed.

Many mainline denominational congregations represent the "graying of Christianity." The median age of those in worship is, simply, rising! When we provide an assessment for these churches, we ask them, "What do you think should be emphasized more?" From a list of more than twenty issues that a church could "emphasize more," the response from those in the aging churches reveals a *high priority* for issues that should not be surprising. The members know their church is dying!

The graph below depicts the top five issues listed by a graying church in Washington state. Notice what the majority of the people want emphasized "more" and "the same," from a list of twenty-five potential ministry priorities.

■ Emphasize More	■ Emphasize the Same	■ Emphasize Less
Ministry to Younger Generations	71%	
Growth in Numbers of People	65%	
Activities for Youth	64%	
Outreach to Unchurched People	56%	
Activities for Children	55%	

158

Congregations attracting younger families have a different profile. These churches attract families with children and youth as well as single adults. Some have a median age of thirty-five. These congregations usually use an electronic sign. They have an inviting, easy-to-navigate website. The facilities reflect contemporary architecture. You see screens throughout the building, sharing opportunities for ministry and spiritual growth. The worship utilizes contemporary instruments. They use screens in the sanctuary as well. Language is translated, even though the meaning is the same. In mission terminology, these churches are a form of *indigenous* Christianity. Together, these elements represent Kingdom atmosphere for contemporary culture. If your church is one of the many aging congregations, look around. Does it feel out of date?

INDIGENOUS CHRISTIANITY

Indigenous Christianity is faith that carries the integrity of Scripture. Do not make the tragic error of changing the message to fit the culture. This, in missionary terminology, is called *syncretism*. It occurs when you try to "sync up" with the culture, to the extent that you abandon biblical theology. This does not work. Eventually, this brand of Christianity dies because it is void of spiritual power. Some trends and fads in secular culture do not, and will never, fit Kingdom culture.

Indigenous Christianity packages the faith into *forms* matching the culture you are trying to reach. For years, I have consulted a wonderful group of Pakistanis who lead a ministry called POBLO International—People of the Book Ministries. They are reaching and discipling Muslims. They target Muslims who have moved to the United States. POBLO helps Christian churches reach Muslims in an indigenous approach.

Sometimes, well-meaning Christians do not understand the culture of the people they are trying to reach. Though well intentioned, they often use wrong approaches. Jesus called us to be fishers of men and women, but it does make a difference *how* you fish, with sensitivity to the culture.

Indigenous ministry is an incarnational approach. Unfortunately, many churches are indigenous in their outreach to a target audience that has been dead for three or four hundred years. Obviously, that is not very effective! To develop indigenous ministry to your community, you must first stop, look, and listen to your target audience.

My friend Tony Steinbronn was a missionary in Botswana in southern Africa. We were in a remote village in the Kalahari Desert. I asked, "How does a missionary come here and reach people who are so different?" Watching the people in the busy marketplace, he said:

> You *stop*. You don't bring your own ideas on how to reach out. You *look*. You must become a student of the culture. You *listen*. You listen to how they mourn and celebrate. What is important to them? What challenges them? These are your cues for how you will effectively reach them with the gospel.[33]

As you think about distant Africa, you may feel, "Well, yeah, of course you have to do that there. Those people are so different." In truth, if you want Kingdom culture to penetrate wherever you are, the approach for a healthy church to thrive is identical. It is just as important for you in Greenville, Tampa, Nairobi, Lhasa, or Walnut Creek. It is also important for this year, next year, and every year until Jesus returns.

CHANGE, AND THE HEART OF A SERVANT

Your willingness to accept meaningful change is unconditionally connected to your attitude. In Luke 9:1–6, Jesus sent His disciples into the villages to announce the Kingdom of God. His instructions were interesting. He started by telling them to "travel light." Think about your church. Is it so top-heavy with "stuff" that your ability to change is inhibited by all the clutter? Jesus says, "Don't worry about how you will pay for this mission." Really? Think about your church. Does discussion about financial resources inhibit change for mission? Jesus says to the disciples, "If people are receptive, stay with them. If they aren't receptive, move on." In other words, focus where the harvest is ripe. For many, the harvest today is ripe. If the harvest is ripe, why is it that your church may not be growing? Though it is hard for many to hear, the primary reason you are not effectively reaching the lost may be selfishness. "Take it or leave it." Many leave it.

What is a tradition, according to Scripture? Actually, a tradition is the living faith of the dead. Hebrews 11 describes the heroes of the Old Testament. It is a Who's Who of great believers who performed awesome acts, powered by their faith and trust in God. Noah built a huge boat on dry land. Abraham wandered all over, not knowing where God was leading. Sarah received the power to give birth as an old woman. These and all the heroes of Hebrews are cheerleaders of faith for people like you and me. This is tradition: the living faith of the dead.

One of the three people God used to inspire me for ministry was my dad. He died at an early age, while I was in college. His passion for sharing the gospel lives on in my memory. I was young when a new translation of the Bible was published. Called *Good News for Modern Man*, it was first released as a New Testament paperback. My dad bought a shopping-bagful of them. I asked, "What are you going to do with all those Bibles?" He answered, "I'm going to give them to those where I work—many of them are not Christians." His faith is a testimony for me. It is one of my traditions—a living faith that lives in me. It is the living faith of my dead father. It still inspires me.

"Tradition is the living faith of the dead. Traditionalism is the *dead faith of the living*," said Jaroslav Pelikan, a professor at Yale.[34] What about those favorite hymns you partially understand at Christmas? Many call them tradition, but that isn't tradition. It is traditionalism. Jesus stated, "If anyone would come after me, let him deny himself and take up his cross and follow me."[35] Who said anything about change? Jesus did!

CHAPTER NINE

Turn Your Strategy into God's Math–Breakthrough Strategy #5

Ceiling #5: Addition Addiction

> Movements have narratives. They tell stories…they…
> *rearrange meaning*…figuring out what is good….They
> have this *culture* piece….Movements require risk-taking,
> uncertainty…against all odds….That takes hope. Where
> do you go for hopefulness?…Moral resources…within
> the narrative, and *faith*.
>
> —Marshall Ganz[1]

What does it mean to experience breakthrough? The word is not used much in sermons. It isn't the subject of many prayers. Most aspiring pastors don't hear much about breakthrough at seminary or Bible college. The word rarely occurs in contemporary Christian books. A dictionary describes breakthrough as "The act, result, or place of breaking through against resistance, as in warfare; a strikingly important advance or discovery."[2]

Perhaps you have noticed some breakthrough events from the Bible: Moses leading God's people out of Egypt; senior citizens

Abraham and pregnant Sarah; the first Christmas with God in a diaper; a wedding in Cana with 120 extra gallons of wine; Lazarus lives again; Jesus attends his own funeral; blinded Saul sees the light.

If you were the enemy of Christianity, what would you do to move the movement in reverse, from breakthrough to mediocrity? This enemy messes with our minds, twists reality, and ever so subtly tries to undermine the movement of the Master. However, "He who is in you is greater than he who is in the world."[3] One of the enemy's most sinister tricks is to rob you of God's breakthrough mathematical strategy. Say a prayer for clarity, and do the math. The DNA of God is designed for multiplication.

A Swiss professor once calculated that if nothing hindered a single grain of wheat, in only eight years, it would sufficiently multiply to feed all the inhabitants of earth for one year.[4] If there were no bugs to eat the grain, no bad weather, and no drought, it would feed everyone on earth for a year. This is how God works.

HEAVENLY MATH

God's plan to fill earth is to be "fruitful and multiply."[5] Jesus' commission to fill heaven is identical: "Go and make disciples… baptizing… and teaching."[6] This commission wasn't given to a bureaucracy. This commission was given to *every* Christian. Making disciples is God's strategy of multiplication. This is the genius of the movement.

> One of the enemy's most sinister tricks is to rob you of God's breakthrough mathematical strategy.

In Matthew 25:14–30, Jesus tells a story about some servants who were given a piece of the master's property to manage. The story, in older translations, speaks of one man who was given five "talents," another given two "talents," and another, one "talent." You can think of this as different amounts of money or responsibility. You can also consider this to be your church, your life, your time, your gifts, or your energy. All of it belongs to God, and each is a piece of His Kingdom to manage by multiplication.

In the story, each servant was to manage a piece of property for the master until he returned. As you consider this story, focus on the importance of multiplication. The master returned and called the servants to report. In the Kingdom, low control is balanced by high accountability. As low control, the master did not look over his shoulder at the servants while he was gone. He practiced high accountability when he returned. He asked for a report.

The servant with five talents *multiplied* what he had. The one with less responsibility, two talents, *multiplied* also. However, the servant with even less responsibility, one talent, dug a hole and hid it. The Master, Jesus—said to each multiplier, "Well done, good and faithful servant...enter into the joy of your Master." He then turned to the one who did not *multiply*, with harsh words: "Wicked and lazy...a worthless servant."

Someday, you will leave this earth and be with Jesus. You will be there because you believe in Him as your Savior. He died for your sins and paid for them on the cross. This is the sure promise of eternal life. However, when you get there, would you like to hear Jesus say, "Well done, good and faithful servant"? On what basis will He say that? I'm sure it won't be on how many church meetings you attended. It's quite certain it won't be how many Sunday school classes you taught, or how many sermons you preached. It won't be based on how much money you gave back to God through your church.

In creation, God's call is *multiplication* to fill the earth. Jesus' heavenly math is to *multiply*: make disciples—to fill heaven. The movement genius is to multiply multipliers who disciple others who disciple others. Jesus modeled this. He multiplied Himself in three years, to twelve. One of them didn't make it, so Jesus' ratio of discipleship was 1:11. That was the group "close in" around Jesus. Of course, countless others were followers, who also became disciples. Then there was Saul, also called Paul, to make the ratio 1:12 again.

The real *breakthrough* occurred when His followers began to disciple. This multiplication propelled the movement that rocked the Mediterranean world. There is breakthrough wherever disciples disciple others who disciple others. Would you like to see that in your life? In your church? In your community? In your nation? In our world? Whether or not this is your passion, I promise you it is the passion of Jesus. He was passionate enough about it to suffer and die. We even call that "the Passion." Some Christians reenact it through passion plays.

CEILING #5: ADDITION ADDICTION

I glanced at my phone. It was 9:00 a.m. Then, in the reception area of the restaurant, I saw my appointment for breakfast. Pastor Bob was right on time.

"Good morning, Bob," I said. We meet for breakfast about five times a year.

> The real *breakthrough* occurred when His followers began to disciple. This multiplication propelled the movement.

"You know," he said, "you have more influence on my ministry than anyone." I took that as a compliment and a responsibility. My passion is to help Christians and churches become more effective for the Great Commission. However, with Bob, it is more personal. He is the pastor where my wife and I worship.

Bob graduated from a seminary that modeled the staff-led church. I had been encouraging Bob to practice discipling. I urged him to multiply Christians in ministry by mentoring one-on-one.

"The last time we met, Bob, we talked about discipling another person," I said, displaying gentle accountability. "How is it going?"

"Not very well," he replied. "I don't think...I don't really know how to start. I think I'm just not wired to disciple another person one-on-one. Besides, my schedule is already full."

I see this everywhere. (1) So many don't know how to disciple. Why? No one ever discipled them. (2) It takes time, and most Christians have a life too cluttered with nonessentials. Let's look at the second issue first.

At the heart of the issue is major Kingdom drift about how we do church. For the vast majority of Christians, church is *inverted*. Their church is staff-led—pastor-led in smaller churches. The worldview is that the church staff exists to do ministry. When I mention inverted churches, most Christians look at me like I came from a different planet. That planet, if it had a name, would be called the Bible. The New Testament church comes from this planet, too.

To grasp this concept, try an experiment. Train a few people to perform hospital ministry. Ask them to act as the primary group serving those in the hospital. The first reaction they will encounter from a patient sounds like this: "I appreciate the visit, but where is the (real) pastor?" In their minds, they are thinking, "We have a pastor. What do we pay him for, anyway?"

The answer to that question depends on whether you operate from the perspective of Kingdom culture or not. According to Scripture, you pay the minister to "equip the saints for the work of ministry."[7] Due to serious drift, you may pay the minister to call on people at the hospital. Discipling leads to multiplication, Kingdom style. Drift from Kingdom culture is the enemy's delight! This is the enemy's plan: Change the Jesus epidemic from multiplication to addition, burn out staff, make the movement a program, and stall the growth of God's Kingdom.

If you want to multiply hospital ministry through this biblical approach, *invest a few years*. Guide your church into Kingdom culture. Get people into Scripture. Let *God* make them Kingdom people. (There's a novel idea!) Then, they will want to be equipped to do ministry of all kinds. Before long, those you train will be training others, who will then train others, and the Jesus epidemic is on its way. So many people will find their calling, you'll be reaching people beyond your church membership.

Now, let's take on Bob's other issue: "I'm too busy." There are literally two antidotes for the chronic busyness in most churches. The first is easy to comprehend, yet hard to do. The way to do it is to have a program rummage sale. Offload activities that fill the church calendar but do not fill the Kingdom of heaven. Bob could just drop some activities, but that would come back to haunt him. Some people rebel against those who kill the activities they love.

The second approach is difficult to comprehend but easier to do: Teach, model, and develop Kingdom culture. When Christians catch it, many activities that sap their time and energy will die a natural death. The approach is woven into the fiber of discipling. Bob doesn't have to give up hospital ministry. As a discipler, he should take someone with him. Discipling occurs on the job. For Bob to say, "I don't have time" is a cop-out. All he has to do is repeat the words of Jesus: "Come, follow me." C'mon Bob! How hard is that?

The fine art of discipling is quite simple. Bob should begin with prayer. After all, Jesus did say, "The harvest is great, but the workers are few. So *pray*."[8] It's amazing how many Christians moan about how hard it is to get help. You ask, "Have you prayed about it?" They look at you, as if to say, "Pray? No, you don't get it, we need help, not prayer." Really? Bob should pray and look until he finds someone with the spiritual gifts and personality for hospital ministry.

Let's take the next step. Bob prays and looks, until God provides Mary. Bob doesn't have to say, "Come, follow me." He could say, "Mary, I see you have gifts of mercy and service. I've heard you pray. You have good people skills. Since you're now retired, would you join me on a hospital call? You don't have to do anything, just come along." The spiritual translation? "You don't have to do anything AT FIRST; UNTIL YOU CATCH FIRE, just come along."

Jesus recruited disciples by saying, "Come, follow Me." As far as we know, He didn't say much about what they were getting into, yet. Jesus wasn't practicing "bait and switch," either. He was sensitive to how much they could handle at that time. Remember, they were baby Christ-followers. If He told them everything, it would be like feeding a steak to a two-month-old child. What crazy person would do that? (Most church program leaders would!) Jesus graciously and lovingly respected their spiritual early childhood. So did Bob.

When Bob invited Mary to watch, he demonstrated the first of four steps of discipling a Christian into ministry: *I do / you watch.*[9] Mary goes along with Bob. He briefs Mary on who they will see, shares a little bit about the person, and transparently tells Mary how he prepared for this visit.

After the hospital visit, Bob debriefs. He uses the Kingdom

culture dynamic of interrogative influence: asking questions. "Did you see the tear in Mr. Langwell's eye when I read the Scripture?" "Did you notice I held his hand when I prayed?" "Did you catch how the Scripture I read focused on assurance of forgiveness?" "Do you know why I used that verse?"

When Mary shows comfort and enthusiasm, Bob senses she may be ready for stage two of discipleship. This may be after two hospital visits, or it could be after two years. It depends on Mary. Bob says, "Tomorrow afternoon, I need to make some hospital calls. Can you come along?" She says she is available. Bob continues, "Mary, as you think about tomorrow, would you be willing to share the Scripture? I will give it to you so you can read it in advance and prepare." This second step is *I do / you help.*

In time, Mary has helped Bob on enough hospital visits, and he feels a sense of confidence in her work. He moves to the third stage of discipleship: *you do / I help.* "Mary," Bob says, "You've been on a number of hospital visits. You really seem to do well. Why don't you take the lead on this one? You can do everything and I'll close in prayer. If you feel uncomfortable at any time, or feel surprised by anything that occurs, just look at me, and I'll take over." By this time, Mary has watched and helped Pastor Bob so many times, in so many situations, she easily moves into this third stage of ministry discipleship. As she leaves the hospital, she feels a strong sense of God using her, and she is growing in confidence.

In the fourth stage of discipling, Bob recognizes Mary is ready for anything that might occur on a hospital visit. They may have been working together for a few months or a few years. I repeat this because the effective discipler is sensitive to how the Holy Spirit works in the person's life. This isn't a secular training program; this is God at work in Bob, multiplying in Mary. This is God at work in Mary, who is becoming a disciple for hospital ministry. Bob moves to the fourth stage: *you do / I watch.*

At this point, Bob talks with Mary on the phone. He says, "Mary, you've done this so long, and you're doing such a great job, I can tell God has gifted you for this ministry. Today, when we go into each hospital room, I will say hello and goodbye to the person, but you do the rest. If, at the end of the visit, the person appears to be uncomfortable—not because of your ministry, but because I sat silent—I'll explain to them that you have been training for this ministry. I'll say, 'Doesn't Mary do a great job?' "

The Discipling Steps

Step #1: **I do/you watch**

Step #2: **I do/you help**

Step #3: **You do/I help**

Step #4: **You do/I watch**

Three weeks later, a great opportunity comes for Pastor Bob. "Mary, I'm going to a conference next week. How would you feel about making the hospital calls? By the way, Mary, begin to pray about, look for, and see if you can find someone to go with you. Over time, take them through the four steps we've followed before: *I do / you watch*; *I do / you help*; *you do / I help*; *you do / I watch*." Way to go, Bob!

Pastor Bob has not only trained Mary for hospital calls, but even more important, he has also trained Mary to disciple while she does it. In this moment, in God's math, the miracle of multiplication is birthed. Mary starts making hospital calls on her own and begins a multiplication process. Having caught the Kingdom culture, she now disciples another person as she serves in hospital ministry. She follows the four steps. She has learned how to *disciple*.

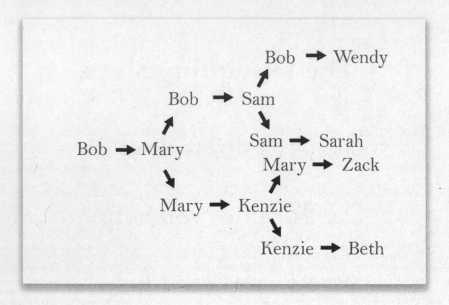

As Mary conducts her ministry, Bob is in contact with her occasionally and holds her accountable through short, written reports each week. Pastor Bob, who is now committed to discipling, has invited Sam to follow him in the church's prison ministry. Meanwhile, Mary is discipling Kenzie in hospital visits.

Fast-forward five years. What ministry effect do you expect from Bob's discipling? The church has ceased adding paid staff (and robbing God's people of the privilege of ministry). We will look at this issue from a different angle in the next chapter, "Turn Your Service into Dignity."

INVERTED OUTREACH

When Jesus said to "make disciples,"[10] He had a greater vision than plodding along with two hundred people in worship for decades.

This is a significant issue, since there could be twenty thousand people around your church untouched by the gospel. The Great Commission vision is to make disciples of all nations. That takes an army, not a few burned-out professionals.

The target for the Great Commission (all nations) sounds like a focus overseas. However, the words in the original Greek are different. The best translation may not be "nations." The word is *ethne*, from which we get the word *ethnics*. Translated directly, it means "peoples." This is rendered more smoothly as "people groups."

What are some of the people groups in your community? Anglos, Hispanics, African Americans, Asians? White-collar business leaders? Retirees? Millennials? Second-generation unchurched people? Those suffering from addictions? Unwed mothers? Singles? Those in the food service industry? Who do you think can reach them best for Christ? Pastors? Those on an evangelism committee? To focus on organizational structure and ignore natural relationships is *inverted outreach*. *Inverted outreach is killing the explosive potential of Christians.*

At some point, the Great Commission was hijacked. It became *isolated* and *insulated*. It became *isolated* as the work of church staff or evangelism committees—the organization. When it becomes the passion of the organization, it is the passion of no one. The Great Commission becomes perverted to the few reaching the many. This Kingdom culture drift cuts the Great Commission off at the knees. It cripples the body of Christ. The power and potential of the Christian movement are decimated. Multiplication is reduced to addition.

> Inverted outreach is killing the explosive potential of Christians.

Should anyone be surprised that churches are plateaued and declining? Can you grasp this reality? Most churches reach a pittance of their potential!

For centuries, much of the Christian church has promoted the role of clergy not as *equippers* of masses, but as *doers* of ministry. Churches reflect a culture that allows anyone to put away chairs and wash dishes in the kitchen, yet they empower almost no one to reach out. If you want everyone in worship to look down at their shoes, ask for a show of hands of those who feel called to evangelism!

In Kingdom drift, we have *isolated* outreach as the work of staff and the organization. In the same stroke, we have *insulated* the mission from a people-group-sensitive approach. Who reaches out to retirees better than retirees? Workers to fellow workers? Business owners to business owners?

Christians share the gospel more effectively with those who speak their language, have similar lifestyles, work similar jobs, and like the same music. This is an extension of the incarnation. Jesus became a person because God wanted to show His love for people. If God wanted to save penguins, Jesus would have been born a penguin. If God wants to save a waiter at Applebee's, who could be better to reach that waiter than a fellow waiter who is on fire for Christ? That waiter's introduction to Christ *could* come from anyone. God can do anything, but the relationship established between one waiter and another is usually the most productive way to share the good news of Jesus. The Christian waiter has a relationship with Jesus and a relationship with his fellow waiter.

This relational principle reflects the wonderful Kingdom potential of a multicultural, diverse church. If your church has people from every people group in your area, and they are equipped to reach those in their social networks, how effective is that? However, if they are not equipped, the church is crippled in potential for mission. Many churches have inherited a system that *isolates* and *insulates* the potential for the Kingdom. They have emasculated the power of the Jesus epidemic.

Every church leader should study epidemiology. Epidemiology is the science of epidemics. Jesus, the genius who started the Christian movement, focused entirely on a multiplying form of movement. Christianity is built to grow exponentially. This is God's math. This movement is a spiritual epidemic. You catch it like you catch the flu: up close and personal.

You don't get the flu by reading a book about the flu. You don't catch the flu by hearing a sermon about the flu. You catch the flu by being up close and personal with someone who has it. You catch Christianity from contagious Christians who have hearts burdened for those who don't know Jesus. That is Kingdom culture: on-fire

Christians up close and personal with those who have not yet met the Master.

Through *isolation* and *insulation*, many churches successfully quarantine Christians. Many churches inoculate the carriers of the Jesus movement by professionalizing the contagious: "That's the pastor's job." "The staff does that." "Who, me? I'm not into evangelism; I work in the kitchen."

> Christianity is built to grow exponentially. This is God's math. This movement is a spiritual epidemic.

KINGDOM OUTREACH

As epidemics spread, they reach a tipping point. They take on a life of their own. This is what happened in the New Testament church. It occurs in great moves of God (revivals). Jesus, the brilliant Master, marked the movement with God's math: *multiplication in geometric progression.*

Jesus is the *Word* who became flesh.[11] This Word, Jesus, gave us *the* Word, the good news—the saving story of God's love. Think about this: You are on your deathbed. Your family and closest friends are gathered around. It is your last chance to say your last words. It is unlikely you're going to say, "Julianna, do you think the Colts are going to win the Super Bowl next February?" You're probably not thinking, "Kailyn, that was a great dance recital in June." Last words are important.

Jesus had three big moments to say something really important. (1) Just before He died on the cross: "Father, forgive them; they don't know what they're doing."[12] (2) After the Word was resurrected: "As the Father has sent me, so I send you."[13] (3) Just before His ascension into heaven: "You will be my witnesses...to the end of the earth."[14]

His words were not the last word! You have the last word! You have *the Word* in you to share *the Word* with the world. The movement rests on your tongue, in your hands, and on your life. You have the power of multiplication, a tipping point for the most important movement on earth.

In his book *The Tipping Point*, Malcolm Gladwell focuses on mass movements. Social epidemics, he says, are "driven by the efforts of a handful of exceptional people," and one of the key factors in a social epidemic is "stickiness."[15] Does the Word of God stick with you all week long? Is it sticking when you visit Vi and Thom?

Contagion is the important element of messages. Are you a contagious Christian? Will others catch the holy infection from you? The hard part, according to Gladwell, is figuring out how to make sure a message does not go in one ear and out the other. "Stickiness means that a message makes an impact." That's why the evidence of a healthy church is changed lives. Gladwell concludes, "Stickiness is a critical component in tipping."[16] This is the power of the Christian movement.

Before you say, "That could never happen in my church, in our city, or in this country," remember, this is exactly what happened in the early church. It is occurring today in Ethiopia, South Korea, Communist China, and in some areas of the United States and Europe.

A JESUS EPIDEMIC

How can this occur in your church? First, pray for a God-sized worldview. Breakthrough is not exceptional. Exponential, transformational growth is normal. Ask God to help you get out of the way, beginning with your mind, your puny vision. There's nothing special about being a large church. There are lost people out there. Jesus died for them. He's dying for you to reach them. That's the point.

Next, stop freaking people out about evangelism. The spiritual gift of evangelist is given to about 10 percent of Christians. Equip those who have the gift, for sure. Encourage them to share the faith with strangers, developing good presentations supported by Bible passages.

Witnesses come forward to testify, or give a testimony. *They simply tell their story.*

For the 90 percent, teach them to witness. Jesus says, "You will be my witnesses."[17] Most everyone knows what it means to be a witness: "I was there; I saw it. It happened to me." Witnesses come forward to testify, or give a testimony. *They simply tell their story.*

Parables are stories. Stories gently nudge people to receptive insight. Every Christian has stories. Even new Christians have some. Jesus modeled storytelling. Your stories are not about you. They are "God stories." They are true stories about God's work in your life.

• A God story might reflect a time when you were financially devastated. In the process, you went back to church for the first time in years. Through your regular worship, God restored your hope. You got through it. That is a God story.

• Maybe your spouse failed you. You went deeper into Bible study, you learned a new level of forgiveness, and your marriage was restored. That is a God story.

• Perhaps you lost your job. Your Christian neighbor encouraged you, prayed for you, and prayed with you. You joined a Bible study and became a Christian. You believe God got you through the hard time. That is a God story.

How do you develop a culture of storytelling in your church? Every time a small group meets, no matter what the agenda, the leader starts by asking, "Does anyone want to share what God has done in your life lately?" At first, it is likely no one will respond. Don't be concerned. Remember, the power of asking questions is incredible. Just keep asking. You are building culture, and culture takes time. You are developing this culture of God storytelling, which is witnessing. You don't have to use the word *witnessing.* You don't have to explain what you're doing. Culture building is spontaneous. Don't program it. Let it happen!

In time, you will see the birth of a culture of sharing God stories. It will begin in and around church. It will spill into everyday lives as Christians interact with those in their social networks. It may take a few years, but it will occur. This is the beginning of a movement toward God's math of multiplication.

Imagine what God would accomplish if twelve people in your

church shared their God stories with an unchurched person at work, in their neighborhood, seven days a week, 365 days a year. Do the math. Twelve times 365 is 4,380. What if that group, in two years, expanded from twelve to a hundred? One hundred times 365 equals 36,500. How do you think God would use that to grow His Kingdom? What if 10 percent of the churches in the United States caught this vision? What if that influenced 10 percent more? This is movement thinking. This is how great moves of God occur. Do you understand how this could begin *with you*?

You could also encourage Christians to develop what we call a *sociogram*. On a sheet of paper, put a rectangle in the middle. Put your name in the rectangle. Draw arrows from your name to the four corners of the paper. In the corners, list those in your social network who are *not yet Christ-followers*. In one corner, list friends. In a second corner, put unchurched relatives. In a third corner, write non-Christian neighbors. In a fourth corner, list those at work or school who show no outward signs of faith in Jesus.

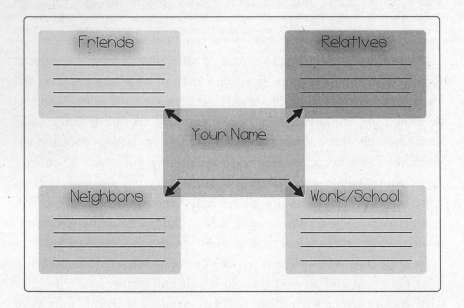

Put this sociogram somewhere you visit every day, such as on the bathroom mirror. Every day, pray these people will, by God's power, grow in receptivity and become people of faith. God reaches people through people like a contagious epidemic. Jesus said, "The harvest is great, but the workers are few. So pray."[18] Don't be surprised if your prayers are answered and God uses *you* to be the one to reach those in your social network. This is not a program. It is a prayer lifestyle. You are praying for the harvest. God will honor those prayers.

RECEPTIVITY

The harvest concept is about receptivity, when the crop is ripe. When do people show receptivity to spiritual issues? (1) When they ask spiritual questions. (2) When they appear to be hopeless. (3) When they feel stress. (4) When they experience discomfort. (5) When they are going through a transition, such as marriage, divorce, death in the family, job change, retirement, or birth of a child.

Receptivity is not rocket science. You might wonder, "Why doesn't every Christian know about these easy-to-learn markers of receptivity?" "Why don't many pastors know about harvest receptivity?" These are basic elements of Kingdom culture. God's math comes from returning to harvest thinking, praying, and multiplying workers for the harvest.

This may sound odd, but be cautious about bringing people to worship. When you are nurturing a new Christian, wait until she expresses interest in worship. Focus on personal, one-on-one interaction. Nurture the seeds God is planting through your relationship. Ask permission before you pray. Let her be the barometer of how deep and how fast you move to disciple. Be like a farmer who goes out to the field several times to check when the crop is ripe.

After a while, invite her to a social gathering at your home or some other neutral setting (not a church building). We call these "Outreach Clusters."[19] Help her to become acquainted with other Christians. Warn the others not to talk about church, the organization. Ask them to be themselves. Before the gathering ends, ask your friends if anyone would share what God is doing in his or her life. This will show your new disciple you are not the only one who has experienced the power of God. Experience beats academic content every time. That is not to say the content of the Bible is unimportant.

It is to say that your experiential sharing or witnessing in the early outreach stages of mission are more appropriate. That is why Jesus said we should be witnesses, not professors of religion.

Continue meeting with Christian friends. If, when you ask, "What is God doing in your life?" your new disciple shares, it is a sign she *may* be ready to visit worship. If she shows interest in worship, do not invite her; bring her. Sit with those in your Outreach Cluster. In this process, your disciple assimilates into a network of Christians before she attends church. Christians spend too much effort trying to assimilate others into church, the organization. Assimilation is first relational and, much later, organizational.

As you continue discipling a new Christian, don't rush to get her into a membership class. Membership classes are important, but the more you disciple her prior to organizational exposure, the better. Be sure to nurture her to the point where she can disciple.

If she has been a non-Christian, it is unlikely many in her social network are Christians. The potential for exponential Kingdom growth is huge. If all you do is put her through a membership class, she becomes part of the organization. This approach could inoculate her from her own social network. However, if she is discipled first, her social network becomes her mission field. Do you see the potential for geometric progression? Can you feel the movement? Do you see how Jesus put this movement together? Do you see how far churches have drifted? Are you shocked by the minimal growth of most churches?

Think about Jesus and the woman at the well.[20] She had a poor reputation in the village. As she was a woman, a man should not even talk to her in public. When she went back to her village, however, she became a conduit to Jesus and salvation for many. This is the power of (1) reaching the least, the last, and the lost, and (2) discipleship multiplication through social networks.

DO THE MATH

Suppose two hundred people worship at your church. Consider that one in ten of them (not counting staff or those on the evangelism team) is equipped to reach out with God stories. One in ten is 10 percent of two hundred, which equals twenty people.

What if, over the next ten years, those twenty people would reach and disciple sixty others for Jesus Christ? For most churches, it may seem impossible. Remember, when you disciple a non-Christian, her social network includes unchurched people, and the dynamic begins a geometric progression.

If the twenty people would reach only one person each in the first year, that would be twenty new people. If those twenty people were discipled (not just became church members), it would become forty people. The next year, the forty people would reach forty more. Project that out, without considering any outreach by the two hundred original members, the staff, or anyone else. In ten years, the size of the discipleship impact is 20,480.

Recognize that we live in an imperfect world, and there is attrition for all sorts of reasons. Therefore, cut that number in half. At that point, your outreach would be "only" 10,240 people! It doesn't matter, of course, if they don't all end up belonging to your church. It is all about the growth of God's Kingdom. As you see, geometric progression equals an amazing movement. Can you hear Jesus saying, "Well done, good and faithful servant"?[21]

Consider what really matters. Are you doing what counts? Is your life dedicated to significance? The *Guinness World Records* book has a section about a man who grinds up metal and glass to eat it. Over several years, this man ate six bicycles and four chandeliers. In Caracas, Venezuela, he ground up and ate a Cessna airplane![22]

Now, can you imagine when this guy stands before the Lord (whether it is a welcome or in judgment) and the Lord says, "Well, what did you do with your life?" The man replies, "I ate an airplane." Do you think the Lord will say, "Well done, good and faithful servant?"[23]

God's math is not a program. Don't make it into a program. It only works in the context of Kingdom culture. Without Kingdom culture, discipling would die out in the second or third year. You would never see the Kingdom grow in geometric progression. God's powerful seeds are supposed to be planted in fertile soil.

Like many, you may be tempted to grab the idea of writing your social networks on a sheet of paper and asking everyone to pray every day for those who are not yet Christ-followers. I know it is tempting to start a program by asking people, "What is God doing in your life?" It might be that you want to start Outreach Clusters, involving many in your church.

I beg you, *don't* do it—unless you first build Kingdom culture. If these programs would grow God's Kingdom, someone would already have put them in a box and sold it a long time ago. Everything else you read in this book would be unnecessary. I promise you, it is not about what you do. Primarily, it is about who you are and who you become. That is the way God changes everything.

If you ask Christians who is to fulfill the Great Commission, many would name the pastor and the staff. In our research, we surveyed those who attend church. We asked them to identify the goal of the Great Commission.

The issue behind this survey question is not the goal of the Great Commission, but about how many will answer, "Preach the Gospel." This is a subtle way of discovering whether they identify it as the role of the staff or whether they see the commission as their personal mission. From clinical observation, interviewing those who answer this question with "Preach the Gospel," we have discovered that the answer reflects a staff person.

Our database on this issue, which includes 24,654 respondents, reflects that 36 percent (more than one-third) see the goal of the Great Commission as to "preach the gospel to all nations." This reduces the mathematics of the Great Commission from multiplication to addition among more than one-third of those in the churches that were surveyed. The concepts of "teach" and "baptize" may reflect even more.

Look around our world and see how God operates. God is a creator of brilliance. He is a sustainer by multiplication. He told our first parents to be fruitful and multiply. All of creation works this way. Does your church?

The Goal of the Great Commission

Choose the statement which *best* describes the goal of
the Great Commission. (Mark one.)

   ①   Make disciples of all nations
   ②   Preach the gospel to all nations
   ③   Teach all nations
   ④   Baptize all nations

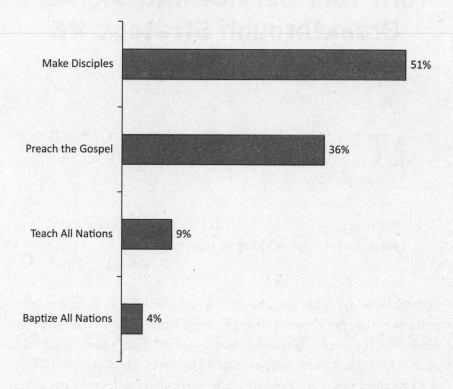

CHAPTER TEN

Turn Your Service into Dignity– Breakthrough Strategy #6

Ceiling #6: Identity Theft

> Intrinsically motivated people usually achieve more
> than their reward-seeking counterparts.
>
> —Daniel H. Pink[1]

In Matthew 9:35–36, Jesus visits several towns and villages, "proclaiming the good news of the kingdom.... When he saw the crowds...they were harassed and helpless, like sheep without a shepherd." Jesus "had compassion."[2] How would you respond?

The disciples were probably not surprised by Jesus' assessment that "There is a large harvest, but few workers to gather it in."[3] The disciples learned, early on, what every active Christian has discovered: God's work always needs more help.

"That's why we started our volunteer program," said Julie. "We don't have enough people involved. We've got a lot going on. It takes a larger number of people to keep this church going." Julie paused and thought to herself, "I just wish we could get more people to volunteer. People are so busy these days."

When Jesus recognized the large harvest and few workers, He didn't recommend a volunteer program. He told His disciples, "Pray to the owner of the harvest that he will send out workers to gather in his harvest."⁴ Really? That's Your plan, Jesus? Pray?

If you have prayed for help, as Jesus suggests, how has the Lord answered? What is the Kingdom culture? You will be hard pressed to fit the "ministry of volunteerism" into Kingdom culture. This is a challenge. The use of volunteers is so prevalent that the concept is considered sacred.

CEILING #6: IDENTITY THEFT

Most Christians are shocked to learn that the idea of a "volunteer" is foreign to the ethos of the Christian church. In the New Testament, the word *service* comes from the word *servant*. "That's just semantics," you might say. "You can call it anything." It is not that simple.

Jesus modeled servanthood in John 13:14–15. It is a posture, an attitude of the culture of the King. Jesus says, "If I then, your Lord and Teacher, have washed your feet, you too ought to wash one another's feet. For I have given you an example—you should do just as I have done for you."⁵ When Jesus washed His disciples' feet, He wasn't launching a program. He was modeling an attitude. It is the posture of servanthood. It is the culture of being a servant of Jesus, as Jesus was a servant Himself.

In my work with churches, I have been increasingly troubled with the posture of volunteerism from a Kingdom culture perspective. The call for volunteers is most always the way Christians are asked to serve, with the purpose of getting the job done and making sure the program is successful. This makes the program the *priority*.

The challenge is this: God does not *use* people for programs, even those we call "ministries." The concept of volunteerism is grounded in a program that needs help. The approach *is program centered*. The culture of the Kingdom is *person centered*. In the Kingdom culture, God's people do not *volunteer* for ministry; God *calls* people into ministry. God called Moses; the job didn't call Moses. Jesus Christ called Paul. His transformation to become a missionary was not an offer to volunteer. Henry Ford came remarkably close to this cultural attitude when he said, "The whole secret of a successful life is to find out what it is one's destiny to do, and then do it."[6]

Volunteers focus on "There is a job to do. We [the institution] need your help," or, "It [the job] needs your help." This is the issue between a career and a calling. You drive your motivation for a career. However, a calling drives you. Serving God is not a duty. God can accomplish anything. God doesn't need you. God doesn't need anyone. Kingdom culture is not a system in which God is begging for volunteers. He doesn't *need* you—He *wants* you. This is a big deal. It is the difference between law motivation and gospel motivation.

Law motivation is "God needs you. If you don't help, God's work won't get done." This is law, because it is motivation by threat, such as: "If you don't help with crafts for vacation Bible school, the kids won't have crafts."

From the Kingdom perspective, it is a privilege and an honor to serve God. In my book *Burn On or Burn Out*, I have said, "We see Christians going around in circles, confusing activity with accomplishment. So many are near burnout they suffer from ecclesiastical exhaustion."[7] God gives us the privilege to join hands with Him. This is gospel motivation. This is not "Somebody has to do it." It is "I get to do this!" Donald Miller, in his fascinating book *Blue Like Jazz*, says, "By accepting God's love for us, we fall in love with Him, and only then do we have the fuel we need to obey."[8]

Think of Simon from Cyrene. On Good Friday, he was just a face in the crowd. He didn't get up that morning and say, "Today I will go down in history as the guy who volunteered to help Jesus carry His cross." He didn't have a clue. However, he was called to help carry the redemptive load of the Savior. When Jesus says, "Take up your cross, and follow Me," it is a calling, a divine appointment, and an opportunity to do something great—as a servant. Jesus didn't say, "Can I get a volunteer?"

God gives the privilege of service so Christians like you and me can experience the joy of partnership. It is the thrill of being a conduit for God's power in Jesus Christ. Partnership—isn't that what being part of the body of Christ is all about? Isn't that the joy of having an important role in the life-changing work of the Savior of the world?

> From the Kingdom perspective, it is a privilege and an honor to serve God. God gives us the privilege to join hands with Him.

The motivation is not to help get a project completed. It is not described as a Kingdom-level motivation to usher in church, just because "we need another usher." John Maxwell in his book *It's Just a Thought...But it Could Change Your Life* writes, "People will work eight hours a day for pay, 10 hours a day for a good boss, and 24 hours a day for a good cause!"[9] The cause of Christ has fueled Christian service for centuries.

What is the end game for a *volunteer*? It is a job well done. What is the end game for a *disciple*? It is multiplying Jesus' movement by discipling another person and discovering divine fulfillment by using your spiritual gifts to achieve a job well done. What is the end game of an *ambassador*? It is multiplying Jesus' movement by discipling another person and using your spiritual gifts to achieve a job well done, influencing the world for Jesus Christ. "Well done, good and faithful servant."[10] In other words, "Way to go—you multiplied as you served the cause of growing the Kingdom!"

As we have seen, the Great Commission is not a commandment we must obey. It is a commissioned privilege. Is there any greater privilege a human can experience? Hugh Thomson Kerr is quoted by George Peters in his excellent book *A Biblical Theology of Missions*:

> We are sent not to preach sociology but salvation; not economics but evangelism; not reform but redemption; not culture but conversion; not progress but pardon; not a new social order but a new birth; not revolution but regeneration; not renovation but revival; not resuscitation but resurrection; not a new organization but a new creation; not democracy but the gospel; not civilization but Christ. We are ambassadors not diplomats.[11]

The New Testament calls Christians a holy priesthood."[12] Our service in the body of Christ is a gift from God. It gives us the privilege to experience God working through us. This grows our faith. The Kingdom culture worldview is not the utilitarian approach of volunteerism. The call of God to partner with the King of the universe is your highest honor and greatest challenge. As you step out in faith, you grow in faith. God demonstrates that you cannot do this alone. It is a miracle. God has chosen you. You have faith in God, and God has faith in you!

Mark Marxhausen puts the Kingdom worldview in perspective so well:

There are many reasons why God would not want you. But don't worry, you're in good company. Moses stuttered. David's armor didn't fit. John Mark was rejected by Paul. Hosea's wife was a prostitute. Amos' only training was in the school of fig tree pruning. Jacob was a liar. David had an affair. Solomon was too rich. Abraham was too old. David was too young. Timothy had ulcers. Peter was afraid of death. Lazarus was dead. John was self-righteous. Jesus was too poor. Naomi was a widow. Paul was a murderer. So was Moses. Jonah ran from God. Miriam was a gossip. Gideon and Thomas both doubted. Jeremiah was depressed and suicidal. Elijah was burned out. John the Baptist was a loudmouth. Martha was a worrywart. Mary was lazy. Samson had long hair. Noah got drunk. Did I mention that Moses had a short fuse? So did Peter, Paul—well, many folks did.

But God doesn't require a job interview. He doesn't hire and fire like most bosses, because He's more our Dad than our Boss. He doesn't look for financial gain or loss. He's not prejudiced or partial, not judging, grudging, sassy, or brassy, not deaf to our cry, not blind to our need. As much as we try, God's gifts are free. We could do wonderful things for wonderful people and still not be...wonderful. Satan says, "You're not worthy." Jesus says, "So what? I AM." Satan looks back and sees our mistakes. God looks back and sees the cross. He doesn't calculate what you did in '78. It's not even on the record. Sure. There are lots of reasons why God shouldn't want us. But if we are in love with Him, if we hunger for Him more than our next breath, He'll use us in spite of who we are, where we've been, or what we look like. Step out of your limitations into the limitless nature of who God is.[13]

THE VOLUNTEER SCENARIO

Richard Exley says, "God has a history of using the insignificant to accomplish the impossible."[14] All the time in churches, we see volunteerism, a well-oiled machine to "plug people in" to the programs of the church. In most congregations, it is so far from biblical Kingdom culture that it is unrecognizable.

> As you step out in faith, you grow in faith. God demonstrates you cannot do this alone. It is a miracle. God has chosen you. You have faith in God, and God has faith in you.

You have probably witnessed an approach like this. The Sunday school, a program/ministry of the church, needs another Sunday school teacher. The superintendent asks the teachers, "Do you know anyone who might help teach Sunday school?" The teachers shake their heads, "No." The Sunday school superintendent then asks the pastor and staff. They shop through a list of people who seem to be exceptionally committed to church and who might not be too busy already. When that step reaches a dead end, the superintendent asks the pastor to make an announcement in church. On Sunday morning, the pastor works through the announcements. "We [the congregation] need your help in the Sunday school [program]." Ebbie Smith in his book *Balanced Church Growth* points out how this type of approach doesn't fit Kingdom culture: "The people are not there to help the minister run the church. The minister is there to help the people be the church."[15]

Volunteerism is backward to the Kingdom culture of *being*

a servant of God. Serving is a privilege for you to experience the fulfillment of God working through you. Can that fulfillment be achieved through volunteering? Possibly. However, it teaches a system backward to Kingdom culture. It promotes a culture that represents Kingdom drift.

Often, the volunteer approach faces resistance from the words, "I'm too busy." This, to be honest, is the most frequent public lie around church. Admittedly, people feel pressured, so they try to be gracious in their rejection of the request to volunteer.

How many burned-out church leaders have you heard say, "I've called so many people to volunteer. All I get is 'I'm too busy,' or 'Not at this time.'" This is discouraging for leaders. The reaction is often to cheapen the calling: "Look, you can just help out for three months while the fourth grade Sunday school teacher is on maternity leave." Often, the person is still teaching twenty years later!

This approach is so mundane it could be followed by any secular organization. Volunteerism reflects *devotion* to a cause, like Sunday school. We are called to be *devoted* to Jesus Christ, not to a cause. Our primary calling is not to *do*, but to *be* and *become*. In *The Present Future*, Reggie McNeal says, "Christians (evangelicals especially) emphasize that our connectivity to God is through a relationship with Jesus. We talk about giving Him our hearts or inviting Him into our hearts. We use love language to talk about committing our lives to Him. Then, as soon as the deal is done, we switch the language and go to head stuff."[16]

Consider for a moment that Cindy responds to the pastor's plea to teach fourth grade Sunday school. Cindy meets with the Sunday school superintendent, who hands her a teacher's guide and shows her the fourth grade room—and that's the end of Cindy's preparation. The Sunday school superintendent smiles, shakes Cindy's hand, and says, "Don't worry, you'll be fine." If you know much about churches, you know this happens a lot.

> Volunteerism reflects *devotion* to a cause.... We are called to be *devoted* to Jesus Christ.

The next Sunday, Cindy experiences trauma. She has never

taught a Sunday school class in her life. Now she steps into her first classroom experience with ten fourth-graders. Cindy has no experience. She has received no mentoring, no coaching, and no discipling in the process. Here she is, with ten kids and the responsibility of representing God. (No pressure, Cindy!)

The volunteer approach is disrespectful. Often, there is total disregard for the spiritual gifts God has given to Cindy. This is disrespectful to Cindy, to the Holy Spirit, and to Scripture.

Most volunteer efforts do not include a ministry to help people discover, develop, and use their spiritual gifts. In Kingdom culture, this is the *primary* way people discover where God wants them to serve. The biblical approach is not program centered, merely filling the spot in the Sunday school. It is person centered, with high respect for the person. This is the respect God has for people.

Kingdom culture works like this: "Cindy, if you're willing, I'd like to help you (by serving you) discover the gifts God has given you. We have a little survey you can take. It will help you discover your dominant and subordinate gifts. It will also tell you about what spiritual gifts God has not given you. It will show you which gifts you perhaps have not yet experienced and don't know about. Then, as you want to confirm some of your gifts, I can connect you with a ministry that will allow you to use these gifts. You can be a 'helper' to someone who has these gifts and explore your gift mix further." Spiritual gifts and discipling are the way, in Kingdom culture, people find their niche in the body of Christ. In Kingdom culture, the focus is to help every Christian discover their spiritual gifts. The most important records for a church—the gift mix of each of the members—aren't found in most church offices.

As a consultant, I have heard a story like this more than once: "I was on the nominating committee. We were looking for elders for the upcoming election. I bet I called twenty people to find one that let us put his name on the ballot. We had to have at least two names, according to the bylaws of our constitution. I guess we have to have one that is voted in and one that loses the election. I had one man ask me what the qualifications were for elder before he would let me add his name to the ballot. I just told him, 'Check your pulse.' We just needed a warm body to fill the slot." How does this approach honor God?

If you want to be part of a thriving church, you will change whatever is not in harmony with a biblical approach. Service begins in the atmosphere of humility. In *My Utmost for His Highest*, Oswald Chambers writes,

> Do you say, "But He has been unwise to choose me, because there is nothing good in me and I have no value?" That is exactly why He chose you. As long as you think you are of value to Him He cannot choose you, because you have purposes of your own to serve....
>
> It is not a matter of our equipment, but a matter of our poverty; not of what we bring with us, but of what God puts into us; not a matter of natural virtues, of strength of character, of knowledge, or of experience—all of that is of no avail in this concern. The only thing of value is being taken into the compelling purpose of God and being made His friends (see 1 Corinthians 1:26–31)....As Christians we are not here for our own purpose at all—we are here for the purpose of God, and the two are not the same.[17]

Jesus modeled how people are invited into ministry. Not once did He look for a volunteer. His approach was not to recruit help to usher in the Kingdom. He invited others to follow Him. He did not take from them; He gave to them. The immediate objective was not to put them to work but to disciple them. They were not invited to do but to become. "But our volunteers are already Christians," you say. Ephesians 4:12 says that God's people are to be equipped—not with a manual, but through on-the-job discipling. Consider the approach modeled by Jesus.

Suppose I am a Sunday school teacher, and I want to live my life from the perspective of Kingdom culture. I am clear about my responsibilities: (1) Prepare the lesson. (2) Show up on time to teach Sunday school. (3) Teach the children. (4) Follow up on any absent child. (5) Pray for the children. (6) Participate in ongoing teacher training twice each year.

In the Kingdom culture, as a Sunday school teacher, I would begin with my number one priority: to multiply myself by discipling another Sunday school teacher while I taught Sunday school. This is not just another check-off on the responsibility sheet. This is in my DNA. This is my worldview as a Christian and, therefore, as a Sunday school teacher. I would see this as my privilege and my calling: to pray for and look for, until I find, a person to disciple as a Sunday school teacher, while I teach Sunday school.

I would check at the church office for those with the dominant gift of teaching and perhaps subordinate gifts in knowledge, wisdom, and possibly other gifts that might meet the unique challenges and opportunities with the children in my class. Since my Kingdom culture has influenced me to recognize the value of *relational* discipling, I would consider if there is anyone I already know at church who might have the right gift mix. I would not consider it important if a person is already involved in another ministry. I would not simply look for someone who is not involved yet. I would submit to Christ, the head of His body the church. I would not limit my search by human variables.

As I continue to pray for guidance, I would ask God to direct me to someone. I would approach that person in the model of Jesus, who said, "Come, follow Me." However, since I am clearly not Jesus, I would modify it and say, "I've been praying about inviting someone to join me in my teaching, as Jesus tells us to do. I ask you to pray about joining me. If you love children, ask God if this might be worth considering. I'll check back with you. Is two weeks okay? I just want to know if you would join me in the class. I don't have any specific tasks for you, for now. And at this point, I'd just like to acquaint you with this ministry."

My motivation to multiply myself is *not* because the Sunday school (program) needs help. It doesn't matter, for my motive, whether help is needed or not. I do this because *this is who I am.* This is what Kingdom culture is. This is what Christ-followers do. I am a disciple who disciples. My desire is to help another Christian

(1) experience the fulfillment of partnership with the King of Kings, and (2) help another Christian exercise his spiritual gifts for the benefit of the Kingdom. Albert Schweitzer said, "I don't know what your destiny will be, but one thing I know—the only ones among you who will be really happy are those who have sought and found how to serve."[18]

As a Christ-follower, I follow the four steps of discipling (considered in chapter nine): (1) I do / you watch; (2) I do / you help; (3) you do / I help; and (4) you do / I watch. This is, in every respect, a desire to multiply myself. This is not simply teaching another Christian. This is not just training another Christian to do Christian work. This is discipling. It is raising another person to experience the joy of Kingdom service. In this way, the Kingdom is caught. I've heard John Maxwell say, "We teach what we know, we reproduce who we are....People do what people see." This is what we see Jesus do in Scripture. Healthy churches thrive when Christians live in the Kingdom culture of one-on-one relational multiplication.

At some point, I observe proficiency in my disciple. At that point, I invite my disciple to teach her own class. I would continue to teach Sunday school, and while I teach, I multiply myself again. My disciple does the same. Discipling never ends. I remain a mentor and friend to my disciple.

Together, we begin a *movement* of Sunday school teachers in our church. This changes the approach from volunteer recruitment to discipling, from addition to multiplication, and from program to movement. Jesus launched this movement. Multiply this for every ministry in your church, and you will see why healthy churches thrive. You will never focus on volunteerism again.

The real fruit of an apple tree is not apples, but another apple tree. Volunteers add to church programs. Disciples multiply the movement. This is legacy leadership. It is what Jesus did. It is what the church does in revival mode. The New Testament church caught it from the apostles, who caught it from Jesus. Sadly, most churches today have drifted from it.

Over the last four decades, I have interviewed hundreds of Sunday school teachers during consultations at their churches. I ask them, "What is your job description as a Sunday school teacher? What are you supposed to do?" Not once have I heard a Sunday school teacher say, "To equip another Sunday school teacher." Not once! These are not bad people. They are dedicated teachers who sacrifice their time and energy in the service of the Lord and in service to their church.

Do you see the drift? Do you see why so many churches are often begging for Sunday school teachers and other workers? Do you see the power of Kingdom culture? Can you see the vision for a thriving church? Can you see the breakthrough potential?

GIFTED TO GROW

Kathy was livid. "Listen, Church Doctor. The reason I requested an interview is our new pastor."

"Okay," I said, with a sensitive voice and an I-can't-wait-for-this attitude. "Go ahead, Kathy. Tell me what's on your mind."

> This changes the approach from volunteer recruitment to discipling, from addition to multiplication, and from program to movement.

"You do know we had a pastor serving here for thirty-five years, right?" she asked.

"Yes," I replied, "I've heard quite a bit about him. He must have been a great pastor."

"Yes, he was!" Kathy smiled.

I interrupted her next thought to share some genuine empathy. "I understand he died quite suddenly."

She sighed. "Yes, he did."

"That's a hard experience for Christians," I said, with a merciful tone. I meant it. It's a shock to lose a pastor most everyone loved.

"Well, I want to talk about Pastor Paul," she said.

"I understand he's been here not quite two years," I reflected. I knew that already but wanted to remind her he was trying hard to fill big shoes.

"Well, he's so difficult. He's not the preacher Tim was, I'll tell you that. He teaches his sermons more than preaches them."

"Yes, I understand he has the spiritual gift of teaching," I added. "We always ask each staff member to take the Spiritual Gifts Profile before we arrive at the church for a consultation."[19]

As the conversation continued, I thought, "Here is another church leader on the church council who has no clue about spiritual gifts." Kathy could not grasp that the new pastor, who has different gifts, might be who God intends for the next chapter of history.

I'm amazed how many Christians approach ministry as a job description, with no understanding about spiritual gifts. This is also true of many who serve in staff positions. Christians everywhere are operating without access to the Kingdom culture dimension that helps you know your spiritual calling. Do you know your spiritual gifts? If not, attend a spiritual gifts workshop or read a book about gifts. Your experience will open a new worldview for you.

My colleagues and I have worked with churches in the process of adding new staff. Some of these churches have systems that include input from a denominational leader. Many of these leaders review résumés with no information about spiritual gifts! How can you add a pastor, like Paul, and not help those, like Kathy, know he is gifted in different areas than the previous pastor? The apostle Paul said, "Now concerning spiritual gifts, brothers, I don't want you to be ignorant."[20]

Your church will not thrive unless you get back to the Bible and use Scripture as the blueprint for the work of the church. Spiritual gifts are the way God has miraculously designed the royal priesthood. Add this to a discipling process, and the difference is phenomenal. You simply cannot improve on God's plan.

My friend Don Flatau had a great teaching about the different spiritual gifts. We were consulting a parachurch ministry that is growing. In order to grow to the next level, this ministry needed to add a leader with the gift of administration. This would free up staff to work in the areas where they were gifted. Don created square coasters made of OSB board with EPHESIANS 4:16 printed on the side. He explained, "OSB stands for 'oriented strand board.' It is wood, but stronger than wood." Don passed a coaster to each of us. As we inspected our OSB coasters, Don explained. "Notice, this is like God's plan for the body of Christ. All the chips of wood are different sizes. Builders have discovered that if all these pieces were the same size, it wouldn't be nearly as strong. However, *because* they are different from one another, the whole board, when it is glued together, is stronger. It is now one piece of board, but it consists of many very different parts. This is how the body of Christ is supposed to work: many different gifts, glued together by the Holy Spirit."

When a church operates in the framework of Kingdom culture in every area of ministry, recruiting volunteers, as an approach, simply evaporates. Discipleship multiplication will accelerate, and operation by spiritual gifts saturates the ministry.

It is an honor, a privilege, to serve Jesus Christ. As ambassadors of the King, we serve with dignity. In Kingdom culture, life is very different. Being last is to be first, dying to self is living, operating as Christ's slave is the way to freedom, giving is how you receive, service leads to influence, humility results in exaltation, and spiritual gifting, not effort, generates productivity. This is Kingdom culture. It is one more dimension of church life that supports what Jesus said: "My kingdom is not of this world."[21] God will use Kingdom culture to help your church thrive. It is your privilege to serve with dignity. You serve the King Jesus!

In our research, we have asked those in worship about how often they serve the Lord through their church.

The focus here is on those who say they serve "regularly" or "once in a while." After six months of exposure to Kingdom culture, the jump among those who serve grows from 67 percent to 83 percent, representing an additional 16 percent in the six-month time frame. This not only represents a mindset of *willingness* to serve, it demonstrates those who are actively serving. Congregations perpetuating volunteerism will continuously be looking for workers. Congregations operating in Kingdom culture will experience more involvement. Six months is a small beginning. In three to five years, the growth in the number of those who serve will increase as the size of the church grows. Once the discipling engine multiplies

Serving in Ministry

Do you serve in a ministry of this church?

①	Yes, regularly	③	Not now, but I did in the past
②	Once in a while	④	Never

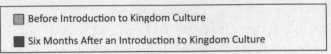

■ Before Introduction to Kingdom Culture

■ Six Months After an Introduction to Kingdom Culture

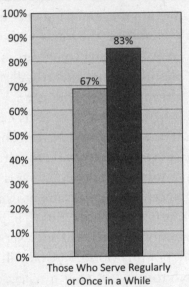

Those Who Serve Regularly
or Once in a While

through three or four generations, increasing numbers of Christians will serve. Kingdom service will begin to appear beyond the boundaries of the congregation, extending the impact of the church into the community and beyond. This leads to future Kingdom growth. Christian service is also an element of the lifestyle of generosity, the subject of the next chapter.

CHAPTER ELEVEN

Turn Your Life into Generosity– Breakthrough Strategy #7

Ceiling #7: Recession Impression

> Seek first his kingdom and his righteousness, and all these things shall be yours as well.
>
> —Matthew 6:33[1]

The atmosphere of generosity permeates Kingdom culture! Generosity among God's people is a visible litmus test of spiritual health and a characteristic of healthy churches. Generosity is not a program, habit, or activity. It is a selfless attitude—a posture you reflect to God and your world. It is about living generously. It is powered by a God of generosity who gave you Jesus. It is about Jesus who generously gave His life on the cross. It is about the cross that generously gives you grace. Grace fuels generosity. In 2 Corinthians, Paul references the amazing generosity of the Christians in Greece (Macedonia) who were poor but generous to the Christians in Jerusalem. It was about grace: "The grace of God that has been granted to the churches of Macedonia."[2]

Not everyone is generous, not in any church. I've never consulted a church where everyone radiated a spirit of generosity. Any growing church will have new Christians, younger in faith. And generosity comes as Christians mature. Some long-term members, of course, haven't grown into Kingdom culture generosity. They are mature in membership but young in spirituality.

In grad school, I read a fascinating book by Wilbert Norton and James Engel called *What's Gone Wrong with the Harvest?* One of their insights is the Engel Scale.[3] It is a measurement of behavioral characteristics among those on the journey of faith. The Engel Scale demonstrates elements of receptivity before a person becomes a believer and dimensions of growth as they mature in faith. A life-style of generosity, stewardship, is listed at the high end of the maturation process (along with sharing the faith and discipling).

Here is how it works:

God is generous to you. God is generous in you. God is generous through you.

God is Generous *to* You ⟶ God is Generous *in* You ⟶ God is Generous *through* You

God is the giver. God gives life, Jesus, forgiveness, new life, ambassador status, and eternal life. Generosity is caught from God.

Generosity influences every area of life: time, energy, financial resources, use of spiritual gifts, hospitality, wise stewardship, compassion, and gracious openness to those who are not yet Christians. Perhaps the most tangible and identifiable area in most churches is financial giving. Guess what? God and His church do not need your money. God owns it all anyway. God wants you to grow in Kingdom culture. You become a citizen of the Kingdom by transformation. God wants a transformed you. The life of generosity is a byproduct.

When our children were young, I'm sure we told them more than two thousand times to say "thank you." I wondered if the culture of giving thanks would ever catch on! You might think we were teaching them to be polite. More than that, we were teaching them Kingdom culture, the culture of generosity. The culture of gratitude is only the first step. When it catches on, you learn what Paul said: "It is more blessed to give than to receive."[4]

CEILING #7: RECESSION IMPRESSION

During a consultation at her church, Pastor Ann boasted, "I never preach about money." This interested me, because Jesus spoke about money more than He discussed prayer. Why? Money is a tangible measure of a generous life. Generosity takes many forms. It is the way we treat others, help one another, serve others, care for others, accept others, pick up litter, and protect our environment. Generosity is demonstrated when you drive your car in heavy traffic! Or not!

> Generosity is caught from God.

When Jesus taught about the Kingdom, he reflected on the fruit of faith. Money is our crystallized sweat. It is easy to measure, and its use reflects priorities. It is surprising the amount of attention money gets in churches. Think about how many decisions have money as a central issue! Money is important but overrated. Jesus' main thing isn't giving away money. It's giving away your faith—which miraculously doesn't reduce your faith but increases it! Next to that, His priority is to care for others. When you do, it is often an opportunity to share your faith.

Many churches seem to be ruled by the "almighty buck." Isn't that interesting terminology? Knowing all God teaches about money, would you be willing to open a joint bank account with Jesus Christ? It comes down to a matter of trust, an issue of faith. The power of financial resources is undeniable. Finances can make or break any enterprise, even the church.

Would those who know you best identify you as a generous person? How would they describe that? Would they reflect on your generosity of time with them? How would your Father in heaven report your generosity of time with Him reading the Bible and conversing in prayer?

The management of money, time, energy, and spiritual gifts is called "stewardship." Some think stewardship is just another word for fundraising. When I was a young pastor, one of the encouragers in my life was Paul Foust. Paul liked to say, "Stewardship is raising people, not money. To raise money is being a pickpocket. Raising people is the Lord's work."[5] How do you raise others spiritually? Do you provide emotional support? What about encouragement? Do you know anyone who could use a little more encouragement? I tell pastors, "When three people thank you for a great sermon, there are probably thirty others who felt the same but didn't tell you." It is, sadly, the one-in-ten rule. Remember the ten lepers? All ten were healed. Only one said, "Thanks!"[6]

Someone once told me that money in the Kingdom of God is like fertilizer: no good until it is spread around. It is true, finances release more Kingdom effort. Lack of finances diminishes ministry. For most church expenditures, the money is always there. It is simply untapped. Faith influences generosity, which starts the flow of money for ministry. Paul wrote the Corinthians, "Whoever sows sparingly will also reap sparingly, and whoever sows generously will also reap generously."[7]

Your attitude toward generosity is a spiritual issue. John Maxwell explains: "Most people want resources to flow to them without making a commitment. They say, 'God, if You'll take care of me, I'll serve You.' God says, 'No, you just serve Me and I'll take care of you.' They say, 'If You'll just bless me, then I'll obey You.' He says, 'No, if you'll just obey Me, I'll bless you.' We spiritually tend to get the cart before the horse."[8]

This is the way the Kingdom works. You can't outgive God. It is a miracle you will never understand and always have difficulty explaining. This generosity is not just about money. It is about generosity of time, service, caring for others, and sharing your faith. "God loves a cheerful giver,"[9] and so do others! Generous living multiplies generous living. How much do you think our world needs that?

MONEY MATTERS

The congregational meeting focused on one agenda item: adding to the facilities—a $1 million project. The pastor and leaders had spent a year in prayer and study with guidance from a consultant, an architect, and a builder. After their thorough presentation, it was time for questions.

Bill immediately raised his hand. He stood and said, "We can't afford that!" It felt like a dark cloud entered the room. The mood changed to doom and gloom. Has this ever happened at your church? From the Kingdom culture perspective, what are the real issues?

Issue #1: Bill was out of order, biblically speaking. His immediate negative response was irrelevant. The first order of Kingdom business is never about the cost—never. The primary issue is: "Is this God's will for our church at this time?" (This is the appropriate issue in any area of generosity. Should I thank that person? Should we help that family? Should we work in the homeless shelter? Should we go on that mission trip? Should we live generously?)

Arnold Glasow said, "To know the will of God is the greatest knowledge, to find the will of God is the greatest discovery, and to do the will of God is the greatest achievement."[10] Every decision in Kingdom culture, large or small, should be put under the lens of God's will. You can't be simplistic and say, "Where in the Bible does it say we should build this million-dollar addition to our facilities?" However, you can ask, "How will this building be used? What is the Kingdom impact on the mission of this church?" Bob Pierce defined the centerpiece of God's will: "Let my heart be broken by the things that break the heart of God."[11]

When you are faced with decisions of any magnitude, it is helpful to keep the conversation focused on what God wants. "What would God want? Why? What would Jesus do?" Here is a useful prayer, as you wrestle with decisions: "Lord, I want to be in Your will, not in Your way."

In Bill's church, the leaders jumped the line of biblical culture. They responded to Bill, "We need the space." This is a rational argument but the wrong response to Bill. This is so common. It demonstrates how easy it is to drift from Kingdom culture. This type of approach can become emotional. Relationships get strained, and Christians become discouraged. When that occurs, the enemy wins. Victory for the enemy is never God's will.

Jesus said in John 5:19, "The Son can do nothing by himself. He does only what he sees the Father doing."[12] Did the disciples immediately grasp this incredible Kingdom principle of Jesus? Many Christians seem to miss it. Two ways to make decisions as a Christian are: (1) Get an idea and pray like crazy God will bless it. This is most common, yet it does not represent Kingdom culture. (2) Seek God's will. Identify where God is blessing, and go there. See what God is doing, and do that. *Seeking God's will is the Kingdom approach to decision making.*

If you are convinced it is God's will, the decision is over, whether it is about use of time, a new direction, involvement in service, or money. The key is to demonstrate why you believe it is God's will. The cost (in time, discomfort, energy, or money) is irrelevant if it is what God wants you to do. It doesn't have to be "the way we've always done it" if you can demonstrate, to the best of your ability, the decision is God's will.

In Kingdom culture, God pays for what He orders. What God decides, God provides. Following God's will is generosity issue number one. God's work done in God's way will never lack God's supply. Perhaps the most difficult Scripture is Acts 20:35, "It is more blessed to give than to receive."[13] One way to translate that verse might be: "It makes you happier to give than it does to receive." Kingdom drift is evident when you pray to receive. Instead, pray for the ability to give.

> Seeking God's will is the Kingdom approach to decision making.

Issue #2: It is an undeniable truth that you cannot outgive God. This Kingdom culture is not like this world. Human math works like this: When you give time, energy, and money, you have less. In Kingdom math, when you give time, energy, and money to God's cause, you have more.

This doesn't make sense. Why? It is a miracle. My friend Jim Manthei likes to say, "The safest place is in the center of God's will." In a consumer-driven world, our math is ruled by subtraction. However, in the Kingdom of God, the math is multiplication. You can't outgive God.

As a boy, I learned this from my grandmother. When I was ten years old, I started giving her presents for her birthday. However, every time I gave her a present, before long she would give me a gift. It was always worth more than what I had given her. She learned generosity from God. She was one of the wealthiest people I have ever met. She was not wealthy in money but in generosity, which means more.

Generosity can be described very simply as changing your focus from self to others and from self to God. According to Virgil Hensley, "Karl Menninger of the Menninger Clinic points out: 'Generous people are rarely mentally ill.' (On the other hand, stingy people are often neurotic.)"[14] Generosity gives birth to generosity. Like every dimension of Kingdom culture, generosity is more caught than taught. You catch it from others. You catch it when you try it. You do it, and then you want to do more. It grows.

Malachi 3:8 is an unusual challenge from God. It says God feels robbed when we are not generous. Then He throws out this challenge: "Be generous, and see if I don't open the windows of heaven and pour out My blessings upon you."[15] I have never met Christians—not ever—who took God up on the challenge and then went back to their old mediocre, selfish, and chintzy lifestyle. I've met many Christians, however, who never trusted God enough to try it.

Many people say you can't prove the existence of God. That's not even close. Take God at His word, and you will know He is for real. What I can't understand is why more people don't take Him at His word, even those who claim to be His people. It gives you an idea of how far the drift from Kingdom culture can take you from the heart of God.

How many churches have declared bankruptcy? I know of none, except in rare situations where criminal activities were involved. In how many churches has God given a vision that stretched to the outer limits of risk? Those churches usually seem to make it, even in instances where they struggle for some time. Churches in which a large percentage of the people live generously, in every dimension, are healthy churches. They thrive!

This is not an invitation to become fiscally stupid about your time, energy, service, or money. The Scripture says to test God, not tempt God. This is a challenge for many Christians operating from a low ceiling of potential.

> The Scripture says to test God, not tempt God.

They say they trust in God, but their intolerance of risk demonstrates faith a hundred times smaller than a mustard seed.[16] Seek God's direction for faith-filled balance.

It is difficult to comprehend the number of Christians (or churches) sitting on piles of money. What would you say to the Lord if He were to return tomorrow? The Lord would say, "What were you thinking? You are the church, not a bank. Why didn't you spend that money to reach the thousands of people around your church who don't know Me? Now it's too late. How could you?"

This is Kingdom drift. It is belief in a "God of scarcity." Jack Hayford said:

> There is too much of a tendency to have a poverty mentality in today's church.... Our outlook is too small, but that small-ness can be shaken off in answer to our Lord Jesus, who has called us to be *big* people. Big in our world view. Big in our love for the lost. Big in our giving.[17]

2 Corinthians 9:8 says, "And God is able to make all grace abound toward you, that you, always having all sufficiency in all things, may have an abundance for every good work."

This scarcity mentality sometimes shows up in sports. You see a football team get one field goal ahead late in the fourth quarter. The team then slows down in intensity. They are no longer playing to win. They are playing not to lose. What happens? Quite often, the other team will stop them, and they will have to punt. The losing team is behind, so they are playing to win. They continue to play with aggressiveness, end up getting a touchdown, and win the game. Playing not to lose is a scarcity mentality.

I see this in churches. Christians play it safe. They are so conservative that their approach does not resemble the Kingdom culture. Mark Pfeifer in his book *Breaking the Spirit of Poverty* remarks:

> The spirit of poverty infects individual believers, entire congregations, whole cities and even nations of the earth.... It infects them with an attitude that believes not losing is winning; not giving up ground is taking ground; not being defeated is victorious; not dying is living. This is why, when people ask how their church is doing, they will often give you an answer like: "Boy, we're doing great. We haven't lost anybody this year. We're running the same amount that we did last year, praise God!"[18]

God is a God of abundance. He owns the cattle on a thousand hills.[19] This is the Bible's way of saying God is not broke. The Bible talks about storing up treasures in heaven.[20] There, in heaven, it is safe—no risk, ever. Martin Luther said, "I have held many things in my hands and I have lost them all. But whatever I have placed in God's hands, that I still possess."[21]

Generous Christians give beyond themselves. This is an abundance mindset as opposed to a scarcity mindset. If you want a big harvest, you have to be on the giving side. The Proverb says, "One person gives freely, yet gains even more; another withholds unduly, but comes to poverty. A generous person will prosper; whoever refreshes others will be refreshed."[22]

Many churches develop a poverty or scarcity mentality because they can't get enough workers. The leaders beg for helpers. However, Jesus says in the Kingdom culture, "Pray to the Lord of the harvest to send out workers."[23] Church leaders should beg less and pray more. Christians should moan less and disciple more. It is all about multiplication. Christians should never hesitate to be generous with God's work and should trust Him more. The God of abundance has untapped resources beyond your wildest imagination. Deal with it. Call it what it is: a faith issue.

Issue #3: A key element to understand generosity is the truth that

God owns it all. He owns everything. He owns the money you give. He owns the money you keep. He owns your every heartbeat. He owns every second of your existence. This is not scary. It is awesome! As the song says, "He's got the whole world in His hands."

Human nature tempts you to focus on what you *give* to God and others. Kingdom culture teaches you to celebrate how much you get to keep. A Kingdom worldview ignites you to enthusiasm for how generous you can become. Kingdom culture identifies you as a manager. You are the manager of your time, health, intellect, finances, and spiritual gifts. You are the manager of your church, your family, your work, your community, and your world. You can become a manager of generosity. This is how you experience greatest fulfillment.

Kingdom culture is not about giving but *returning*. You can't give what is not yours. It all belongs to God. Why don't more Christians get this? The answer is Kingdom culture drift. Think of how much faith God has in you, to let you manage the world. This perspective would greatly increase the spiritual health of every Christian and every church.

Issue #4: Generous giving is an exciting privilege. The Kingdom approach is not by dollars, pesos, or rubles. It is not time, energy, or effort spent. God values the amount of what you return in the percentage you give back. God measures everything as a percentage of what you have been given. Remember the widow's offering?[24]

From a Kingdom culture perspective, the only way you can decide how much to give back is by a percentage. This is called "proportionate giving." Unfortunately, many Christians, according to our research, do not give proportionately. (Our research survey demonstrates a relatively low level of proportionate giving. This is reported at the end of this chapter.) The difference between percentage giving and dollar giving is significant when it comes to resources for Kingdom purposes. The same is true of time giving, thanksgiving, and service giving.

Consider your retirement someday as a *refirement*. If you have been generous, God blesses you. You have, perhaps, been blessed with skills, wealth, wisdom, and time. What a great period of life to be a generous blessing to others!

Issue #5: Generosity is closely connected with spiritual vision. *Vision precedes provision.* Most churches focus on the lack of workers and finances. However, the real issue may be a lack of vision. The grand vision of Kingdom culture is to make disciples. Where Great Commission vision is strong, generosity is strong. Where this vision is weak, churches struggle in all areas of generosity. God does not call Christians to give *to* anything, including a vision. Christians give *from* what God has given. Vision clarifies and energizes *generosity* from what God has given *generously.*

Vision leak is a challenge faced by every Christian, every church. Like Kingdom culture drift, vision leak occurs in your life, or in the life of your church, when you are so cluttered with activities you do not reflect the mission priority of the King. It is difficult for Christians to connect the cause and effect of generosity. Routine maintenance enthusiastically motivates no one. It is the role of leader-

> Vision leak occurs in your life, or in the life of your church, when you are so cluttered with activities you do not reflect the mission priority of the King.

ship to keep the compass on the mission and cast the vision for Kingdom causes. Nothing builds the fire for generosity like the cause of Christ.

Issue #6: Generosity can be leveraged by incremental distribution. This is tied to the law of large numbers. Church leaders may identify God's will for a project requiring generous giving of skills, money, and energy at a level that seems overwhelming. Leaders must break the project down using the incremental distribution approach. For example, let's say the vision is to support a mission in Africa, which includes a hospital clinic, a primary school, and building a new church. The cost to the church is $600,000, which will be matched by a mission agency. The way to break down the $600,000 cost is something like $25 per month (less than $1 a day) for five years. Ultimately, $25 per month times twelve months, for five years, times four hundred families equals $600,000—less than $1 per family per day!

What about the number of those who serve? Consider six teams of ten people, times five years. Of course, there will always be those who have been blessed with more money, more time, and more skills. They will have the capacity to provide large chunks of money and labor at the beginning. Add to a great vision the incremental generosity of many people, and sprinkle it with faith and God's will, and you can experience what Jesus said: "The one who believes in me will also do the works that I do and, in fact, will do greater works than these."[25] Really?

Issue #7: Financial generosity includes several different dimensions. One dimension is beyond *special giving*. This is usually project giving, like the mission effort in Africa mentioned above. Another dimension of financial generosity is the *tithe*. This was required of God's people in the Old Testament. It became a minimum-giving goal for many Christians in the New Testament. Tithing is not a bill you owe. Tithing is a seed to grow. A tithe is 10 percent of what God gives you. According to George Barna, church-attending Christians in the United States give back about 3 percent of their income in a typical year and consider this "sacrificial" generosity. Less than one out of every ten Christians donates 10 percent or more of their income to church and other nonprofit organizations combined.[26]

Anything above a tithe can be called an *offering*. If you hear an announcement in church, "We will now collect tithes and offerings," it implies the 10 percent tithe and anything given over that amount. If you return 12 percent of your income back to God, you give a tithe and a 2 percent offering.

Another dimension of financial generosity is *alms*. In modern terminology, this is a special, need-focused offering. If a family in your city lost their house to fire, the local churches might provide a door offering to help the family. The door offering is a spontaneous response to a sudden need. In my perception, most cities have a special need of some kind every week. I have always wanted to belong to a church with a door offering every week. Why? If a church were so generous, what would it say about the people? I would like to attend a church with that level of generosity. I just can't find one. Look at it this way: The Christian is forgiven, forgiving, and for giving. I believe such a church would be equally generous in acts of service. It is my belief that their outreach to non-Christians would be generous. I think their encouragement and thanksgiving would be greater. Generosity builds generosity.

Issue #8: An important part of generosity includes management of time and energy. Think about time. For many of those in developed countries, time may be more valuable than money. Many Christians have become sophisticated about the management of time. Two disciplines stand out: multitasking and the ability to say no. Every Christian should have a personal system to guard time. Some use block time—a period of uninterrupted concentration. The use of caller ID and blocked cell phone numbers are mechanisms to manage time in this interruptible world.

Roger is one of those Christians I admire for his spiritual wisdom. He is a successful owner of a software company and budgets his time carefully. Occasionally, I like to tap his spiritual wisdom. One of the challenges is how to get to him. My assistant contacted Roger by e-mail and gave him four dates in which I would be in his area. I was interested in setting up a breakfast or lunch appointment. Roger told my assistant I should phone him instead. He had no time to meet face-to-face during the following eight weeks. I tried all of his phone numbers: work, personal cell, and home. I left messages, with no response. I finally e-mailed him to explain my complex issues. This required a long e-mail. He replied within two days. I learned the best way to communicate with Roger is through e-mail.

Jim is an extremely busy businessman who has been another great source of wisdom for me for decades. Jim's style is different. He does not use an assistant. Jim told me, "I get fifty e-mails a day. If you send an e-mail, don't make it longer than four or five lines, or I'll delete it. I'd rather you pick up the phone and call." Each person has his or her own profile for managing time. The management of your time includes knowing what works for you and for those around you.

Poet Carl Sandburg said, "Time is the most valuable coin in your life. You and you alone will determine how that coin will be spent.

Be careful that you do not let other people spend it for you."[27] How often do you consider the management of time from the biblical perspective? Colossians 4:5 says, "Walk in wisdom...redeeming the time."[28] It has been said you can accomplish more in one hour with God than in one lifetime without Him.[29] The good management of time is a discipline allowing opportunities for generosity. As Christians come together in churches, time can be wasted through lack of focus, unclear purpose, and unwise decisions. Many churches are filled with Christians suffering from death by meetings.

The management of energy overlaps with time. It is also related to health and stamina, which is management of your body. Do you know someone who has boundless energy? From where does that come? Some of it comes from factors such as age, health, and genetics. However, there are Kingdom culture elements that trigger energy as well.

A positive attitude generates energy. Attitude is your posture toward God. Faith in Christ gives you hope. Divine hope fuels energy to do the impossible, overcome obstacles, and persevere through challenges. Read Hebrews 11. The chapter begins, "Now faith is being sure of what we hope for, being convinced of what we do not see."[30] The apostle Paul said, "I can do all things through Christ who strengthens me."[31] Faith in Jesus is a spiritual energy drink of divine power. The dark side of a positive attitude is a negative attitude. Those with negative attitudes have plugged into a dead battery. It drains their energy and the energy of those around them. How is your attitude?

Can you believe God for the impossible? Those who catch the attitude of Kingdom culture have the vision that God changes lives, churches, communities, and nations. What greater vision is there? This vision ignites energy. When you have the passion of Christ, you have the energy for generosity. For centuries, this passion has provided energy to millions of Christians—missionaries, reformers, church leaders, evangelists, and ordinary Christians God uses in extraordinary ways. God's love touches others through that passion. Those who are abandoned are loved. The homeless find a place to live. The hungry are fed. When, as a person of faith, you operate in Kingdom generosity, the people of this world touch the face of God. The King of the universe lives through you.

GENEROSITY DNA

Kingdom culture is the stimulus for spiritual generosity. The spirit of generosity blossoms into healthy churches. It works both ways: Healthy churches stimulate a culture of generosity. Generosity is contagious. Glen Zander, writing for *Preaching Today*, shares this story:

> Those who catch the attitude of Kingdom culture have the vision that God changes lives, churches, communities, and nations.

> The owner of a drive-through coffee business in southwest Portland, Oregon, was surprised one morning to have one of her customers not only pay for her own mocha but also for the mocha of the person in the car behind her. It put a smile on the owner's face to tell the next customer her drink had already been paid for. The second customer was so pleased that someone else had purchased her coffee that she bought coffee for the next customer. This string of kindnesses—one stranger paying for the mocha of the next customer—continued for two hours and twenty-seven customers.
>
> That's how it is with God's love—it starts with His unexpected love for us and then it is passed on to others, who in turn pass it on.[32]

In 2 Corinthians 8:1–7, Paul reports to the believers at Corinth about "the grace that God has given the Macedonian churches." In verse 2 he writes, "In the midst of a very severe trial, their overflowing joy and their extreme poverty welled up in rich generosity." Paul concludes, "But since you excel in everything—in faith, in speech, in knowledge, in complete earnestness and in the love we have kindled in you—see that you also excel in this grace of giving."[33]

This is Kingdom culture. It begins with trust that God will supply all your needs, not all your wants. Sometimes what you want isn't good for you. Jesus says you shouldn't worry about food or

clothes. "Now if that's the way God clothes the grass in the field...
how much more will he clothe you—you who have little faith?...
Instead, *be concerned about his kingdom*, and these things will be
provided for you as well."[34] We live in a consumer-oriented, materi-
alistic world. How important is a refreshment of Kingdom culture?

The best future for your church is birthed in the Kingdom culture
of people like you. No wonder Jesus spent so much time teaching, "The
Kingdom of God is like..." If you want your church to generously influence your community, it begins in Kingdom culture. It begins with you.

Trust in God generates a spirit of generosity. In Luke 6, Jesus tells
His followers how radically different the Kingdom of God is: "Love
your enemies, do good to those who hate you, bless those who curse
you, pray for those who mistreat you....If someone takes your coat, do
not withhold your shirt from them. Give to everyone who asks you."[35]

Martin Luther said, "Possessions are not given that we may rely
on them and glory in them but that we may use them and enjoy them
and share them with others....Our possessions should be in our
hands, not in our hearts."[36] The spirit of generosity recognizes that
we make a living by what we get, but we make a life by what we give.

GENEROSITY FOR THE WORLD

Two age groups in North America that are most receptive to a generosity lifestyle are the baby boomers and the millennials. The boomers continue to retire in large numbers. They have made a living, and
now many want to make a difference. As boomers approach the end
of their lives, many want to invest in legacy efforts. The millennials,
at the younger end of life, want to make the world better. Through
the Internet, they are the most aware generation in history. Many
millennials want to make a difference more than they want to earn a
paycheck. They love a challenge, the greater the better.

From both ends of the age spectrum, and everyone in between,
churches have an opportunity to help others experience the joy of
service and support in a lifestyle of generosity. The spirit of generosity is evident in many aspects of society. "Layaway angels" continue

to surprise shoppers at Christmastime. Many groups provide energy for causes like Habitat for Humanity, mission projects, and humanitarian efforts around the globe. Crowdsourcing has become an Internet opportunity for nonprofits through sites like Kickstarter.

The environment is increasingly receptive to the Kingdom culture of generosity. If your church is ready for breakthrough, help Christians grow into a lifestyle of generosity. If you want to make a difference, you have to start out being different. The Kingdom of God is not like this world; it is different. It requires courage. Jesus said, "You will have suffering in this world. Be courageous! I have conquered the world."[37] Corrie ten Boom said, "The measure of life is not its duration but its donation."[38]

DO YOU CHOOSE BY A DOLLAR AMOUNT OR A PERCENTAGE?

The approach to financial giving is based on the concept of a percentage, rather than a monetary figure. This represents *proportionate* giving. It reflects the biblical worldview that "Each man must bring a gift in proportion to the blessings the LORD your God has given him."[39] The apostle Paul in 2 Corinthians 9 supports this Kingdom concept using the farmer's language of sowing and reaping. You sow much, you reap much. You sow sparingly, the result is much less.[40] The only scriptural way to approach giving is by percentage, or proportionate giving (discussed earlier). While often overlooked by many Christians, this approach has significant impact over your lifetime. Since most Christians increase in earning power from their early years until retirement (excluding fluctuations in the economy), proportionate giving results in far greater revenue given for Kingdom purposes. When Christians operate from a mentality of "giving a few dollars more" each year or respond only to funding appeals, the impact of giving is far less. How you look at giving is a key element in God's design for funding the mission and ministry of the church. Church Doctor Ministries' research probes the approach to giving.

In this research, only 26 percent of the worshipping Christians

Approach to Financial Giving

When you figure how much money to give to God through your church, do you decide the amount by choosing a percentage to give or just a dollar amount?

①	A percentage	②	A dollar amount

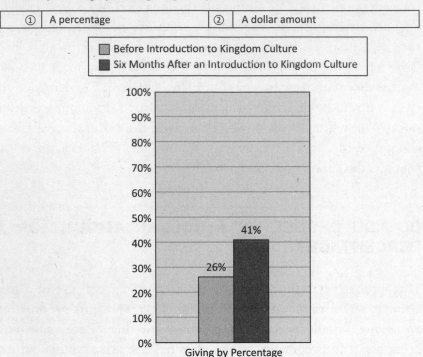

Legend:
- Before Introduction to Kingdom Culture
- Six Months After an Introduction to Kingdom Culture

Giving by Percentage

follow the biblical approach of percentage giving. After six months of Kingdom culture change, there is an increase from 26 percent to 41 percent. This equals an additional 15 percent. This increase, compounded over time, helps God's work reach greater potential. It provides greater financial stability. Further, as this Kingdom approach to giving becomes a pattern of life, it influences others in the congregation. As Christians are given the opportunity to share the experience that "you can't outgive God," more people experience the God of abundance.

BUILDING THE RIGHT CULTURE THE RIGHT WAY

CHAPTER TWELVE

Organic Launch

> The vast majority of organizations [churches][1] today have more than enough intelligence, expertise, and knowledge to be successful. What they lack is...health.
> —Patrick Lencioni[2]

Does developing Kingdom culture in your church seem overwhelming? It shouldn't. Scripture says, "With God all things are possible."[3] Of course, that does not mean it is easy. The greatest challenge is believing the promises of God, not just in theory but also in the trenches of Christian life. It takes serious effort to change the way you do church. You know the saying, "We've always done it that way." It is heard more often than you want to admit. It takes time and effort for God to change the culture in you and in your church. Remember that one of the characteristics of the fruit of the Spirit is *patience*.[4] If you are thinking about a quick fix, patience will be a challenge and a good discipline.

The path to health—a thriving church—takes time. It takes patience, discipline, perseverance, and a long-term commitment. It is a journey. Some in your church are eager and ready. It could take months, even years, before others show interest. Some, of course, will never get it. Do they lack faith in Jesus? Probably not. It could be they are just not ready. Love and accept them. Jesus does! *Your patience is the path for the organic growth of a healthy church.*

Are you willing to focus? Focus reflects a priority for spiritual growth in Kingdom culture. You and your church can't grow spiritually and continue all the activities shouting for your attention. This applies to most people in the church, especially leadership and staff. You cannot add a movement for Kingdom culture without cutting back. Kingdom culture does not include killing people from overwork. If you're not willing to make some adjustments in the schedule, you are not ready.

Christian leaders are not given a license to become dictators. Don't try to kill the aging and shrinking women's group. They generally shoot back! Readjust slowly. Operate with a commitment not to lose anyone. Each one is someone for whom Christ died!

In mission school, I had a professor who asked if I ever thought about leaving my declining church. He said, "You know, Kent, you could always plant a church." The idea of starting from scratch has always been appealing. Over the years, I've worked with a number of church planters in the United States and abroad. My professor said, "There's a saying among church planters: 'It's easier to give birth than to raise the dead.'" After we both chuckled, I thought, "My church may be declining, but it's not dead." At the same time, I realized the strategy of church planting is an important part of the Great Commission mix.

Think of the thousands of struggling churches that are losing members and aging. People who are not yet Christ-followers surround every one of those churches. If Kingdom culture really does make a difference, it should be honored as a viable strategy. Our Lord is a Master at resurrection. By the grace of God, I saw my church turn around. Later, I pastored another failing church. I witnessed how God brings life. I know firsthand the power of Kingdom culture. The body of Christ can rise to life!

As a consultant, I've seen churches with enormous challenges experience turnaround. I've also seen growing churches become healthier and grow exponentially. Since Jesus established Kingdom culture, don't be surprised when it occurs. Expect it! The return to Kingdom culture works. God brings an awakening. Healthy churches thrive!

Your greatest hurdle is to let God begin a slow, organic movement and watch it blossom into an awakening, according to His timetable.

In the coming years, I pre-
dict this will occur in thousands of churches. All the
signs point to a move of God
already started.

> *Your patience is the path for the organic growth of a healthy church.*

This chapter focuses on the elements of an organic movement
toward Kingdom culture. *The greatest obstacle is failure to let God
grow the garden.* Some of the most gifted and eager Christians try to
turn growing a garden into a program. They dig up the young seeds
as they are growing, before they have popped through the surface
of the soil. Leaders destroy what God has begun long before fruit
appears. In our world of Google searches, fast results are normal.
When Kingdom culture is superimposed or forced, the church blows
up from culture shock. Hundreds of crippled churches across North
America are unintentionally maimed by leaders who have the right
goal but the wrong strategy. Why? It is a tough concept to grasp
that Kingdom culture is not a program. Rush it, and Christians go
into shock. Kingdom culture shock can blow up a church. Think
of Jesus, who spent three years with His disciples. Of course, your
church has Christians, not raw recruits such as fishermen, tax collectors, and the like. However, remember, you're not Jesus either! The
movement toward Kingdom culture is likely to take two-and-a-half
to three years, even with guidance from the outside. Jesus did teach
that before you build, "count the cost."[5]

Have you ever experienced an awakening in a church? If so, you
know the cost, the effort, the time required, and the patience. Without question, it is all worth it. For people of faith, nothing is more
exhilarating than a spiritual breakthrough. This gift from God you
will never forget.

PLANTING A GARDEN

In his book *The Strangeness of the Church*, Daniel Jenkins writes,
"The strange thing about the church is not that it grows old, but
that it seems to have discovered the secret of being born again."[6]

Many are focused on leadership in our generation. I have been a student of leadership all my life. I am grateful for everything I have learned. I plan to keep learning for the rest of my life. Leadership is important. However, to launch a movement of the Kingdom, Jesus did not focus first on leaders. This seems unusual. Throughout the history of Israel, whenever God acted, He raised a leader. However, in the new covenant, Jesus does not focus on leadership as a priority. If leadership were most important, He would have never chosen the motley group of twelve disciples. This is an important lesson for Kingdom breakthrough.

Jesus didn't focus on leadership. His primary focus was on discipleship. For this movement, Jesus' priority was to integrate the culture of the Kingdom. Later, in the power of the Holy Spirit at Pentecost, these disciples became leaders. *This sequence is not circumstantial. It is a template for changing a church for breakthrough.*

Developing culture focuses on values, beliefs, attitudes, priorities, and worldviews, as you will remember. The objective is not *doing*; it is developing people into a different culture. The disciples became different people. There was major change in who they were. They were imprinted with Kingdom DNA. This focus is about *being* and *becoming*. This approach doesn't feel natural to most.

Movements are different than programs, yet still some ask, "When is the movement going to move?" The people around you wonder, "When are we going to *do* something?" They are asking program questions, not movement questions. Most Christians have never experienced a movement *within* their church. Most Christians have participated in numerous programs. Yes, the movement is hard to grasp. It may be a challenge to put some programs into a lower priority to make room for growth in Kingdom culture. The disciples dramatically changed their lifestyle priorities to follow Jesus. Are you ready to do the same?

> Jesus didn't focus on leadership. His primary focus was on discipleship.

A movement may seem to be simply a lot of information. In reality, this movement (Christianity) is not limited to content. It is not about information alone. It is about transformation. At the core, Christianity

is not about accomplishment. It is about becoming someone different—
a citizen of the Kingdom and
a follower of the King. Once

> Once people *become* different,
> **everything** they *do* is different.

people *become* different,
everything they *do* is differ-
ent. When that occurs, it defines transformation. The Bible finds us
where we are and, with our permission, will take us where we ought to
go. Other books were given to us for information, but the Bible is given
to us for transformation.

The dynamic approach in a program is for the leader to push the
agenda. That is not a criticism; it is simply different. In a movement,
however, individuals are invited by the leader to be nurtured. They
respond only when they are ready. The movement leader is as patient
as a gardener waiting for seeds to sprout and for plants to produce
fruit. This is organic Christianity. This is a movement.

THE VALUE OF ASSESSMENT

If you garden as a hobby, you till the garden, perhaps add some
fertilizer, and plant the seeds. Professionals who grow food add a
very important component: They take soil samples and ask for an
objective assessment. Why? Soil samples reveal *how* you should treat
the soil: what kind of fertilizer, how much lime. Soil samples also
tell you *where* to treat the soil and what type of treatment should
be placed in each area. The result? Greater yields. In biblical terms,
more fruit.

Your first important step in the journey toward Kingdom culture
is to obtain *a thorough professional assessment of your church.* To
move forward, you need to know the attitudes and worldviews of
those in attendance. You will want to see the overall spiritual health
of your congregation. This is a matter of good stewardship.

The most effective assessment will be conducted by professionals from outside your church. This approach makes the assessment
objective. Most Christians will tell a professional "outsider" more in
a confidential interview than they would ever say to anyone inside

the church. Swallow your pride and ask God for strength to overcome your insecurities and fears. Get professional help. When your body is suffering or not working well, you see a medical doctor. Why? The health of your body is important. How important is the body of Christ, your church?

It is also helpful if the assessment is provided by a group outside your denominational or network family of churches. The more objective and "safe" for your church members, the better results the assessment will deliver. Starting with a professional assessment will provide strategic guidance to your spiritual direction. A report from the assessment raises interest: It "softens the soil." It also provides a catalytic boost as you begin the journey.[7]

SPIRITUAL LEADERSHIP

In *Managing People Is Like Herding Cats*, Warren Bennis identifies a different kind of leader—a transformational leader. He writes about these transformational leaders:

> Leaders inspire and empower people; they pull, rather than push. This "pull" style attracts and energizes people to enroll in the vision and motivates people by bringing them to identify with the task and the goal, rather than by rewarding or punishing them.
>
> I mentioned this once in a lecture at AT&T, and a woman in the audience said, "I have a deaf daughter, so I've learned American Sign Language. This is the sign for manage." She held out her hands as if she were holding onto the reins of a horse, or restraining something. And she went on, "This is the ASL sign for lead." She cradled her arms and rocked them back and forth the way a parent would nurture a child.[8]

Spiritual leadership is not the *approach* to discipleship. The *result* of discipleship is spiritual leadership. Discipled people are not primarily doers. They are influencers. This is an organic approach. It results in organic growth. The best way to grasp this movement approach is to keep thinking about planting a garden. Someone once said, "All flowers of tomorrow are the seeds of today. In a movement, you sow seeds, nurture the plants, but God has been making them grow."[9]

John Maxwell says, "Seek to be a plow rather than a bulldozer. The plow cultivates the soil, making it a good place for seed to grow. The bulldozer scrapes the earth and pushes every obstacle out of the way."[10] It is common to think church health is the result of a top-down, leadership-driven approach. Many Christians have tried this in an attempt to change from maintenance to mission. It usually blows up in their faces because the whole project is approached as a program. The mission of the Kingdom, however, is not the result of people *doing* something different. It is the result of people *being* and *becoming* someone different.

Jesus focused on picture language to describe strategy. He described the process in images like the sower, seeds, and soils. This is gardening language. It is organic change. The direction of change is a paradigm shift, not top-down but bottom-up. Robert Louis Stevenson said, "Don't judge each day by the harvest you reap, but by the seeds that you plant."[11] Jesus focused on action only as a reaction. You don't *act* to make the crop ripe. When God causes the crop to be ripe, you *react*. You harvest what God has done. At Church Doctor Ministries, we have developed a booklet called *Healthy Churches Thrive! The Church Leader's Toolkit for Shaping Kingdom Culture*. This booklet provides various ways influencers can use Jesus' techniques to softly develop Kingdom culture in your church.[12]

A leader can't force others to become receptive. A leader can only respond when people demonstrate receptivity. That is a reaction, not an action. The difficulty with a program superimposed on a congregation? Everyone isn't ripe—receptive—at the same time. A program operates on the false premise that people are receptive in one single instant or even in a relatively short amount of time. A movement works from the ground up, always planting seeds and watching for growth. The development of Kingdom culture is not top-down transactional change. It is bottom-up transformational change, one person at a time. It occurs in each person's timetable. It is the work of the Holy Spirit who, like the wind, blows when and where He wants.[13] Leadership, in Kingdom perspective, is accepting people where they are, then taking them somewhere. This is an organic approach.

> The difficulty with a program superimposed on a congregation? Everyone isn't ripe–receptive–at the same time.

Jesus spoke about yeast.[14] Yeast describes the dynamics of Kingdom culture change. Yeast in dough is slow and gentle, but it changes everything. Jesus also said, "The kingdom of heaven is like a mustard seed."[15] The growth is slow; the results are large.

Many leaders are eager to make the church more effective for the Great Commission. In excitement and enthusiasm, they push top-down Kingdom culture onto a congregation. It is the right goal but the wrong strategy. Some members respond. Most do not. Others become resentful. The church is divided, as some feel judged as "second-class Christians" when they are not as enthusiastic as others. Rather than growing the church, this approach often results in a division.

When a church splits, it is a terrible witness to unchurched people in the community. They misunderstand the tensions in the church. Unfortunately, the situation castrates the church from the objective of reaching non-Christians in the community. Believers, as a church, become impotent to reproduce disciples. Hundreds of churches in North America are suffering the consequences of top-down approaches for change. Sadly, some have the attitude that "It can't be helped." They have not looked closely at Jesus' model.

LEARNING FROM JESUS

Jesus did not develop leaders. He multiplied disciples who became leaders. The primary approach was to build Kingdom culture.

Jesus spent most of His time modeling and teaching the culture of the Kingdom. He invested years of His life into a few people. From a human perspective, it didn't make sense. To many, it may have looked like a failure. It's a strange approach. Jesus made it clear His Kingdom is not of this world[16] and not like this world. By sharing Kingdom culture, primarily with a dozen ordinary people, Jesus launched the most effective movement in history. What can you learn from Jesus?

1. Work organically, from the bottom up. My colleague Dennis Kutzner is an accomplished student of the American Civil War and the early colonial period. His reflection on the celebration of Christmas as a holiday in the United States is an example of a bottom-up movement. The early Puritans rejected the European Christmas traditions. They made Christmas "a serious occasion, introspectively pondering sin and religious commitment." Two hundred years later, Christians reintroduced a festive atmosphere amplifying the joyous season. In 1836, the state of Alabama was the first to make Christmas a holiday. Congress did not make Christmas a federal holiday until 1870—more than thirty years later! Christmas, as an official holiday, is the result of a bottom-up movement.[17]

2. Don't rush people. Nudge them gently and lovingly to receptive insight through relational discipling.

3. Growing Christians is not a program or a class. It is more like raising children—a long, slow, loving process. Each one matures at a different pace. We are called the children of God.

4. Parents who force their children to behave in certain ways experience rebellion. Church leaders who force members into certain behaviors have the same experience with the children of God. They experience rebellion.

5. Jesus is the head of the church. Church leaders are not.

6. Leadership, according to the New Testament, is a spiritual gift given to some Christians by the Holy Spirit. The disciples became apostles only after their Holy Spirit encounter at Pentecost.

7. The apostles provided advice and guidance to early Christians. Their posture toward churches of the New Testament was not hierarchical. They learned Kingdom culture from Jesus, who embedded it into them. The apostles learned what Jesus taught: Influencers (leaders) are "servants." They are not like the Gentile rulers who "lord it over people."[18] The apostles did not flaunt their authority; they influenced through relationships.

In Kingdom culture, leaders do not push. They do not force or superimpose mission thinking on Christians. They continue to invite others to come along when they are ready, as the Holy Spirit moves them. Kingdom culture works like yeast in dough. It is not a quick-fix program, yet it changes everything. It is a movement. The movement approach is gentle and nurturing. In time, it changes everything.

MOVEMENT TIPPING POINT

Kingdom culture in your church eventually reaches a tipping point called *critical mass*. This is when enough people in the church "get it," so the personality of the church begins to change, and the movement takes on a life of its own. Kingdom culture becomes dominant. It becomes a visible movement. It becomes the norm. This is when the growth of God's Kingdom accelerates by geometric progression. Some call this a revival.

Everett Rogers in his book *Diffusion of Innovations* used the bell curve to show how groups change.[19] The concept is universal among organizations, including churches. Long before Rogers, Jesus was the Master of a movement. Jesus' movement in your church has a tipping point as well. However, it, like Jesus' Kingdom, is not the same as the world's tipping point.

Rogers claims once you reach the innovators and the early adopters, there is a tipping point. When it occurs, you have enough momentum to push through. The tipping point is 17 percent of the total group (see Figure #1). This is where the movement of Jesus

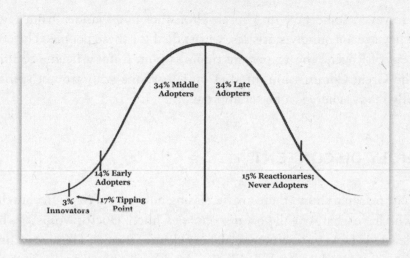

Figure #1

departs from the theory of Rogers. Unfortunately, in hierarchical thinking, many church leaders follow Rogers rather than Jesus.

In a secular organization, like a business, people are hired and fired. The leader has the leverage of a paycheck. In that environment, a 17 percent tipping point is reasonable. In a church, Christians join voluntarily. Christians have two levels of commitment. First, they are Christians. At this level, for centuries, people have given up their lives rather than renounce their faith. The second level is a connection with a particular church. At this level, the primary glue that is holding people is the quality of the experience, denominational/theological loyalty, and their relationships with others. However, if push comes to shove, they will seek another church, even though they remain sold-out Christians. It is traumatic for them, but as you know, it occurs all the time.

In a church, change of culture might occur, in *theory*, with a 17 percent tipping point. However, it will come with many casualties. One of those casualties is usually the pastor, who is looking for another church. Further, the church's reputation in the community is marred, which is especially serious for reaching non-Christians. It adds an element of burden to *any* church trying to reach those in their community.

Members who leave their church are not "collateral damage" or "unavoidable losses." Some of them will find another church.

However, some give up church altogether and wander from faith. They are not simply statistics. Christ died for these people. The concept of Rogers, the 17 percent tipping point, is not a license to force the Great Commission mindset on Christians who are not spiritually ready. There is a better approach.

HOLY DISCONTENT

Our research shows there are increasing numbers of those in churches who have what we call *holy discontent*. Church Doctor Ministries has developed survey instruments to help identify them.[20] These are Christians in whom the Holy Spirit has developed a burning desire to see their church become more effective in making disciples and impacting their community. They are ready and eager for their church to grow. Holy discontent is not the result of some program. This is the work of the Holy Spirit. Who they are in your church may surprise you. They are not always the key leaders and may not include everyone on staff. The quiet widow who sits in the fourth row in worship may have holy discontent. Again, the Holy Spirit is like the wind: it blows anywhere He wishes, and is full of surprises for the rest of us![21] Those with holy discontent already exist in your church.

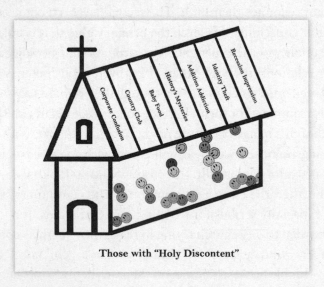

Those with "Holy Discontent"

A church is a spiritual organism with voluntary membership. As Church Doctors, it is our perception that a tipping point is, at a minimum, more than twice the size of Rogers's 17 percent. Our research shows that before a movement becomes visible in a church, a critical mass of 40 to 50 percent is a viable tipping point. We call this a level of *breakthrough potential*. At this level, we define a church's potential for this movement as being minimal. It is even more viable when it reaches above 65 percent, which we describe as *breakthrough readiness*.

If your church does not have a minimum of 50 percent of active worshippers eager to grow in Kingdom culture, we suggest you continue to cultivate until God moves in the lives of more worshippers. In John 5:19, Jesus taught believers to do what the Father is doing, move where God is moving, and focus where God is blessing.

By tapping those God has already prepared, you gently begin the movement of growing Kingdom culture. Using Jesus' metaphor of yeast, those with holy discontent or spiritual restlessness are like a "starter batch" for certain types of bread. This is a portion of dough with unique characteristics. When joined to regular dough, its distinctiveness grows. Before baking, you hold back a portion, another starter batch, for the next time you want to make bread with those characteristics.

Notice in the illustration, some with holy discontent are closer to the outside walls of the church than others. This signifies they are, at this moment, more eager to reach out to those outside the church. They could be considered early adopter missionaries.

Christians with holy discontent can be gathered into a Kingdom community to grow in Kingdom culture. They learn and serve together. They are encouraged to invite others in the church to participate in this Kingdom community. They do this through relational networking, inviting those with whom they already have a relationship. This is the way the Kingdom moves most effectively. Those invited never feel rushed or forced to join the Kingdom community. They are never made to feel "less" or "inferior" as believers if they don't show readiness to join the movement.

In the movement, there are never public approaches in the worship service, posters, or bulletin announcements. When Jesus worked with the disciples, posters were not on display around Jerusalem inviting every Tom, Dick, and Harry to come to learn what they could. In truth, Jesus died for Tom, Dick, and Harry (though these were likely not their Jewish names). Every aspect of influence is through relational invitation. While the movement is completely transparent—not a "secret"—it is not strongly visible on a corporate level of the church either. It's not a program!

Relational invitations work best when you use the power of story, as we have seen before. Those Christians involved in the growth process are encouraged to share their personal testimonies. They share what God is doing in their lives as they grow in Kingdom culture. As the movement expands, new Kingdom communities are formed along the lines of relationship networks. As the movement continues to grow, some middle and late adopters become part of the Kingdom communities. As they become Great Commission champions, they share their stories in relational settings. They influence other middle or late adopters with credibility that early adopters could not have. Early adopters seem a bit strange or radical to some middle and late adopters. However, when one of their own shares a positive response, other middle and late adopters more eagerly respond. They recognize that "one of us" is experiencing something beneficial. This raises interest. At this point, you may feel the momentum of a breakthrough for the first time. This movement approach is like throwing a pebble in a pond and watching the concentric rings continue to expand until they reach throughout the entire pond.

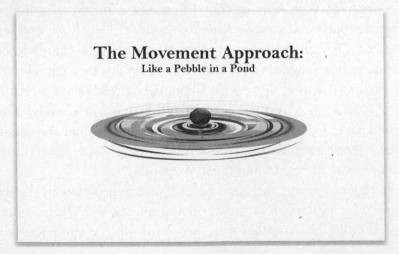

The Movement Approach:
Like a Pebble in a Pond

When this occurs, your church is on the verge of a wake-up call—an awakening. The movement approach works so well in Christianity because Christianity is born to be a movement!

A "train wreck" occurs in so many churches when top-down change agents superimpose Kingdom culture on the congregation all at once in a church-wide public program approach.

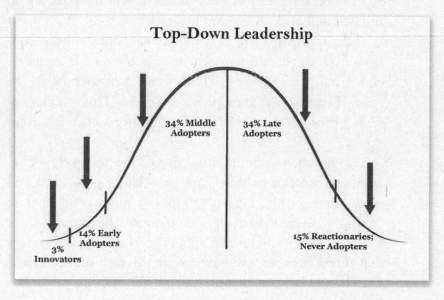

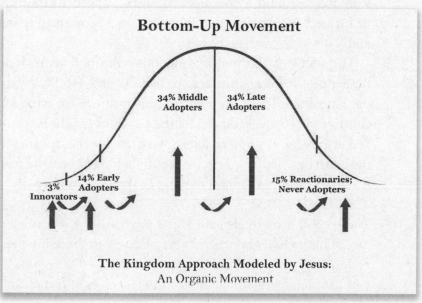

KINGDOM CULTURE

The Kingdom communities continue to grow in Kingdom culture. They learn more about Kingdom culture through two approaches:

(1) They learn through group studies organized as a flat learning experience. A flat learning experience emphasizes discussion and de-emphasizes dominant leadership.

The participants are exposed to Kingdom culture concepts and asked to discuss them in a congenial "roundtable" atmosphere. It works best when no expert is in the room. The emphasis is on group discovery. This is a journey among those who are ready and eager, not a class led by an expert.

The Kingdom communities should be relatively small. They can meet anywhere. They are able to pick when and where they gather. No superimposed amount of content "must be covered" each time they meet. Therefore, if there is a great deal of discussion about a certain topic, no one is shut down because "we have to get through the material." This should be seen as a journey rather than an event. If a Kingdom community becomes too large, another group can be formed. Structure is not important in a movement. Kingdom culture growth is the key.

The focus of learning is Kingdom culture. This includes the values, beliefs, attitudes, priorities, and worldviews of the Kingdom. There are two original sources for Kingdom culture: the Gospels (especially the parables taught by Jesus) and the New Testament letters written by the apostles to the churches. These letters frequently address the drift from Kingdom culture that is occurring in those churches.

(2) The second growth element is the practice of Kingdom culture. This includes efforts that may be new to those involved:
- Sharing what God is doing in your life.
- Offering to pray for waiters and waitresses at restaurants.

- Developing a list of unchurched friends, relatives, neighbors, fellow workers, or students and praying for them on a regular basis, that they may come to know Jesus as their Savior.
- Watching for receptivity signs in those in your social network; discussing this with others in your Kingdom community.
- Developing Outreach Clusters.
- Praying as you walk through your neighborhood.
- Increasing personal prayer time focused on reaching your area for Jesus.
- Identifying the level of hopelessness in those who are part of your social network by asking them, "What do you think it will be like for your grandchildren?"
- Discovering your spiritual gifts.
- Discipling another Christian in an area of ministry, using the leadership steps.

THE SEVEN CEILINGS

Inevitably, the Kingdom communities will begin noticing and discussing areas of your church's life that may not be entirely in line with Kingdom culture. The holy discontent that rises to the surface is not a complaining attitude but one of desire for change.

Holy discontent aimed at the seven ceilings is the beginning of breakthrough. Change is hard, but it doesn't have to be negative or critical.

As the critical mass grows in your church and the seven ceilings are clearly identified, your church will begin to experience transforming action toward the seven ceilings.

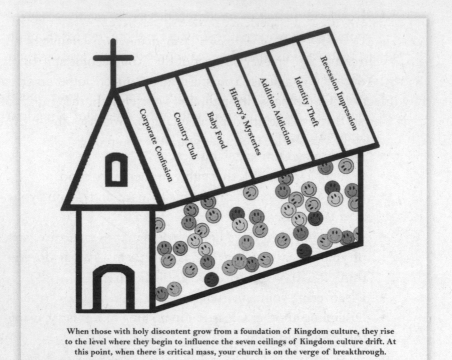

When those with holy discontent grow from a foundation of Kingdom culture, they rise to the level where they begin to influence the seven ceilings of Kingdom culture drift. At this point, when there is critical mass, your church is on the verge of breakthrough.

BREAKTHROUGH

The breakthrough occurs when God begins to use you to transform your ceilings toward Kingdom culture. This does not occur all at once, but over time. The growth of Kingdom culture is a critical mass of those in your congregation who are involved in removing the ceilings that have held your church back. The breakthrough is not an event. It is more like a process. As it occurs, God uses your church, your fellow Christians, more effectively to influence those around you. Through this breakthrough, you effectively penetrate those in your community who are not yet Christ-followers. You begin to move beyond the walls of your church. Your church is no longer a destination but a launch pad. Your congregation becomes a mission because your people have become missionaries to your community.

You will never improve on Jesus' approach. When you grow in Kingdom culture, it changes you. You become a different person. You are transformed. You experience a life with different values, beliefs, attitudes, priorities, and worldviews. Your behavior is changed, not just in church but also in every aspect of life. You become spiritually healthy. You are contagious. You spiritually "infect" others with a holy infection. God breaks through, and your church, the church of Jesus Christ, thrives. The atmosphere changes. God uses this movement to change the world. God uses you. Are you ready?

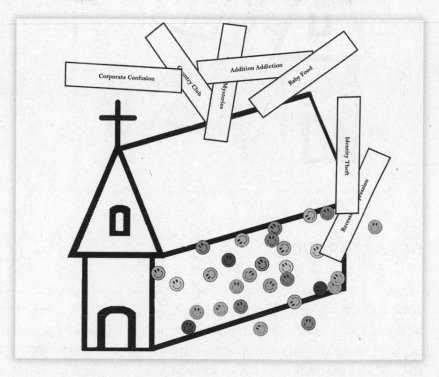

Jesus Culture is a musical group (interesting name—*culture*). In 2012, they produced a song, "Holy Spirit," featuring Martin Smith. Here are a few lines to sing as you travel your spiritual journey:

> Let us become more aware of Your presence.
> Let us experience the glory of Your goodness.
> Holy Spirit, You are welcome here,
> Come flood this place and fill the atmosphere.[22]

ACKNOWLEDGMENTS

The research and development of this fifteen-year project includes many people. This project required 75,000 surveys completed by church members in hundreds of congregations. We thank all of you for your input. We are grateful for the 5,500 church members who participated in one-on-one interviews. We appreciate our Church Doctor colleagues who joined us in the interview process: Chrysanne Timm, Alan Chandler, Rupert Loyd, and Barry Kolb.

Both Church Doctor Ministries and North American congregations in general will forever owe a debt of gratitude to our friends in England. For the last fifteen years, we have learned so much from this "classroom of the future" for North American Christianity. We are especially grateful to Andy Hawthorne at The Message Trust and Anthony Delaney, Strategic Leader at the Ivy Church—both in Manchester, England. We are also grateful for our several friends in the desperation church planting work of Holy Trinity Brompton in London. Our thanks go to those at Worship Central in Birmingham. The whole world is blessed by your music. We also owe much to our colleague Peter Brierley of Brierley Consultancy, in Tonbridge, Kent, an area outside London. Your analysis of Christian movements is amazing. Most of all, I thank Mick Woodhead, our friend and hero of church leadership at St. Thomas Crookes, Sheffield. Thank you, Mick, for your formal teaching to our groups and the informal insights as we talked into the late night and early morning so often, sharing our mutual passion for healthy and thriving churches.

No one could complete a project like this without a great support staff. We thank God for the privilege of working with Church Doctor Ministries' core group: Jason Atkinson, Dennis Kutzner, Carol Kutzner, Dawn Hammer, Michele Ellison, Brian Tew, David Beare,

Acknowledgments

Terry Atz, Beth Knoll, Kathy Parks, Wendy Kratzman, Sarah Kolb, Meghan Ulrich, Mariah Passalacqua, John Wargowsky, and our colleagues Mackenzie Ritchie and Jonathan Hunter, who lead the young adult training mechanism SEND North America. Thank you, John Rudow, for your communication insight and strategies, and Laura McIntosh for your editing skills.

We are grateful for the excellent guidance for this project from Greg Johnson and WordServe Literary Group as well as the great people at Hachette Book Group. The teamwork Jesus modeled continues through servant leaders working for Kingdom objectives. Thank you all for your partnership in this project.

Our gratitude also goes to Rob Olson, Robert Shriner, Esther Hunter, Steve Peterson, Luann Heffelfinger, and Paul Stratton, who read and critiqued early drafts of this work, and to our friends and colleagues who shared endorsements.

It takes a supportive family for writers to work so long on such a big project. We thank God for Kent's wife, Janet, daughter, Laura, and her husband, Jason, as well as Kent's son, Jonathan, and his wife, Esther. We are grateful for Tracee's husband, Matt, for his generous patience. Thank you for your continued support, encouragement, and shared commitment to reach the world for Jesus Christ.

ENDNOTES

CHAPTER ONE

The Gift of Holy Discontent

1. Acts 17:11 (NIV).
2. John 15:5 (NIV).
3. John 15:16 (GWT).
4. Genesis 1:22 (KJV).
5. John 18:36 (NIV).
6. Isaiah 55:8 (NASB).
7. Holmes, Oliver Wendell, Jr. Shared on his 90th birthday, March 8, 1931. Library and Information Services for the 21st Century, Vol. 1991, Part II, p. 272.
8. John 15:2 (NLT).
9. John 10:10 (ESV).
10. Adapted from John 8:32 (NASB).
11. McNeal, Reggie. *The Present Future: Six Tough Questions for the Church.* San Francisco: Jossey-Bass, 2003, p. 1.
12. Matthew 16:18 (NIV) [Emphasis mine].
13. Blanchard, Ken, and Terry Waghorn. *Mission Possible: Becoming a World-Class Organization While There's Still Time.* New York: McGraw-Hill, 1996, p. 178.
14. Adapted from Matthew 13:33.
15. John 14:12 (NIV).
16. Adapted from Matthew 6:10.
17. Matthew 7:29 (NLT).
18. Chambers, Oswald. *My Utmost for His Highest.* Grand Rapids, MI: Discovery House Publishers, 1992, October 26.
19. Manthei, Ben, and Ruth Manthei. *In His Majesty's Service: From Success to Significance.* South Charlevoix, MI: Creative Cottage Publishing Partnership, 2002, p. 32.

20. Knutson, Gerhard. *Ministry to Inactives: A Manual for Establishing a Listening Witness to Inactive Members.* Minneapolis, MN: Augsburg Fortress, 1979, pp. 30–31.
21. Shibley, David. *Challenging Quotes for World Changers.* Green Forest, AR: New Leaf, 1996, p. 87.
22. Isaiah 40:31 (NLT).
23. Ephesians 3:20 (NLT).
24. Hall, Mark, and Matthew West, composers. "Thrive." (Performed by Casting Crowns.) Arranged by Dan Galbraith. ©Sony/ATV Tree Publishing, My Refuge Music, Songs for Emily Music Publishing, 2014.

CHAPTER TWO

Health Wins

1. Filson, Floyd V. *The Layman's Bible Commentary: The Gospel According to John, Vol. 19.* Richmond, VA: John Knox Press, 1972, p. 173.
2. Matthew 28:19 (ISV).
3. 1 Chronicles 12:32 (RSV).
4. www.brierleyconsultancy.com.
5. www.thrivent.com.
6. The instrument developed is *The Church Health Assessment (fully revised).* Corunna, IN: Church Doctor Ministries, 2014. www.churchdoctor.org.
7. Chambers, Oswald. *My Utmost for His Highest.* Grand Rapids, MI: Discovery House Publishers, 1992, January 7.
8. Kaiser, John Edmund. *Winning on Purpose: How to Organize Congregations to Succeed in Their Mission.* Nashville, TN: Abingdon Press, 2006, p. 1.
9. John 10:10 (ESV).
10. Pierson, Paul E. *The Dynamics of Christian Mission: History through a Missiological Perspective.* Pasadena, CA: William Carey International University Press, 2009, p. 39.
11. Bryant, David. *The Hope at Hand: National and World Revival for the Twenty-First Century.* Grand Rapids, MI: Baker Books, 1995, p. 79.
12. See Matthew 28:19.
13. Acts 1:8 (NLT).
14. Gladwell, Malcolm. *The Tipping Point: How Little Things Can Make a Big Difference.* New York: Little, Brown, 2000, p. 11.
15. 1 Peter 4:1 (MSG) [Emphasis mine].
16. Matthew 3:10 (NIV).
17. Heidler, Robert. "The Counterfeit Kingdom," in *Freedom from the Religious Spirit: Understanding How Deceptive Religious Forces Try to Destroy God's*

Plan and Purpose for His Church, edited by C. Peter Wagner. Ventura, CA: Regal, 2005, p. 63.

18. John 18:36 (NRSV).
19. John 8:23 (ESV).
20. John 8:23 (MSG).
21. www.churchdoctor.org.
22. Lencioni, Patrick. *The Advantage: Why Organizational Health Trumps Everything Else in Business.* San Francisco: Jossey-Bass, 2012.

CHAPTER THREE

Outreach: An Inside Job

1. Miller, Darrow, in conversation with the author, referencing his book *Discipling the Nations: The Power of Truth to Transform Cultures.* Seattle: YWAM Publishing, 1998.
2. Cymbala, Jim. *Fresh Wind, Fresh Fire: What Happens When God's Spirit Invades the Hearts of His People.* Grand Rapids, MI: Zondervan, 1997, p. 78.
3. Mark 1:15 (ESV).
4. Pattison, Gregory Scott. "Principles of Renewal and Revitalization Based Upon the Doctrine, Spirit, and Discipline of the Wesleyan Revival of the Eighteenth Century." (Doctoral dissertation), Anderson University School of Theology, Anderson, IN, 2011.
5. www.htb.org.
6. www.worshipcentral.org. Worship Central is now located at St. Luke's Church in Birmingham, England.
7. www.alpha.org.
8. www.brierleyconsultancy.com.
9. Psalm 23:4 (ESV).
10. Roxburgh, Alan, and Fred Romanuk. *The Missional Leader: Equipping Your Church to Reach a Changing World.* San Francisco: Jossey-Bass, 2006, p. 16 [Emphasis mine].
11. Lindsey, William J. *The Will to Be: Becoming More Than What You Are.* Bloomington, IN: WestBow, 2014, p. 117.
12. www.goodreads.com.
13. 1 Peter 3:15 (NIV).
14. Maxwell, John C. "94 Leadership Quotes for You and Your Church," www.sermoncentral.com.
15. www.sendnorthamerica.com.
16. Anderson, Leith. "The Church in the 21st Century Conference," Irving, TX, June 14–17, 1992.

17. Matthew 27:2ff.
18. Matthew 16:24 (NLT).

CHAPTER FOUR

The Culture of the King

1. Hunter, George G. III. "What is Your Main Business?" *Great Commission Research Journal* vol. 6, no. 2. La Mirada, CA: Biola University (Winter 2015): p. 183.
2. John 3:16.
3. Luke 2:14 (MSG).
4. http://www.quotes.net/quote/48425.
5. Acts 15:5–21.
6. Rainer, Thom S., and Eric Geiger. *Simple Church: Returning to God's Process for Making Disciples.* Nashville, TN: B&H Publishing Group, 2006, p. 26 [Emphasis mine].
7. John 18:36 (ESV).
8. John 18:36 (NIV).
9. John 20:21 (NRSV).
10. Tertullian. *On Idolatry.* Paris, France: Bibliothèque Nationale, Codex Agobardinus, Parasinus, 1622.
11. Matthew 28:18 (NASB) [Emphasis mine].
12. Matthew 28:19 (NIV).
13. Acts 1:8 (BSB).
14. See Romans 8:28 (BSB).
15. See Matthew 14:13–21.
16. Matthew 14:25–32.
17. See Mark 6:7–13.
18. See Matthew 17:27.
19. Matthew 13:10 (GWT).
20. Matthew 13:13 (MSG).
21. See Philippians 2:1–5.
22. Matthew 16:24 (NLT).
23. Romans 12:2 (NLT).
24. Acts 9:2 (NIV).
25. Matthew 6:33 (NIV) [Emphasis mine].
26. John 8:32 (NASB).
27. See 2 Corinthians 5:20 (ESV).
28. Warren, Rick. "Our Convictions Determine Conduct" (Sermon). www.pastorrick.com.

29. Philippians 2:5 (GWT).

30. 1 Corinthians 15:3–4 (ESV) [Emphasis mine].

31. Matthew 22:37–38 (ESV).

32. Matthew 20:25–27 (ESV).

33. Benson, Ezra Taft. www.lds.org/ensign/1989/07/born-of-god?lang=eng.

34. Covey, Stephen R. *The 7 Habits of Highly Effective People: Powerful Lessons in Personal Change.* New York: Free Press, 2004, p. 101.

35. Warren, Rick. "The Church in the 21st Century Conference," Irving, TX, June 14–17, 1992.

36. Pew Research Center. www.pewresearch.org.

37. *Ibid.*

38. www.poblo.org.

39. Maxwell, John C. "11 Keys to Excellence." *INJOY Life Club* (audio resource), vol. 11, no. 2.

40. Ruhl, Mike. Presentation at Camp Arcadia, Arcadia, Michigan, August 1995; Luke 15:7 (BSB).

41. Luke 19:10 (NIV).

42. Peters, George W. *A Biblical Theology of Missions.* Chicago: Moody, 1972, p. 351.

43. 2 Corinthians 5:20 (ESV).

44. Hunter, George G. III. *Go: The Church's Main Purpose.* Nashville, TN: Abingdon Press, 2017, p. 186.

45. Gibbs, Eddie. *ChurchNext: Quantum Changes in How We Do Ministry.* Downers Grove, IL: InterVarsity Press, 2000, p. 187.

CHAPTER FIVE

Turn Your Church Right-Side Up: Breakthrough Strategy #1

Ceiling #1: Corporate Confusion

1. Gibbs, Eddie. *LeadershipNext: Changing Leaders in a Changing Culture.* Downers Grove, IL: InterVarsity Press, 2005, p. 100.

2. Matthew 16:13–18 (NLT) [Emphasis mine].

3. Matthew 16:18 (NLT).

4. John 1:14 (NIV).

5. See Ephesians 2:8–9.

6. Kolb, Barry. Shared at the Apostolic Council Meeting, Detroit, Michigan, December 2006.

7. See Kent R. Hunter, *Six Faces of the Christian Church: How to Light a Fire in a Lukewarm Church.* Corunna, IN: Church Growth Center, 2017.

8. McManus, Erwin Raphael. *An Unstoppable Force: Daring to Become the Church God Had in Mind.* Loveland, CO: Group Publishing, 2001, pp. 6–7.

9. See Exodus 20:12.

10. John 18:36 (NIV).

11. Matthew 6:10 (NIV).

12. John 4:34 (NET).

13. See 1 Corinthians 2:16 (NIV).

14. See Luke 6:38 (NLT).

15. Hughes, Emmet John. *The Ordeal of Power: A Political Memoir of the Eisenhower Years.* New York: Atheneum, 1963, p. 124.

16. See Mark 8:35.

17. Quoted to the author by Walt Kallestad, Sr. Pastor, Community Church of Joy, Glendale, AZ, 2015.

18. Matthew 16:6 (NIV).

19. See Matthew 20:20.

20. See Matthew 20:25–26 (NLT).

21. See Philippians 2:7.

22. Mead, Loren B. *The Once and Future Church: Reinventing the Congregation for a New Mission Frontier.* Washington, DC: Rowman & Littlefield, 1991, p. 41.

23. Leviticus 26:12 (NLT).

24. See 1 Peter 2:5 (NRSV).

25. Mark 12:31 (GWT).

26. See Matthew 18:15–17.

27. Ephesians 4:15 (NLT).

28. See Psalm 111:10.

29. 1 John 4:8 (ESV).

30. Matthew 11:28 (KJV2000).

31. Survey used in Church Doctor Ministries' Church Government Consultation.

CHAPTER SIX

Turn Your Church Inside Out: Breakthrough Strategy #2

Ceiling #2: Country Club

1. McGavran, Donald A. *Understanding Church Growth*, 3rd ed. Grand Rapids, MI: Wm. B. Eerdmans, 1990, p. 255.

Endnotes

2. Feucht, Oscar E. *Everyone a Minister: A Guide to Churchmanship for Laity and Clergy.* St. Louis, MO: Concordia Publishing House, 1974, p. 70. (Quoting Donald R. Heiges: *The Christian's Calling.* Philadelphia, PA: Board of Publication of the United Lutheran Church in America, 1958, p. 114.)

3. Grenny, Joseph, et al. *Influencer: The New Science of Leading Change.* New York: McGraw-Hill Education, 2013, pp. 67–75.

4. Luke 10:36 (NLT).

5. See Matthew 16:13–15 (NIV).

6. Mark 2:25 (NRSV).

7. Matthew 28:18 (NIV).

8. See 2 Corinthians 5:20 (NIV).

9. See Acts 1:8.

10. John 14:12 (NRSV).

11. Matthew 28:20 (NIV).

12. Matthew 24:14 (NRSV).

13. 2 Corinthians 12:10 (NIV).

14. Galatians 2:20 (NRSV).

15. Ephesians 5:15–17 (NLT) [Emphasis mine].

16. www.alphausa.org and www.alpha.org.

17. Isaiah 49:6 (ISV).

18. See Luke 2:41–42.

19. Isaiah 60:1–3 (ESV).

20. John 8:12 (NIV).

21. John 2:19 (NRSV).

22. John 12:32 (NIV).

23. Matthew 5:14 (NIV).

24. John 20:21 (NRSV).

25. Matthew 28:19 (NIV).

26. Acts 1:8 (NIV).

27. 1 Corinthians 6:19 (NIV).

28. 1 Corinthians 12:27 (NIV).

29. Matthew 4:19 (ESV) [Emphasis mine].

30. Warren, Rick. "The Church in the 21st Century Conference," Irving, TX, June 14–17, 1992.

31. Maxwell, John C. *Thinking for a Change: 11 Ways Highly Successful People Approach Life and Work.* New York: Center Street, 2003, p. 13 [Emphasis mine].

32. McGavran, Donald A. "Still Building the Bridges of God." *Global Church Growth* vol. 21, no. 4–5, 1984.

33. www.evangelismexplosion.org.

CHAPTER SEVEN

Turn Your Faith into God-Sized Potential: Breakthrough Strategy #3

Ceiling #3: Baby Food

---

1. Moore, Beth. *To Live Is Christ: Joining Paul's Journey of Faith*. Nashville, TN: B&H Publishing, 2001, p. 207.
2. 1 Corinthians 3:1–3 (MSG).
3. 2 Peter 3:18 (NIV).
4. Matthew 10:14 (NRSV).
5. See Luke 10:8 (ESV).
6. Mark 10:15 (NRSV).
7. Psalm 119:105 (KJV2000).
8. Matthew 6:33 (ESV).
9. 1 Corinthians 2:16 (ESV).
10. Luke 18:13–14.
11. St. Augustine, source unknown.
12. Emory, John. *The Works of the Reverend John Wesley, A.M. Sometime Fellow of Lincoln College, Oxford*, Vol. 3. New York: J. Emory and B. Waugh, 1831, p. 138.
13. See 2 Timothy 3:16 (NIV).
14. Hybels, Bill. "Leading in the New Reality." Willow Creek Leadership Summit, August 6, 2009.
15. Brierley, Peter. Correspondence with the author, November 20, 2014.
16. Romans 1:16 (NET).
17. Kelley, Dean M. *Why Conservative Churches Are Growing*. New York: Harper & Row, 1972, p. 148.
18. Ephesians 3:20–21 (ESV).
19. Wagner, C. Peter. Peter Wagner used this phrase when explaining *koinonitis*, a term describing inward-focused Christians fixated on fellowship with one another.
20. Van Engen, Charles. *American Society for Church Growth*, November 19, 1994.
21. Cope, Landa. *Clearly Communicating Christ: Breaking Down Barriers to Effective Communication*. Seattle, WA: YWAM Publishing, 1996, pp. 111–112.
22. 2 Peter 3:18 (NIV).

23. Matthew 17:20 (NIV).

24. Acts 2:43 (MSG).

25. Acts 2:47 (HCSB) [Emphasis mine].

26. Swindoll, Charles. "The Value of a Positive Attitude," January 20, 2009. www.insights.org.

27. See Ephesians 4:7–15 (RSV).

28. Stark, Rodney. *The Rise of Christianity: How the Obscure, Marginal Jesus Movement Became the Dominant Religious Force in the Western World in a Few Centuries.* San Francisco: HarperSanFrancisco, 1997.

29. Philippians 1:21 (NIV).

30. von Drehle, David, with Aryn Baker. "The Ebola Fighters: The Ones Who Answered the Call." *Time* magazine, December 10, 2014. Time.com.

31. Philippians 2:2 (MSG).

32. Matthew 26:24 (NLT).

33. Philippians 2:3 (BSB).

34. Maxwell, John C. *Failing Forward: Turning Mistakes into Stepping Stones for Success.* Nashville, TN: Thomas Nelson, 2000, p. 102.

35. John 8:11 (NLT).

36. Hunter, George G. III. The Billy Graham Advanced School of Evangelism. Wheaton College, Wheaton, IL, June 15–18, 1998.

37. This thought is used by numerous writers. Undocumented origin.

CHAPTER EIGHT

Turn Up Your Fire for Change: Breakthrough Strategy #4

> ### Ceiling #4: History's Mysteries

1. Friedman, Thomas L. *The World is Flat: A Brief History of the Twenty-First Century.* New York: Farrar, Straus & Giroux, 2005, p. 451.

2. Matthew 16:24 (NLT).

3. See Romans 9:30–33.

4. Berlin, Jeremy. "Last Call for Pubs?" *National Geographic* (February 2015), p. 12. [The word *community* in the singular is improper. It should be *communities*, but this is the way *National Geographic* reported it.]

5. Tolstoy, Leo. "Three Methods of Reform." In *Pamphlets, Translated from the Russian.* Christchurch, UK: Free Age Press, 1900, p. 255.

6. Revelation 21:5 (KJV).

7. 2 Corinthians 5:17 (ESV).

Endnotes

8. John 3:3 (ASV).

9. Sweet, Leonard. *SoulTsunami: Sink or Swim in New Millennium Culture.* Grand Rapids, MI: Zondervan, 1999, p. 308.

10. Twain, Mark. (Attributed).

11. 1 Corinthians 9:22 (NRSV).

12. Hunter, George G. III. American Society for Church Growth Conference, November 1997.

13. McManus, Erwin. *An Unstoppable Force: Daring to Become the Church God Had in Mind.* Loveland, CO: Group Publishing, 2001, p. 177.

14. Pearcey, Nancy. *Total Truth: Liberating Christianity from its Cultural Captivity.* Wheaton, IL: Crossway Books, 2004, p. 361.

15. John 9:16 (GWT).

16. Pearcey, Nancy. *Total Truth.*, p. 67.

17. See Matthew 16:24 (NIV).

18. Philippians 2:3 (BSB).

19. Matthew 21:16 (KJV).

20. Related to the author by musician Dave Anderson.

21. *Ibid.*

22. Padilla, C. Rene, Ed. *The New Face of Evangelicalism.* London, UK: Hodder & Stoughton, 1976, p. 79 (Quoting Helmut Thielicke, *How Modern Should Theology Be?*).

23. 1 Corinthians 9:19 (NASB) [Emphasis mine].

24. 1 Corinthians 9:21–23 (MSG).

25. John 21:15 (NIV).

26. John 21:17 (NIV).

27. 1 Peter 4:1–2 (MSG).

28. See Matthew 23:24 (KJV).

29. John 1:14 (MSG).

30. Warren, Rick. *The Purpose Driven Church: Growth Without Compromising Your Message & Mission.* Grand Rapids, MI: Zondervan, 1995, p. 248.

31. See Lamentations 3:23 (NIV).

32. Psalm 96:1 (NIV) [Emphasis mine].

33. Shared with the author in a remote village of the Kalahari Desert, Botswana.

34. Interview with Jaroslav Pelikan, *U.S. News and World Report.* June 26, 1989. Also found in the book by Pelikan, *The Vindication of Tradition.* New Haven, CT: Yale University Press, 1989.

35. Matthew 16:24 (ESV).

CHAPTER NINE

Turn Your Strategy into God's Math: Breakthrough Strategy #5

Ceiling #5: Addition Addiction

1. Ganz, Marshall. "Marshall Ganz on Making Social Movements Matter," May 10, 2013. www.billmoyers.com.

2. *Webster's New World College Dictionary*. Boston: Houghton Mifflin Harcourt, 2016.

3. 1 John 4:4 (ESV).

4. Shared with the author by Ernest C. Hinze Jr.

5. Genesis 1:28 (NLT).

6. Matthew 28:19–20 (NIV).

7. Ephesians 4:12 (NRSV).

8. Matthew 9:37–38 (NLT) [Emphasis mine].

9. This concept was originated, of course, by Jesus. In recent history, Ken Blanchard reflected on this in his book *Leadership and the One Minute Manager*. (New York: HarperCollins, 2000). Paul Hersey, a coauthor with Ken Blanchard, wrote *Management of Organizational Behavior: Utilizing Human Resources* (Upper Saddle River, NJ: Prentice Hall, 2012, in its most recent reprint. The earliest edition: 1969). Mike Breen and Steve Cockram have developed this idea, calling it "The Square," in *Building a Discipling Culture* (Pawleys Island, SC: 3D Ministries, 2009).

10. Matthew 28:19 (NIV).

11. See John 1:14 (NIV).

12. Luke 23:34 (MSG).

13. John 20:21 (NRSV).

14. Acts 1:8 (ESV).

15. Gladwell, Malcolm. *The Tipping Point: How Little Things Can Make a Big Difference.* New York: Little, Brown, 2000, pp. 21–25.

16. *Ibid.*

17. Acts 1:8 (NLT).

18. Matthew 9:37–38 (NLT).

19. Outreach Clusters are targeted outreach groups developed in congregations. Development of Outreach Clusters is a teaching in the video series *The Damascus Road*. It is also explained in the Outreach Clinic taught by Church Doctor Ministries.

20. See John 4.

21. Matthew 25:23 (NIV).
22. Lotito, Michel. Lotito was born in Grenoble, France, in 1950. He was known as Monsieur Mangetout. He ate metal and glass throughout his lifetime, beginning in 1959. His diet after 1966 included eighteen bicycles, fifteen supermarket carts, seven TV sets, six chandeliers, two beds, a pair of skis, a Cessna light aircraft, and a computer. By October 1997, he had eaten nearly nine tons of metal. Lotito died of natural causes on June 25, 2007. www.guinnessworldrecords.com.
23. Matthew 25:23 (NIV).

CHAPTER TEN

Turn Your Service into Dignity: Breakthrough Strategy #6

> ### Ceiling #6: Identity Theft

1. Pink, Daniel H. *Drive: The Surprising Truth About What Motivates Us.* New York: Riverhead Books, 2009, p. 76.
2. Matthew 9:35–36 (NRSV).
3. Luke 10:2 (GNT).
4. *Ibid.*
5. John 13:14–15 (NET).
6. www.usdreams.com/FordW19.html.
7. Hunter, Kent R. *Burn On or Burn Out.* Corunna, IN: Church Doctor Ministries, 2016, p. 2.
8. Miller, Donald. *Blue Like Jazz: Nonreligious Thoughts on Christian Spirituality.* Nashville, TN: Thomas Nelson, 2013, p. 86.
9. Maxwell, John C. *It's Just a Thought…But it Could Change Your Life.* Tulsa, OK: Honor Books, 1997, p. 112.
10. Matthew 25:21 (NIV).
11. Peters, George W. *A Biblical Theology of Missions.* Chicago: Moody Press, 1972, p. 209.
12. See 1 Peter 2:5–9 (NIV).
13. Sent to the author by Mark Marxhausen.
14. Exley, Richard. *God's Little Instruction Book for New Believers.* Tulsa, OK: Honor Books, 1996, p. 67.
15. Smith, Ebbie. Quoted by C. Peter Wagner, Church Growth 1, Fuller Theological Seminary, Pasadena, CA. Expanded by Ebbie C. Smith in *Balanced Church Growth: Church Growth Based on the Model of Servanthood.* Nashville, TN: Broadman Press, 1984, pp. 165–176.

16. McNeal, Reggie. *The Present Future: Six Tough Questions for the Church.* San Francisco: Jossey-Bass, 2003, p. 70.

17. Chambers, Oswald. *My Utmost for His Highest.* Grand Rapids, MI: Discovery House, 1992, August 4.

18. Maxwell, John C. *INJOY Life Club* (audio resource) vol. 14, no. 8, 1999.

19. Hunter, Kent R. Spiritual Gifts Profile. Corunna, IN: Church Doctor Ministries, 2009. www.churchdoctor.org.

20. 1 Corinthians 12:1 (ISV).

21. John 18:36 (NIV).

CHAPTER ELEVEN

Turn Your Life into Generosity: Breakthrough Strategy #7

> ### Ceiling #7: Recession Impression

1. Matthew 6:33 (RSV).

2. 2 Corinthians 8:1 (NRSV).

3. Engel, James F., and H. Wilbert Norton. *What's Gone Wrong with the Harvest? A Communication Strategy for the Church and World Evangelism.* Grand Rapids, MI: Zondervan, 1975, p. 45.

4. Acts 20:35 (NLT).

5. Foust, Paul. Speaking at a conference, November 7, 1974, quoting John E. Herrmann, author of *The Chief Steward: A Manual on Pastoral Leadership.* St. Louis, MO: Lutheran Church—Missouri Synod, Department of Stewardship, Missionary Education and Promotion, 1951, p. 16.

6. See Luke 17:11–19.

7. 2 Corinthians 9:6 (NIV).

8. Maxwell, John C. *INJOY Life Club* (audio resource) vol. 13, no. 11, 1997.

9. 2 Corinthians 9:7 (ESV).

10. Glasow, Arnold. Expanded from George Truett, quoted in "Toolkit," *Cell Church* (Winter 1996): p. 10.

11. Pierce, Bob. Quoted by Henry T. Blackaby and Claude V. King, in *Experiencing God: How to Live the Full Adventure of Knowing and Doing the Will of God.* Nashville, TN: Broadman and Holman, 1994, p. 154.

12. John 5:19 (NLT).

13. Acts 20:35 (NIV).

14. Hensley, Virgil W. "14 Reasons Why Christians Give." Pamphlet, n.d.

15. See Malachi 3:8–10.

16. See Matthew 17:20.

17. Hayford, Jack. *The Key to Everything: Experience the Freedom to Discover God's Purpose.* Lake Mary, FL: Charisma House, 2015, p. 164.

18. Pfeifer, Mark W. *Breaking the Spirit of Poverty.* Kearney, NE: Morris Publishing, 2006, p. 46.

19. See Psalm 50:10 (NLT).

20. See Matthew 6:20 (NLT).

21. Alcorn, Randy. *The Treasure Principle: Unlocking the Secret of Joyful Giving.* Colorado Springs, CO: Multnomah Books, 2001, p. 61.

22. Proverbs 11:24–25 (NIV).

23. Matthew 9:38 (HCSB).

24. See Mark 12:42-44.

25. John 14:12 (NRSV).

26. Barna, George. *Revolution.* Carol Stream, IL: Tyndale House, 2005, p. 33.

27. Maxwell, John C. *Today Matters: 12 Daily Practices to Guarantee Tomorrow's Success.* New York: Center Street, 2004, p. 70.

28. Colossians 4:5 (BLB).

29. Sepúlveda, Art. *Focus: What's in Your Vision?* Tulsa, OK: Harrison House, 2006, p. 225.

30. Hebrews 11:1 (NET).

31. Philippians 4:13 (KJV2000).

32. Zander, Glen. "Multiplication of Kindness," *Preaching Today.* www.preachingtoday.com.

33. 2 Corinthians 8:1–7 (NIV).

34. Luke 12:28–31 (ISV) [Emphasis mine].

35. Luke 6:27–30 (NIV).

36. Attributed to Martin Luther.

37. John 16:33 (HCSB).

38. Marshall, Peter. *Mr. Jones, Meet the Master: Sermons and Prayers of Peter Marshall.* Grand Rapids, MI: Baker Publishing Group (formerly published by Fleming H. Revell), 1982, p. 16.

39. Deuteronomy 16:17 (GWT).

40. See 2 Corinthians 9:6–15 (NIV).

CHAPTER TWELVE

Organic Launch

1. [My addition].

2. Lencioni, Patrick. *The Advantage: Why Organizational Health Trumps Everything Else in Business.* San Francisco: Jossey-Bass, 2012, p. 8.

3. Matthew 19:26 (KJV).

4. See Galatians 5:22–23 (WEB).

5. Luke 14:28 (ESV).

6. Jenkins, Daniel. *The Strangeness of the Church.* London, UK: Victor Gollancz, 1956, p. 14.

7. Several independent ministries offer assessments for congregations. Be sure to ask for references of churches that have used their services. These assessments have different names. The one used by Church Doctor Ministries, for example, is called a *Diagnostic Consultation.* Make sure the assessment tool measures spiritual fruit and Kingdom culture elements. It is important that the assessment uses anonymous surveys and confidential interviews with a cross section of your congregation.

8. Bennis, Warren. *Managing People Is Like Herding Cats: Warren Bennis on Leadership.* Provo, UT: Executive Excellence Publishing, 1997, p. 96.

9. See 1 Corinthians 3:6 (NIV).

10. Maxwell, John C. *How Leaders Gain Influence: Actions.* May 24, 2013. www.johnmaxwell.com.

11. Maxwell, John C. *INJOY Life Club* (audio resource) vol. 12, no. 5, 1996 (attributed).

12. *Healthy Churches Thrive! The Church Leader's Toolkit for Shaping Kingdom Culture* is available from Church Doctor Ministries (www.churchdoctor.org).

13. See John 3:8.

14. See Matthew 13:33.

15. Matthew 13:31 (NIV).

16. See John 18:36 (NIV).

17. Kutzner, Dennis L. "Ho, Ho, Holy Night." Unpublished devotional prayer. December 2014. www.gettysburgcampfires.com.

18. See Luke 22:24–27 (NRSV).

19. Rogers, Everett M. *Diffusion of Innovations,* 5th ed. New York: Free Press, 2003, pp. 150ff.

20. See Appendix I. The Holy Discontent self-reflection tool is one of several assessment resources used by Church Doctor Ministries in a diagnostic consultation.

21. See John 3:8.

22. Torwalt, Bryan, and Katie Torwalt, composers. "Holy Spirit." (Performed by Jesus Culture, featuring Martin Smith.) Arranged by Joel Mott. ©2011, Jesus Culture.

APPENDIX I

Holy Discontent
Self-Reflection Tool

This is a self-reflection tool for you to use before you commit to join the Kingdom Community for Healthy Churches Thrive! Reviewing these few issues should help you make your decision.

On this scale 1 = not at all true of me and 10 = very much true of me.

	Circle your number
1. Are you one who has wrestled with thoughts about how your church could do better at reaching out to those who don't yet know Jesus Christ?	1 2 3 4 5 6 7 8 9 10
2. Have you had concern that the church should have greater impact on your community?	1 2 3 4 5 6 7 8 9 10
3. Are you a person with deep concern about the spiritual deterioration of our nation, its values, and behavior?	1 2 3 4 5 6 7 8 9 10
4. Are you a loyal, committed member of your church?	1 2 3 4 5 6 7 8 9 10

(Over)

5. Do you respectfully support your pastor(s), staff, and leadership?	1 2 3 4 5 6 7 8 9 10
6. Do you pray for your church to do what God wants, following Jesus' direction to "seek first the kingdom of God"?	1 2 3 4 5 6 7 8 9 10
7. Are you optimistic that with God's help, the next few years could be the most exciting years of your church's history?	1 2 3 4 5 6 7 8 9 10
8. While change doesn't come naturally for most of us, are you open to improvements that would make your church more effective for mission and ministry, even though you may be stretched out of your comfort zone?	1 2 3 4 5 6 7 8 9 10
9. Do you consider yourself to be a person with an open mind, eager to know the biblical "mind of Christ"?	1 2 3 4 5 6 7 8 9 10
10. Would you be willing to participate in a movement in your church, not a program where you "do this and that" but a persistent, spiritual growth process focused on who you are and who you become?	1 2 3 4 5 6 7 8 9 10
Total Score:	_____
÷ 10 =	_____

If you scored an 8, 9, or 10, then you are most likely to be experiencing Holy Discontent. If you are experiencing this spiritual restlessness, please watch your church calendar for a special preview event about Healthy Churches Thrive!

www.churchdoctor.org

Nine Categories of Spiritual Fruit, Before and After Kingdom Culture Strategies

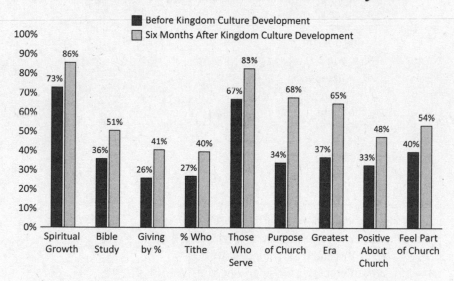

As a result of this church's ministry this past year, my spiritual life has grown (increased by 13 percentage points).

I attend a regularly scheduled Bible class (increased 15 percentage points).

When giving to the church, I decide the amount to give based on a percentage (increased 15 percentage points).

Relative to my household income, I tithe (or more) (increased 13 percentage points).

I serve in a ministry at this church (increased 16 percentage points).

I understand the main purpose of the church as being the Great Commission (increased 34 percentage points).

I am open to meaningful innovation and change (increased 28 percentage points).

I have a positive attitude about this church (increased 15 percentage points).

I feel a part of the church and would invite a friend (increased 14 percentage points).

APPENDIX III

The Use of Many Translations

This book uses many translations of the Bible. Why? Every translation, by definition, has human limitations. Hebrew, Aramaic, and Greek languages are often more precise than English. The original Hebrew, Aramaic, and Greek Bible has 11,280 different words. English translations have typically about 6,000. Different elements of meaning can be missed. It is helpful to compare translations.

In the context of this book, one translation may highlight the intended meaning of a specific point more than another. Sometimes a paraphrase version of the Bible helps to see the meaning of Scripture in a new way.

The following includes the translations used in this book:

ASV	American Standard Version
BLB	The Berean Literal Bible
	www.berean.bible
BSB	The Berean Study Bible
	www.bereanbible.com
ESV	The Holy Bible, English Standard Version
	Wheaton, IL: Crossway Bibles, 2001.
GNT	The Good News Translation
	New York: American Bible Society, 1992.
GWT	God's Word Translation
	Grand Rapids, MI: World Publishing, Inc., 1995.

HCSB	Holman Christian Standard Bible
	Nashville, TN: Holman Bible Publishers, 1999, 2000, 2002, 2003, 2009.
ISV	The Holy Bible: International Standard Version
	Bellflower, CA: ISV Foundation, 1995–2014.
KJV	King James Version
KJV2000	King James 2000 Bible
MSG	The Message
	Colorado Springs, CO: NavPress, 1993, 2002.
NASB	New American Standard Bible
	Anaheim, CA: Foundation Publications, 1995.
NET	The New English Translation
	Garland, TX: Biblical Studies Press, 2005.
NIV	The Holy Bible, New International Version
	Colorado Springs, CO: Biblica, Inc., 1973, 1978, 1984, 2011.
NLT	New Living Translation
	Wheaton, IL: Tyndale House Publishers, 1996, 2004, 2007, 2013.
NRSV	New Revised Standard Version
	Grand Rapids, MI: Zondervan, 1990.
RSV	Revised Standard Version
	Washington, DC: National Council of the Churches of Christ in the USA, 1946, 1952, 1971.
WEB	World English Bible
	worldenglishbible.org

ABOUT THE AUTHORS

Kent R. Hunter is founder of Church Doctor Ministries and developer of *Healthy Churches Thrive!* and SEND North America. Kent received his MDiv from Concordia Seminary, St. Louis, a PhD from the Lutheran School of Theology in Chicago, and DMin in church growth from Fuller Theological Seminary, Pasadena, California. He has pastored churches in Michigan, Indiana, and South Australia. Kent has trained pastors in fourteen countries and is the author of thirty books.

Tracee J. Swank has a business background. She graduated from the University of Toledo with a degree in organizational development and received her master's degree in spiritual formation from Winebrenner Seminary, Findlay, Ohio. She has served on Thrivent Build projects in Central America and is a member of her church in Defiance, Ohio. Tracee is a certified professional ministry coach and a certified Church Doctor consultant. Tracee leads Church Doctor Ministries.

Tracee, Kent, and their colleagues have consulted hundreds of churches from sixty-five denominations, networks, and fellowships in the US and Canada. They are frequent speakers for leadership gatherings and are members of the Great Commission Research Network.

CHURCHDOCTOR
MINISTRIES

Church Doctor® Ministries is committed to helping churches and Christians to become more effective for

The Great Commission

Matthew 28:19-20

Serving churches through...

Consulting • **Coaching** • **Teaching & Training** • **Resources**

Training young adults in spiritual formation and discipleship through SEND North America

www.churchdoctor.org
1-800-626-8515

Connect with the Church Doctors

──────── FOLLOW US ────────

@ChurchDoctorMinistries

@ChurchDoctor

#ChurchDoctor

Read about important issues facing the church today in The Church Doctor Report.

Join our community.

──────── HEAR FROM US ────────

Listen to the Church Doctors where you want, when you want.

Excited and *challenged* by what you read?
Share it with your church and community.
Consider scheduling:

Who Broke My Church?

Reaching the Unchurched **Workshop**

What others are saying about this event:

"Excellent! Great material
presented in a professional manner."

"I wish everyone in our church
could have been here for this!"

"Practical and helped me see
that I can make a difference."

Hosting is simple, and coordinators from our ministry team will
help you plan and market this event. In this one-day workshop,
our certified coaches and consultants will share key insights and
the practical application of the principles in this book.

Visit **www.churchdoctor.org**
Call **1-800-626-8515**
Write **info@churchdoctor.org**